The Catacazy Affair and the Uneasy Path of Russian-American Relations

Library of Modern Russia

Advisory Board

Jeffrey Brooks, Professor at Johns Hopkins University, USA
Michael David-Fox, Professor at Georgetown University, USA
Lucien Frary, Associate Professor at Rider University, USA
James Harris, Senior Lecturer at the University of Leeds, UK
Robert Hornsby, Lecturer at the University of Leeds, UK
Ekaterina Pravilova, Professor of History at Princeton University, USA
Geoffrey Swain, Emeritus Professor of Central and East European Studies at
the University of Glasgow, UK
Vera Tolz-Zilitinkevic, Sir William Mather Professor of Russian Studies at the
University of Manchester, UK
Vladislav Zubok, Professor of International History at
the London School of Economics, UK

Building on Bloomsbury Academic's established record of publishing Russian studies titles, the *Library of Modern Russia* will showcase the work of emerging and established writers who are setting new agendas in the field.

At a time when potentially dangerous misconceptions and misunderstandings about Russia abound, titles in the series will shed fresh light and nuance on Russian history. Volumes will take the idea of "Russia" in its broadest cultural sense and cover the entirety of the multiethnic lands that made up imperial Russia and the Soviet Union. Ranging in chronological scope from the Romanovs to today, the books will:

- reconsider Russia's history from a variety of interdisciplinary perspectives;
- explore Russia in its various international contexts, rather than as exceptional or in isolation;
- examine the complex, divisive, and ever-shifting notions of "Russia";
- contribute to a deeper understanding of Russia's rich social and cultural history;
- critically reassess the Soviet period and its legacy today;
- interrogate the traditional periodizations of the post-Stalin Soviet Union;
- unearth continuities, or otherwise, among the tsarist, Soviet, and post-Soviet periods;

- reappraise Russia's complex relationship with Eastern Europe, both historically and today;
- analyze the politics of history and memory in post-Soviet Russia;
- promote new archival revelations and innovative research methodologies;
- foster a community of scholars and readers devoted to a sharper understanding of the Russian experience, past and present.

Books in the series will join our list in being marketed globally, including at conferences—such as the BASEES and ASEEES conventions. Each will be subjected to a rigorous peer-review process and will be published in hardback and, simultaneously, as an e-book. We also anticipate a second release in paperback for the general reader and student markets.

For more information, or to submit a proposal for inclusion in the series, please contact:

Rhodri Mogford, Publisher, History (Rhodri.Mogford@bloomsbury.com).

New and Forthcoming

Fascism in Manchuria: The Soviet-China Encounter in the 1930s,
Susanne Hohler

The Idea of Russia: The Life and Work of Dmitry Likhachev, Vladislav Zubok

The Tsar's Armenians: A Minority in Late Imperial Russia, Onur Onol

*Myth Making in the Soviet Union and Modern Russia: Remembering
World War II in Brezhnev's Hero City*, Vicky Davis

*Building Stalinism: The Moscow Canal and the Creation of
Soviet Space*, Cynthia Ruder

*Russia in the Time of Cholera: Disease and the Environment under Romanovs
and Soviets*, John Davis

*Soviet Americana: A Cultural History of Russian and Ukrainian
Americanists*, Sergei Zhuk

*Stalin's Economic Advisors: The Varga Institute and the Making of
Soviet Foreign Policy*, Ken Roh

*Ideology and the Arts in the Soviet Union: The Establishment of Censorship
and Control*, Steven Richmond

Nomads and Soviet Rule: Central Asia under Lenin and Stalin, Alun Thomas

*The Russian State and the People: Power, Corruption and the Individual in
Putin's Russia*, Geir Hønneland et al. (eds.)

The Communist Party in the Russian Civil War: A Political History,
Gayle Lonergan

Criminal Subculture in the Gulag: Prisoner Society in the Stalinist Labour Camps, Mark Vincent

Power and Politics in Modern Chechnya: Ramzan Kadyrov and the New Digital Authoritarianism, Karena Avedissian

Russian Pilgrimage to the Holy Land: Piety and Travel from the Middle Ages to the Revolution, Nikolaos Chrissidis

The Fate of the Bolshevik Revolution, Lara Douds, James Harris, and Peter Whitehead (eds.)

Writing History in Late Imperial Russia, Frances Nethercott

Translating England into Russian, Elena Goodwin

Gender and Survival in Soviet Russia, Elaine MacKinnon (trans. and ed.)

Publishing in Tsarist Russia, Yukiko Tatsumi and Taro Tsurumi (eds.)

New Drama in Russian: Performance, Politics and Protest, Julie Curtis (ed.)

The Culture of Samizdat: Literature and Underground Networks in the Late Soviet Union, Josephine von Zitzewitz

Making Ukraine Soviet: Literature and Cultural Politics under Lenin and Stalin, Olena Palko

Family and the State in Soviet Lithuania: Gender, Law and Society, Dalia Lienarte

The Catacazy Affair and the Uneasy Path of Russian-American Relations, Lee A. Farrow

The Catacazy Affair and the Uneasy Path of Russian-American Relations

Lee A. Farrow

BLOOMSBURY ACADEMIC
LONDON • NEW YORK • OXFORD • NEW DELHI • SYDNEY

BLOOMSBURY ACADEMIC
Bloomsbury Publishing Plc
50 Bedford Square, London, WC1B 3DP, UK
1385 Broadway, New York, NY 10018, USA
29 Earlsfort Terrace, Dublin 2, Ireland

BLOOMSBURY, BLOOMSBURY ACADEMIC and the Diana logo are trademarks of
Bloomsbury Publishing Plc

First published in Great Britain 2022

For legal purposes the Acknowledgments on pp. viii–ix constitute an
extension of this copyright page.

Cover image: Top left – Hamilton Fish; Top right – Mme. Catacazy; Bottom left –
Hon. Catacazy Part of Brady-Handy photograph collection. © All images Courtesy of
Library of Congress, Prints and Photographs Division, Washington, D.C.

A catalogue record for this book is available from the British Library.

Library of Congress Cataloging-in-Publication Data
Names: Farrow, Lee A., 1966– author.
Title: The Catacazy affair and the uneasy path of Russian-American relations / Lee Farrow.
Description: London ; New York : Bloomsbury Academic, 2021. |
Series: Library of modern Russia | Includes bibliographical references and index. |
Identifiers: LCCN 2021012390 (print) | LCCN 2021012391 (ebook) |
ISBN 9781350107182 (hb) | ISBN 9781350107199 (ePDF) |
ISBN 9781350107205 (ebook)
Subjects: LCSH: Catacazy, Constantin. | Russia–Foreign relations–United States. |
United States–Foreign relations–Russia. | Russia–Foreign
relations–1855-1881. | United States–Foreign relations–1865–1898. |
Ambassadors–Russia–Biography. | Diplomatic privileges and
immunities–United States–History–19th century. | Fish, Hamilton,
1808-1893. | Perkins, Benjamin W.
Classification: LCC DK223 .F37 2021 (print) | LCC DK223 (ebook) |
DDC 327.4707309/034–dc23
LC record available at https://lccn.loc.gov/2021012390
LC ebook record available at https://lccn.loc.gov/2021012391

ISBN: HB: 978-1-3501-0718-2
ePDF: 978-1-3501-0719-9
eBook: 978-1-3501-0720-5

Typeset by Newgen KnowledgeWorks Pvt. Ltd., Chennai, India

To find out more about our authors and books visit www.bloomsbury.com
and sign up for our newsletters.

Contents

Acknowledgments   viii

Introduction   1

1   "There is a great sympathy between the people of the two countries
which is a delusion": Russian-American Relations before 1869   7

2   "Two-Penny Machiavelli": The Early Life and Career of Constantin
Catacazy   25

3   "The Intermeddling of the Russian Minister"   31

4   "Falsehood, Intrigue and Hostility": Catacazy's Breaches of Protocol   51

5   "She Had a Story and a Past": Olga Catacazy and the Washington
Wives   61

6   "A Thorough Mischief Maker": The Recall of Catacazy   77

7   The "Industrious Flea": Catacazy and the Visit of Grand Duke Alexis   101

8   "He ... Smirked Too Much to Be Dignified": The Departure of
Constantin Catacazy   125

Conclusion: "The Catfish War" and Its Legacy   141

Notes   157
Bibliography   191
Index   201

Acknowledgments

This book was researched over several years, but the bulk of the writing took place in 2020 while I was locked in my house during the first months of the COVID pandemic. During this period, I was fortunate in many ways: I had a job that continued to pay me, none of my family members got sick, and I was in lockdown with someone I enjoyed spending time with. But I feel it is necessary to mention that the first six months of the pandemic in the United States were not so easy for many people, financially or emotionally, and many thousands of people died and lost loved ones. I am dedicating this book to one of those lost to the pandemic, Dr. Joe King, professor of biology and former provost at Auburn University at Montgomery. Joe was a good man and a friend and would have been happy to see this book become a reality.

There are many people who helped make this book possible. Funding for research in the United States, Russia, and England came from various sources, including my own university, Auburn University at Montgomery, and a generous grant from the Kennan Institute at the Woodrow Wilson Center. I am grateful also to Louisiana State University Press and University of Alaska Press since in publishing my previous two books, they in essence helped me research and write some of the material contained here. Of course, I received assistance from the librarians and archivists at each place I researched and I am grateful to all of them, but I would like to single out Alla Viktorovna Abramenkova at the Arkhiv Vneshnei Politiki Rossiiskoi Imperii (Archive of Foreign Policy of the Russian Empire), in Moscow, Russia (AVPRI). Not only was she extraordinarily helpful and efficient, but she was very kind and understanding regarding some special needs I had at the time. As always, I must thank the librarians and staff at the AUM library who have now seen me through numerous research projects.

I want to thank two students, Adam Montgomery and Elizabeth Meads, and one dear friend, Mike Samerdyke, for proofreading the manuscript and giving me their feedback. Mike's feedback, in particular, was incredibly helpful in identifying rough passages in the text. I also have a wonderful group of girlfriends, near and far, who regularly offer me inspiration, encouragement, and support. Among these are Heather Adams, Dana Bice, Angela Mitchell, Karen

Racine, and Heather Thiessen Reily. It is important to surround yourself with smart and kind people and I have been lucky to have these women in my life.

My children, Benjamin and Camille, are always supportive of their mom, and I hope they are proud of me. I am very proud of them and all they are accomplishing as young adults. Lastly, I would like to thank my friend, Chris Bartlett, who has been my proofreader and biggest cheerleader over the past few years and, I hope, for many years to come.

Introduction

Edwin Heath, a member of the British Parliament for fifty-one years and prime minister from 1970 to 1974, is widely credited with having once said, "A diplomat is a man who thinks twice before saying nothing." Constantin Gavrilovich Catacazy, Russian minister to the United States from 1869 to 1871, could have used such sage advice. In fact, he did receive similar counsel from friends and colleagues, but Catacazy was stubborn and certain of himself, and would not listen. Nor did he have much tact for someone entrusted with securing and enhancing the relationship between Russia and the United States, two of the world's most powerful nations. Instead, he was brash and abrasive, meddling and dishonest. Contemporaries called him mercurial, offensive, intriguing, and "odious and disagreeable." In his short tenure as the representative of Russia he was directly responsible for numerous newspaper articles in the American press that were misleading about the current state of Russian-American relations or critical of the Grant administration and its top officials. He attempted more than once to interfere with American diplomatic negotiations and sent false and deceptive reports back to his own government, always presenting himself in the best light. He resorted to name-calling and implied that certain members of the US government were engaged in corruption. While the administration of General Ulysses S. Grant would indeed be labeled by historians as corrupt and riddled with nepotism, it was not the place of the Russian minister to make those public accusations.

As one of his first charges, the Russian government had instructed Catacazy to investigate a financial claim against Russia by the American citizen Benjamin Perkins over an alleged defaulted contract during the Crimean War; Catacazy, with his usual indelicacy, declared the claim fraudulent and worthless and called those associated with it plunderers and scoundrels. In addition, a document appeared in the *Washington Morning Chronicle*, an unsigned dispatch addressed to the tsar, that attacked the reputation of the American secretary of state Hamilton Fish, calling him a "very weak and vacillating man." Fish and others suspected Catacazy was the author of the document and the one who leaked it.

Catacazy's involvement in this claim was not his only misstep with the US government, however. The Russian minister also had been suspected of interfering in the resolution of the *Alabama* claims, a protracted and heated dispute between the United States and Great Britain after the Civil War that at various points seemed beyond resolution. In early 1871, rumors mushroomed that Catacazy was attempting to derail the settlement, hoping to drive a wedge between the two English-speaking nations. Catacazy denied any meddling, but Fish believed he was guilty of the charge and there were others who shared his conviction.

Finally, Catacazy had a scandalous personal life. The Russian minister had been the secretary of the Russian Legation in Rio de Janeiro and, while there, he fell in love with, and wooed away, the wife of the Italian minister from Naples. When he became secretary to the Russian Legation in the United States in 1851, he brought her with him to Washington, though their marital status was not entirely clear. A decade and a half later, when he returned to the United States as Russian minister, she accompanied him as his wife, and her appearance in this role set teacups rattling. If Madame Catacazy's checkered past were not enough of an obstacle to her acceptance by the other Washington wives, her renowned beauty was apparently the last nail in the coffin. The American press was convinced that this "tea-party intrigue" was a significant factor in the Catacazy imbroglio, and other sources hint at this as well. By June 1871, Secretary of State Fish and President Grant could take no more of Catacazy, and the US Cabinet requested that the Russian government recall the unwieldy diplomat. The expulsion would not be so easy, however. Preparations had already begun for the tsar's son, Grand Duke Alexis, to visit the United States in the fall of 1871, and the Russian government made it clear that such a visit could not occur without the presence of a Russian representative. Though Grant and Fish were eager to be rid of Catacazy, they were persuaded by the American minister in St. Petersburg, Andrew Curtin, to compromise, and Catacazy was permitted to stay until the end of the Grand Duke's visit. He would be allowed to travel with Alexis and fulfill his official duties, but he would be persona non grata in official Washington circles. This uneasy resolution solved the matter for the purposes of the Russian visit, but the conflict remained an object of scrutiny and speculation, and there were many who criticized Grant and Fish for their failure to better navigate the scandal, and many others who worried about the future of the Russian-American friendship.

The Catacazy Affair may on the surface seem like a minor tempest, but in reality it had broad implications in both domestic and international arenas. Domestically, the scandal raised a variety of important questions about Congressional purview, the legal rights of American citizens in suing foreign entities, and diplomatic protocol. The lawsuit of Benjamin Perkins and his heirs pushed (or exceeded) the appropriate boundaries of Congressional influence and many in Washington disagreed with the notion of a private dispute impacting national affairs, for example, the appropriations for Alaska. Though the US government did request that the claim be examined and given due consideration, the matter was not clearly one that required government intervention. In fact, there was some debate about the American government's responsibilities in supporting its citizens who engage with a foreign government, a question that still resurfaces today. Catacazy's methods in the case, specifically his habit of taking confidential or private matters to the press, highlighted the importance of diplomatic protocol and the old saying about discretion being the better part of valor.

American historians will appreciate this story as another example of how the personalities and behaviors of individuals in a government can influence policy at the highest levels of power. Most scholars of American history have likely never heard of this diplomatic disaster; consequently, a full discussion of the Catacazy Affair will add to the overall portrait of Grant's administration of one that was rife with turmoil and corruption. At the time, it was front-page news, offering readers the excitement of political intrigue and the salaciousness of social scandal. His choice of the American press as his medium for his efforts at diplomatic deception, political interference, and self-aggrandizement reminds us of the power of the press to influence opinion and craft "reality," then and now. Though American newspapers were becoming less partisan toward the end of the nineteenth century, political news was still central, and a story of this magnitude with such high-level players was bound to attract attention.

Finally, the episode was reminiscent of the "Petticoat Affair" of 1829-31. In that fascinating episode, the wives of President Andrew Jackson's cabinet members played a critical role in the collapse of the government. Jackson had appointed John Eaton as secretary of war, but the wives of the other cabinet members disapproved of his wife Peggy, her family background, and the circumstances of their marriage. Their pressure on their husbands led to the resignation of all but one cabinet member, contributing to Martin Van Buren's rise to the presidency. In the Catacazy Affair, it was widely reported that Olga Catacazy's relationship with her husband, as well as her notable beauty, made her a target of gossip and social exclusion. The other wives of Washington snubbed her and their disapproval influenced their husbands, especially Secretary of State Hamilton Fish, who had the most contentious interactions with the Russian minister. The Catacazy Affair can be seen as yet another example of the unofficial and unacknowledged power of women in politics in the decades before they could vote.

For Russia, the affair left a bad taste in the mouth of Tsar Alexander and the Russian government. An attempt to recall the Russian minister just as the tsar's son was due to depart for America seemed a clear case of sabotage, an intentional insult to stop the visit from occurring and damage the long-standing Russian-American friendship. Russia was particularly sensitive at this moment about which countries it could count among its friends and which were its enemies. Less than a year earlier, during the instability created by the Franco-Russian War, Russia had renounced the restrictions placed on the Black Sea after the Crimean War, limitations that had forbade the maintenance of a military fleet there. The announcement had caused concern and tension in Europe, and so the clash with the United States over Catacazy's behavior was unwelcome to say the least.

This study will explore the complex intricacies of the Catacazy Affair and its immediate and long-term impact on Russian-American relations. The episode was the first scratch on the shiny veneer of the Russian-American friendship that, at the same moment, was being widely proclaimed during the visit of the Grand Duke Alexis. In the wake of the American Civil War and Russia's own domestic upheavals, including the abolition of serfdom, the United States and Russia sought to redefine and strengthen their relationship. The Grand Duke's visit was part of this effort, and throughout his travels in the United States as he was wined and dined, the importance of the Russian-American friendship was a constant refrain. The unpleasantness of the Russian minister's recall represented the exact opposite of the goodwill declared by both countries. It cast a pall over Alexis's visit to Washington; while in other American cities Alexis was the honoree at balls and dinners, in the Capitol he received a brief and formal reception. It also led Alexis to decline an invitation to return to Washington to witness Congress in session. For years after, the conflict with the Russian minister would be viewed as a failure of democracy and a mark of the declining friendship between the two nations. Over the next decades, as the two great nations found less common ground, Russian-American relations grew more tenuous, culminating with the United States' opposition to and intervention against the new Bolshevik regime established by the Russian Revolution of October 1917. The Catacazy scandal and the sore feelings it generated was but one early stumble in the uneasy path of Russian-American relations.

1

"There is a great sympathy between the people of the two countries which is a delusion": Russian-American Relations before 1869

In the second half of the nineteenth century, Russia and the United States had a significantly different and warmer relationship than the one that future generations would come to know.[1] Situated on opposite sides of the globe, they were an unlikely pair in many ways—one a conservative monarchy, the other a young republic—yet over the course of a century the relationship had developed from hesitant and uncertain beginnings to a mature and complex friendship that both countries sought to protect and expand. Repeated encounters in trade, diplomacy, and technological matters had brought the two countries closer, while events on the international scene—war, trade disputes, and the shifting power balance in Europe—often pushed them together as well. Nonetheless, the Russian-American bond was frequently tested by those same events and encounters and, occasionally, the much-revered friendship seemed to be fraying.[2]

Following the abolition of serfdom in Russia and slavery in the United States, both countries were experiencing social transformations and trying to redefine themselves and their relationships with other nations. As the United States recovered from a brutal civil war, tensions continued between North and South, and new problems emerged with the birth of the Ku Klux Klan. On the international scene, the United States was embroiled in conflict over the possible annexation of San Domingo and engaged in a battle of wills with Britain over the *Alabama* claims, an unsettled dispute from the Civil War that charged Britain with failure to enforce its own laws of neutrality. Though both situations were resolved without violence, many had feared war. Meanwhile, Russia faced its own challenges of domestic reform and the growth of an increasingly radical, revolutionary-minded intelligentsia. Russia was also threatened on the international front, confronted with the birth of new European alliances and rivalries. In particular, Russia faced a Polish uprising, the ominous emergence of a newly unified Germany, and a contentious relationship with the Ottoman Empire. While the rumors in the American press that Tsar Alexander II was seeking an alliance with the United States were probably untrue, the tsar certainly viewed the Russian-American friendship as one worth retaining and the visit of his son, Grand Duke Alexis, in 1871–2 was clearly part of that effort. The American government's request for the Russian minister's recall at virtually the same moment, however, threatened not only the visit itself but also the friendship that it was intended to display and enhance.

Russia and the United States already had a surprisingly long and active relationship by the time the Grand Duke set foot on American soil. To a large extent, this marriage of convenience must be understood in a broader diplomatic context—since the end of the eighteenth century, Russian-American relations were both a reaction to and a facet of other relationships, particularly those between Great Britain and Russia and Great Britain and the United States. The constant, if sometimes simmering, tension between these pairs over maritime power, fishing rights, and territorial expansion repeatedly drove Russia and the United States into one another's arms. Though separated by an ocean and the great land mass of Western Europe, Russia and the United States found common interests more than once at the expense of and in opposition to that imperial powerhouse of the nineteenth century, Great Britain.

The first diplomatic contact between Russia and "America" was actually a decision to avoid contact. When the American Revolution began, Catherine the Great (1762–1796) had no desire to get involved in this faraway conflict, but she issued a Declaration of Armed Neutrality in March 1780, which effectively aided the colonies by declaring the right of neutral ships to enter American ports. The declaration also encouraged leaders in the American colonies to give Russia a closer look, and ultimately resulted in a formal mission to Russia.[3] In 1781, Francis Dana, accompanied by a fourteen-year-old John Quincy Adams, traveled to St. Petersburg. Though the complexities of the war and Catherine's hope of convincing Britain to accept her mediation of the conflict prevented Dana from being received in any official capacity, he did meet with important Russian and foreign diplomats and tried to alleviate concerns that an independent United States would be harmful to Russian commercial interests, specifically its trade in naval stores. Dana's efforts at persuading Russia to assist the colonies were a failure, however, and it would be twenty years before the United States could establish an official representative at St. Petersburg.[4]

There were other contacts during Catherine's reign as well. In 1788, the famous American seaman John Paul Jones secured an appointment in the Russian Navy and served in the Black Sea under the talented soldier and leader Prince Grigorii Potemkin, one of Catherine's favorites. Jones's period of service, however, did not go well. He did not speak Russian, did not get along well with the British officers in the Russian Navy, and in the spring of 1789, was accused of raping a twelve-year-old girl. Whether or not the accusation was true, Catherine took the opportunity to get rid of Jones; he was given a leave, made his way as far as Paris, and died there three years later.[5] Despite this rather disastrous episode, Russian-American commercial ties continued to grow in other areas. At the end of the eighteenth century, at least four hundred commercial ships from Boston, New York, Philadelphia, and other American ports brought goods to Russia, and by 1800, "most New England houses and ships were put together with Russian nails, and it would be a rare vessel that did not have sails, tackle and anchors of Russian origin." However, more formal commercial relations were hindered by the lack of an official diplomatic relationship.[6]

Russia and the United States finally established full diplomatic relations in 1809. Alexander I, the liberal grandson of Catherine the Great, had become tsar in 1801, and he and his small circle of liberal friends were more receptive to establishing a diplomatic friendship with the United States. There were practical diplomatic reasons, as well. When President Thomas Jefferson proposed the idea of an official minister in 1807, both the United States and Russia had become increasingly isolated as France proved its superiority on land and Great Britain dominated the seas. In June 1809, the US Senate approved the nomination of John Quincy Adams as minister to Russia, while Alexander had selected Andrei Dashkov as the first Russian minister to the United States.[7] This new diplomatic bond was strengthened when in 1813, Alexander I offered to mediate an end to the war between Britain and the United States. Britain refused and so it was not until the Treaty of Ghent in early 1815 that the war ended, but the Russian offer of assistance impressed the American government as a sign of goodwill.[8]

The following year, however, saw a series of small complications threaten the developing friendship. In November 1815, in an episode oddly reminiscent of the John Paul Jones affair, the Russian consul general in Philadelphia, Nikolai Kozlov, was accused of raping a twelve-year-old girl. A Pennsylvania court denied Kozlov's claim of diplomatic immunity and decided that crimes by foreign diplomats fell within the purview of federal courts. Meanwhile, the outgoing consul general, Dashkov, continued to argue in favor of diplomatic immunity and demanded that Kozlov be cleared of all charges, and when these demands fell on deaf ears, he declared that he was ceasing all communication with the US government. In retaliation, the Russian government in St. Petersburg declared the American chargé d'affaires there, Levett Harris, to be persona non grata, though he was permitted to carry out his official duties. The crisis settled in late 1816 when Alexander I and his cabinet, eager to maintain good relations, came to accept the argument that diplomats were answerable to the laws of the country where they resided at the time of the offense.[9]

In the 1820s and 1830s, the principal Russian-American interaction was trade. Though no official commercial treaty regulated trade between the two countries, an impressive number of American ships traveled to Kronstadt and St. Petersburg with a variety of valuable goods, including sugar from the West Indies.[10] In 1829, Nicholas I sought to modernize the Russian Navy and sent a mission to the United States to visit various shipyards and naval facilities. The visit led to the purchase of one steam corvette, but anti-Russian sentiment in Washington after the Russian government's suppression of the 1830–1 Polish uprising nearly wrecked the deal and interfered with an expansion of trade that might otherwise have followed.[11] The two countries finally signed a commercial treaty in 1832, by which time many Americans had lost interest in the Polish cause.[12] In 1838, Nicholas I sent another mission to the United States to tour shipyards and port facilities, resulting in the purchase of one steam frigate that was delivered to Kronstadt in 1841.[13] Russia also looked to the United States for help in railroad construction. In 1841, a group of Russian railroad proponents persuaded Nicholas to create a special committee to consider ideas for a Moscow–St. Petersburg rail line; subsequently, the tsar approved a proposal to bring an American railroad expert, George Washington Whistler, to oversee construction. Similarly, the Russian government brought in American locomotive manufacturers, including Joseph Harrison, Jr. of Philadelphia, to set up a factory and train locals in the trade. These men all lived in Russia for several years, and Whistler even brought his family, which included his son James, the future painter.[14]

The Crimean War, which broke out in 1853 between Russia and an alliance of the British, French, and Ottoman Empires, posed a serious challenge to Russian-American relations. Though the theatre of war was far away and not an area of interest for the United States, there was much about the conflict that proved relevant. On the one hand, American officials saw Russia as a friend and Britain as a constant irritant; on the other, British trade was too profitable to cast aside easily. Soon, however, American ambiguity shifted in favor of Russia. In the summer of 1854, the United States offered to mediate the conflict between Russia and Britain, but the effort came to nothing. Russia and the United States did, however, sign a maritime neutrality agreement that was so friendly that it "bordered on a quasi-alliance." This did not stop the British from actively recruiting in the United States, however, an activity that angered Russian officials who viewed it as a violation of the American position of neutrality. In fact, several British recruiters were arrested and put on trial and the British minister to the United States, John F. Crampton, was dismissed over the matter.[15] Many Russians would have welcomed a fallout between the United States and Great Britain. Constantin Catacazy, who was serving as secretary to the Russian Legation in the United States, advocated encouraging American merchant vessels to set sail for Russia, hoping that if they were stopped by the British it might push America into the war.[16]

The American government had no intention of getting drawn into the Crimean War, but it did take the opportunity to study the military tactics being used in the conflict. In the summer of 1854, the War Department sent a team of military observers to St. Petersburg, where they stayed for six weeks, touring military installations and learning about the Russian Army, as they waited for permission to head south. Ultimately, the American mission never made it to the Russian front, refused under the official claim that other groups had been denied the same request, so the Americans were forced to observe the war from the British side.[17] A considerable number of private citizens traveled from the United States to the Crimea, as well. Thirty-five American doctors from various places traveled to the region to offer medical aid, some out of sympathy for Russia, others for adventure, experience, or money. Pure profit was the motive for many other Americans. Though the United States remained neutral, a number of individuals took the opportunity to sell guns, powder, coal, and cotton to Russia and, in some cases, to its enemies as well.[18]

The Crimean War concluded in March 1856 with the Treaty of Paris. Tsar Nicholas I had died in 1855 and his son, the more liberal Alexander II, took the opportunity to remove Russia from a war that had exposed many of its weaknesses, particularly the poor physical condition of its peasant conscripts.[19] Russia's attitude toward the United States, however, remained positive, and the person who deserves the most credit for this is the Russian minister Eduard de Stoeckl. Serving as head of the Russian Legation in the United States between 1854 and 1868, Stoeckl was personally popular, having married an American woman, and was active in the social activities of the capital. He also made sure to report all examples of American friendliness and sympathy to his government.[20]

At the same time, the period between the end of the Crimean War in 1856 and the beginning of the Civil War in 1861 was one of the most active periods in Russian-American trade relations, with the continuation of old business deals and the development of many new contracts. In 1857, for example, about 45 percent of Russia's cotton imports came from the United States and that figure rose to 80 percent in the following year. Russia also imported American sugar, rice, and logwood. Military trade flourished as well. In the late 1850s, the William H. Webb Shipyards began building warships for the Russian Navy, and Samuel Colt, who had already been selling guns to Russia, secured a lucrative business deal to supply machinery and designs for Colt-style revolvers to be manufactured there.[21]

The next decade proved to be a more challenging time for Russian-American relations as both countries confronted reform and the opposition it aroused. In early 1861, civil war erupted in the United States over the issue of slavery at the same moment that Alexander II declared an end to the centuries-old practice of serfdom in Russia. American newspapers praised the tsar for this liberal reform and for decades politicians and the press would refer to the serf emancipation in discussions about Russian-American relations, especially the speeches welcoming Grand Duke Alexis to America a decade later. Once the United States had emancipated its own slaves, the two nations perceived a new special bond between them. Russian minister Stoeckl placed great value on this mutual understanding of the importance of emancipation and believed that this shared experience facilitated positive feelings.[22]

Sadly, America's path to emancipation was more difficult. While liberal Russians rejoiced at the news of American emancipation, the violence of the American process saddened them. Russian officials, concerned about the fate of the Russian-American friendship, were even more dismayed by the Civil War. Russia needed a strong ally in its ongoing rivalry with Great Britain and in reestablishing itself as a European power after the disastrous Crimean War. By 1862, the Russian minister of foreign affairs, Prince Alexander Gorchakov, and others in St. Petersburg grew frustrated with the American Civil War and worried that a permanent split in the American Union might occur. Consequently, Gorchakov pledged Russia's support for the Union, a declaration that was widely circulated in Washington and published in all the major Northern newspapers.[23] This pledge did not, however, mean that Russia would intervene in the Civil War. Instead Russia refused to join mediation attempts by France and, to a lesser extent, Britain, until the time came when North and South expressed a willingness to negotiate. The possibility of any Russian mediation in America, however, effectively ended with the internal distraction of the Polish revolt of 1863. Despite decades of foreign rule, the Poles of the Russian Empire had retained a strong sense of national identity and Polish nationalists still held out hope for independence. In January 1863, this desire for autonomy manifested itself in a sudden and violent uprising. The Russian government, however, would not consider the creation of an independent Poland and suppressed the rebellion. International reaction to the Polish revolt varied. Though there was some sympathy for the Poles in the United States, especially at the beginning of the rebellion, American support waned as British and French support for the rebels grew.[24]

It was at this complex moment that Alexander II decided to send a squadron of Russia's Baltic fleet to the United States. Though historians have disagreed about his motives, it is widely believed that Alexander wanted to prevent his best warships from being trapped in Baltic ports in the event of a general European war over the Polish issue. Certainly, many newspapers in the fall of 1863 recognized the diplomatic and military advantages to Russia's visit, both for Russia and the United States. Alexander may even have simply wanted to demonstrate Russia's growing naval capability. In any event, when some three thousand Russian sailors and officers arrived in the United States in September 1863, they enjoyed a hearty welcome and over the next two months attended numerous dinners, receptions, balls, and parades in New York, Philadelphia, Baltimore, and Washington. A separate group of ships from Russia's Pacific squadron visited the west coast, docking in San Francisco. These sailors were fewer in number, but their visit was longer, about ten months. Whatever the primary motive may have been, for many Americans, then and later, the arrival of the Russian fleet was a sign of friendship and a show of support for the North, and one that may have discouraged Britain and France from recognizing the Confederate government.[25]

One other point of Russian-American contact during the Civil War years deserves mention—the project to build a telegraph line connecting the two continents. In 1865, Western Union sent four men to Kamchatka in the far eastern region of the Russian Empire to explore the possibility of building a Pacific telegraphic cable. One of these men was George Kennan, the cousin of the later political advisor of the same name who became well-known during the Cold War era as the "father of containment." The men made their way up the Kamchatka Peninsula with the help of native guides to explore the route for the proposed cable, and according to Kennan's memoir of the expedition, the terrain was difficult and uncharted, and the men suffered greatly from the intense conditions. Ultimately, the expedition was a failure; in 1866, when an Atlantic cable was successfully completed, the project was suspended.[26]

Russians and Americans continued to feel connected by other shared experiences, as well. In April 1865, when President Abraham Lincoln was assassinated by John Wilkes Booth, Russia expressed great sympathy for America's loss in both official and unofficial circles, and throughout Russia pictures of Lincoln were displayed next to those of Grand Duke Nicholas, the tsar's eldest and recently deceased son. Not long after Lincoln's assassination, Alexander II had his own brush with death. In April 1866, a suicidal and disturbed student named Dmitrii Karakozov fired a shot at Alexander II near one of the royal gardens in St. Petersburg. Though the attempt was unsuccessful, such an attack so soon after the American president's murder resonated in both nations. In response, Congress approved a joint resolution to congratulate Alexander on his narrow escape and the new president, Andrew Johnson, selected Gustavus Vasa Fox, assistant secretary to the navy, to deliver it. The mission had another purpose as well—to thank Russia for its continuing support and to broadcast this friendship quite publicly by stopping in France and Britain along the way. Fox and the naval officers were received and welcomed in St. Petersburg, Moscow, and several cities along the Volga, celebrated with dinners and receptions. They were, for the moment, minor celebrities, and had their photographs taken many times, and their images were in great demand.[27]

The year 1867 was an active one in Russian-American relations. In the late summer, a pleasure ship called the *Quaker City* dropped anchor in the Black Sea, and for the first time a large number of American tourists had the opportunity to see Russia and its people. Their experiences, moreover, were shared with a large audience back home through the pen of the *Quaker City*'s most famous passenger, Mark Twain. His *Innocents Abroad*, which appeared two years later, would contain Twain's impressions of Russia and his account of the tourists' reception by Alexander II at the tsar's Livadia Palace near Yalta. Twain observed, "Any man could see that there was an intention here to show that Russia's friendship for America was so genuine as to render even her private citizens objects worthy of kindly intentions."[28] At virtually the same time, another group of Americans had arrived in Russia; in August 1867, Admiral David Farragut and a naval squadron of four ships put in at the Kronstadt naval base where they were met by the governor of the fortress, Admiral Lessovskii, the same Lessovskii who had visited the United States with the Russian fleet during the Civil War. In St. Petersburg, Farragut dined with Lessovskii and his family in the cottage once occupied by Peter the Great, and paid a call to Cassius Clay and the other members of the American delegation in the Russian capital. Farragut also met Grand Duke Constantin Nikolaevich, the brother of the tsar and the head of the Russian Navy, who toured Farragut's ship, the *Franklin*, and exhibited great interest in everything about the American steamer. Altogether, Farragut and the squadron spent three weeks in Russia.[29]

The biggest Russian-American event of 1867, however, was the sale of Alaska, or Russian America, as it was also called, to the United States. The idea to transfer this territory long predated the actual sale. Rumors about a possible sale had begun as early as the Crimean War, and a year after that war ended, Grand Duke Constantin officially proposed shedding the Alaskan burden, arguing that Russia's focus should be on strengthening its center. Serious conversations took place between Russian and American officials, but the turmoil of the early 1860s put any such discussions on hold. In the end, however, American expansionism, Russia's desire to concentrate resources elsewhere, and a shared desire to block British interests brought the two nations to the bargaining table. On March 30, 1867, Secretary of State William Seward and Russian minister Eduard de Stoeckl signed the treaty obliging the United States to pay $7.2 million for Alaska. The official transfer of the territory took place in Sitka on October 18, 1867.[30] Even before the United States had officially occupied Alaska, however, one thread of controversy that had run through all the debates about the purchase remained to be settled. Known as the Perkins claim, this financial claim by an American citizen against the Russian government would prove to be a serious threat to the passing of an appropriation bill for the final step of acquiring Alaska, and a major nuisance for Russian minister Stoeckl. For his successor, Constantin Catacazy, however, the Perkins claim would be much more than an irritant; it would be the catalyst for his diplomatic downfall.

* * *

The Perkins affair is a complicated tale. It began in June 1855 during the Crimean War when Benjamin Perkins was in New York City and met Charles Rackelwicz, an agent and courier of the Russian government. According to Perkins's deposition, Rackelwicz told him that Russia was in need of armaments and powder and that it was his mission to procure the desired items. Presenting various documents that seemed to indicate that he was telling the truth, he suggested that Perkins could supply the goods. Perkins replied that if the deal could be arranged and approved by Russian minister Stoeckl, and if it was "sufficiently remunerative," then he would be interested.[31]

Several days later, Rackelwicz invited Perkins and his associate, Dr. Walter Kidder, to the Metropolitan Hotel in New York to meet Stoeckl who seemed fully informed of all that had already transpired. Assuring Perkins that the deal would be profitable, Stoeckl asked him to draft several proposals based on information provided by Rackelwicz, including the desired quantity of arms and powder. The following day Perkins offered Stoeckl two proposals, each with a different arrangement as to who would provide the capital investment and how much Perkins would be paid. Stoeckl asked for the proposals in writing, with costs itemized, since he was headed back to Washington and wanted to get them on the next steamer; he assured Perkins that the Russian government would accept one of his proposals within sixty days. He urged Perkins to begin production immediately since powder of "government strength" in such a large quantity would have to be specially manufactured. Perkins agreed and delivered the written proposals as requested. Perkins then began to fill the order for powder.[32]

In August 1855, Perkins traveled to Washington to talk with Stoeckl. Though the Russian minister still did not have an answer from his government, he indicated that one of the proposals would be accepted. With this assurance, Perkins returned to New York and continued his preparations, purchasing a small ship called the "Sea Breeze." Meanwhile, the powder was packed according to Stoeckl's specifications and waited in Boston Harbor.[33]

It was at this time that Stoeckl withdrew himself from the negotiations, referring Perkins to Rackelwicz and Captain Otto Lilienfeldt, an "ordnance officer" just arrived from St. Petersburg. All of this made Perkins a bit nervous, but he had received so many assurances that he decided to meet with Lilienfeldt. When Lilienfeldt began to change the terms of the earlier agreement, however, Perkins attempted to see Stoeckl again. The Russian minister now seemed determined to avoid Perkins and left New York without leaving him a message. Perkins felt that Stoeckl had defrauded him and violated their contract. Faced with these circumstances, the frustrated businessman proceeded to Boston and began to try and sort the situation out as best he could. Eventually, Perkins met with Stoeckl several times, but all the minister would give were "guarded, evasive remarks." Realizing that his conversations with Stoeckl were going nowhere, Perkins began to make plans to travel to St. Petersburg.[34]

The powder contract was not the only violated agreement, however. When Perkins had first met Lilienfeldt, the latter had indicated that while he could not purchase powder, he was authorized to buy arms and discussed a possible contract. The men had no further contact until after the breach of the powder deal, when Perkins was preparing to go to Russia. At this meeting, Perkins suggested that he might bring with him to St. Petersburg a sample of the arms he could provide. Over the next six weeks, the two men spoke in person several times to discuss the specific needs of the Russian government and Perkins altered the guns accordingly. On January 12, 1856, they met again in Hartford, Connecticut, at which time Lilienfeldt approved the modified muskets; the men agreed for Perkins to alter 35,000 guns within five months, and signed two copies of a written memo to that effect, each man taking a copy.[35]

The signing of this contract ended Perkins's plans to go to Russia, as he devoted all his attention to fulfilling this new deal. On January 19, Perkins telegraphed Lilienfeldt, "Contract accepted;" that same day, however, Lilienfeldt sent Perkins a letter warning him not to proceed, since he thought he might soon be replaced by another agent. Soon after, however, Lilienfeldt did renew contact with Perkins, and met him to examine a large stash of modified arms. Apparently satisfied with the weapons, Lilienfeldt agreed to draw up a formal contract but then, over the next few weeks, evaded Perkins. What ensued was no less than the proverbial wild goose chase, as Perkins looked for Lilienfeldt in Worcester, New York, and Hartford, and the Russian agent stayed one step ahead.[36]

Eventually, Perkins discovered that Lilienfeldt was leaving the country, and was advised that his only recourse was to initiate a lawsuit. On June 7, 1856, Perkins filed a complaint in the Supreme Court of New York and, according to one source, Lilienfeldt was arrested "on the ground that he was an alien and about to leave the country."[37] In subsequent weeks, Lilienfeldt gave his deposition, yet refused an offer for third-party mediation. Meanwhile, Perkins's inability to pay the cost bond of $500 demanded by the Supreme Court of New York, combined with his other debts and obligations, led to his total financial ruin. In desperation, Perkins reluctantly accepted a $200 judgment offered by Lilienfeldt's counsel on March 21, 1857. This was not the end of the case, however. Perkins and his counsel claimed that he was both embarrassed and financially destroyed by the incident and, therefore, expected remuneration from the Russian government. The settlement with Lilienfeldt, they argued, was just that—a settlement with one man. It did not absolve Russia of its liability in the matter. Specifically, Perkins demanded the amount that he would have made had the contracts been fulfilled: for the arms, $301,000.00; for the powder, $72,613.20; interest on the capital invested, $11,618.11; for a grand total of $385,231.31.[38]

Over the next few years, all of the relevant parties in the case were deposed and Perkins's supporters provided letters, telegrams, and contracts to back their depositions. Moreover, a number of witnesses gave testimony, including several men who were present during Perkins's negotiations with the Russian agents.

During this process, Perkins's attorneys offered Stoeckl all the relevant papers for consideration and discussion, but the Russian minister denied the validity of the claim and refused to engage in an exchange of documents. He stated that he had no authority to refer the matter to arbitration and that Perkins would have to approach the Russian government directly through the American minister in St. Petersburg.[39] In the meantime, Perkins and his counsel appealed to higher powers. On April 27, 1858, Perkins wrote to the president of the United States, asking for the help of the American government.[40] Though little seems to have happened on the case following this appeal, it did receive national attention; there were small newspaper reports mentioning it across the country, including several that declared, optimistically as it turned out, that the entire amount would "probably be paid on the return of the Russian Minister … from Europe."[41] In September 1860, the American minister to Russia, John Appleton, submitted the Perkins claim with all relevant documents to the Russian government for consideration. Three months later, the Russian adjunct minister of foreign affairs, Ivan Tolstoy, rejected the claim, declaring that the claim for arms was settled by the judgment in New York and that there was no written contract for powder.[42]

The actions of the American government in submitting the Perkins case before the Russian government were in keeping with legal precedent established over the previous decades: the Department of State would draw attention to a believable and fair claim, but would not pursue it beyond that limited scope. In 1794, the Attorney General of the United States, William Bradford, noted, "A nation ought not to interfere in the causes of its citizens brought before foreign tribunals, except in a case of refusal of justice or of palpable injustice." This principle was reiterated forty years later by Secretary of State John Forsyth, who proclaimed, "It is not usual for the government of the United States to interfere, except by its good offices, for the prosecution of claims founded on contracts with foreign governments." There was also an important distinction between "good offices," which entailed an "unofficial advocacy of interests," and serving as a mediator. At best, the State Department might facilitate arbitration by a disinterested third party. Moreover, if the amount of the claim seemed to have been inflated, the government would not advocate for it. In 1856, Secretary of State William Marcy had declared, "The Department will not present to a foreign government claims for damages which, though based on a wrong actually done, are speculative and exorbitant in amount."[43]

Despite these restrictions, Perkins's attorneys persisted. In 1861, the House of Representatives received a presentation of the Perkins claim with a new timeline that included international events that were pertinent to the case and proposed that Stoeckl's inconsistent actions coincided precisely with the changing circumstances of the war in the summer of 1855. Specifically, the powder contract occurred in June 1855, during a period when Russia had renewed its war efforts after a failed peace conference in April. That same month, however, the allied powers blockaded all of the Russian seaboard; allowing for the time that it would take for that news to reach Washington, this was about the time that Stoeckl began to waffle on the deal. Still, he did not yet cancel the contract as shown by an August 4 letter from the Russian agent in Berlin to Perkins. But on August 7, the allies destroyed the most important Russian fortress on the Baltic Sea and took control of the coast. Stoeckl would have received this news about September 1, the exact time when he breached the contract. Perkins's attorneys presented a similar argument for the arms contract that showed that in early 1856 Russia accepted new negotiations and sent representatives to the congress being held in Paris; soon after, the arms contract was breached. Perkins's attorneys added that on October 16, 1861, Seward wrote to Cassius Clay, US minister to Russia, expressing the Department of State's opinion that the claim was just and ought to be paid; since these efforts had failed, they now requested help from Congress.[44]

Over the next few years, activity on the Perkins claim came to a virtual standstill as the Civil War took precedence over virtually all other matters. When Benjamin Perkins died in 1862, his claim was taken up by his wife, Anna Perkins.[45] This period of relative inactivity was but the calm before the storm, however, for in 1867 the claim was resurrected and over the next few years, it would grow to include many politicians and diplomats in Washington and would ultimately lead to an international scandal that contributed to the souring of Russian-American relations. In 1867, Anna Perkins once again appealed to Congress for help with a very persuasive argument—aware that the United States was in negotiations for the purchase of Alaska, she asked that Congress withhold the amount of $385,231.31 plus interest from the payment to Russia, at least until her claim was evaluated once more.[46]

A number of politicians embraced Perkins's cause. Over the next year or so, as the House of Representatives debated the appropriation of funds to pay for Alaska, advocates of the Perkins claim in Congress raised it again and again—twice in July 1867, once in December 1867, and at least once every month in the spring of 1868. The case was also referred to the Committee on Appropriations and the Committee on Claims. In the fall of 1867, E. Peshine Smith, an examiner of claims in the Bureau of Claims, concluded that Perkins had been, and his estate now was, entitled to payment from Russia for the losses which he sustained "by the fault of her agent in presenting the execution of a valid contract." He did not believe that Perkins had the right to insist that the American government get involved, however. Smith thus concluded that to tamper with the treaty for Alaska would be "inconsistent with our national honor" and "to postpone payment for the further consideration of such a claim, would ... be to renounce for the future any right to the just confidence in our plighted faith which has been exhibited in this instance."[47]

Meanwhile, the Russian minister Stoeckl was alarmed by the growing momentum of this claim and the attempts to link it to the Alaska purchase. Late in the summer of 1867 he wrote to Seward about his concern that rumors about these efforts might reach the Russian capital and "produce some uneasiness there."[48] In late January 1868, he wrote to Gorchakov that he hoped that there were still enough noble men in the House who would come out against the case. He believed that the backers of the claim were well organized and had some kind of agreement to split the settlement with Mrs. Perkins.[49] The *Washington Daily Morning Chronicle* disagreed with Stoeckl's assessment of the case. Shortly after the Russian minister had expressed his hopes to Gorchakov, the *Chronicle* stated,

> to this appeal it is difficult to see how the House can be insensible ... The proceeding asked for is one that, in view of public law and international usages, involves no offence to Russia; but whether it does or not, is a matter which will weigh very little with an American Congress against the duty of securing one of our own citizens so simple an act of justice as a hearing of her case.[50]

When debate over the appropriation bill began in the full body of the House in late June 1868, Benjamin Butler, a great opponent of the Alaska purchase, submitted an amendment asking that $500,000 be withheld until the Russian government agreed to an impartial tribunal to consider claims by American citizens considered valid by the Department of State. Butler's proposal went nowhere. As a compromise, Nathaniel Banks of Massachusetts, who supported the Perkins claim but did not believe it should be linked to the Alaska bill, negotiated a promise to the supporters of the claim "in public session, with the consent of the Secretary of State, and the Russian Minister" that the subject would be considered once the bill passed. Banks later wrote to the new Secretary of State Hamilton Fish, "I do not state that he [Stoeckl] promised the recognition of the claim in any way, but he said it should be considered and settled upon the facts of the Case—We did not debate the merits of the claim." Ultimately, on July 14, the entire House passed the Alaska appropriation bill and several days later, the Senate quickly and harmoniously passed the bill as well. On July 28, Seward sent a requisition for $7.2 million to the secretary of the treasury and four days later Stoeckl received a treasury draft in that amount. Stoeckl subsequently left Washington in October 1868 and retired in January 1869.

Discussion of the Perkins claim did not occur until the next session of Congress. In mid-January 1869, the House of Representatives resolved that "the President be requested to use the good offices of this government for the purpose of obtaining from the Russian government a prompt and just consideration and settlement of the claims of Benjamin W. Perkins and others," originating in contracts made during the Crimean War. Subsequently, in May and June 1869, Banks wrote two letters to the new Secretary of State Hamilton Fish explaining the particular circumstances of the House resolution and its intent to satisfy that promise of the previous year.[51]

In January 1869, however, the retirement of Stoeckl and the appointment of a new minister, Constantin Catacazy, sent the Perkins claim in an entirely new direction. The Russian government had instructed Catacazy to investigate the Perkins claim, and he did so with brash enthusiasm. Catacazy wrote to Fish that the claim was not deemed credible by the Russian government because of its "essentially fraudulent character" and "entire worthlessness." He called the evidence "absolutely fictitious," and denied that any of the Russians involved in the matter had the authority to negotiate such contracts. Moreover, he added, "Unless completely insane, a man in the position of Mr. Stoeckl, does not engage in such an enterprise without a good and sufficient object or motive." According to Catacazy, Rackelwicz did not even work for the Russian government. Catacazy then introduced the testimony of a number of individuals who indicated that Perkins was a man of intemperate habits who intentionally entrapped the Russian agents in an effort to extort money. Furthermore, they insisted that Perkins was a bad businessman and a bad mariner who either by "design or incompetency" had lost several vessels.[52]

Meanwhile, the Perkins claim had taken on a life of its own in the contentious relationship developing between Catacazy and members of the US Administration. While Stoeckl had dealt with the claim through denial, disagreement, and avoidance, Catacazy took an aggressive and offensive approach, one that brought him into direct conflict with Hamilton Fish and President Grant. Despite these complications, there were legitimate attempts to resolve the seemingly unending conflict. In 1870, the US government proposed mediation by mutually agreed-upon impartial persons and selected E. Peshine Smith, now legal advisor to the Department of State, to arbitrate the claim. Catacazy met with Smith and agreed to supply him with all relevant documents though, in Fish's estimation, the Russian minister's agenda was "to convince this

Govt. that Russia has good reasons for refusing to admit the claim." When Fish confronted Catacazy about this, he declared that Russia would fully consider the case, but emphasized that "Russia will not regard it as having any binding or judicial control over her own action."[53]

Smith delivered his second, and more detailed, assessment of the Perkins claim on May 9, 1871. He concluded that Stoeckl's request for proposals for the production and delivery of powder did not constitute a contract, but simply "the expression of a confident opinion as to the action of his Government, and of recommendation to Captain Perkins to put himself in condition to complete a profitable enterprise."[54] That Perkins and Kidder believed otherwise was unfortunate, but irrelevant. Smith believed that while Perkins had been misled "by facts and appearances which might well mislead prudent men of business," any obligation to Perkins relied solely on the conscience of the Russian government.[55] On the other hand, Smith believed the arms contract to be a valid one and supported Perkins's demands to be compensated for the losses deriving from this failed deal. The settlement of $200 with Lilienfeldt was a matter between two individuals, and Perkins did not need to expressly reserve his right to make claim against the Russian government; his right to do so was always there. Smith concluded, "I have arrived at the unhesitating conviction that Mrs. Perkins is entitled to remuneration for all that her husband lost in consequence of being deprived of the opportunity to fulfill his contract." The final amount in Smith's opinion was $285,625. Smith believed that to this sum should be added interest at 6 percent per annum from July 1, 1856, until the amount was paid.[56]

In a letter of June 26, 1871, Fish reported Smith's opinion to Andrew Curtin, US minister in Russia, instructing him to give Smith's conclusion to the Russian minister for foreign affairs, Prince Alexander Gorchakov, and express that the US government expected that this would solve the matter.[57] Six months later, Curtin forwarded the Russian government's response to this; Gorchakov declared that the report of Smith and the other documents in no way altered his opinion, adding, "It was only out of regard for the Federal Government that the Imperial Ministry consented to bring this question on the diplomatic ground … It has never intended to go further, and finds in the papers recently produced no reason for reviewing this decision."[58] He argued that the agreement for arms had been written to include a one-week probationary period and that Lilienfeldt's letter about his possible replacement was tantamount to an official cancellation and could only be overridden by a subsequent contract, which did not exist. Consequently, Gorchakov found the claims to be "without foundation, either legal or equitable, and consequently perfectly inadmissible," and he chided Curtin that if a Russian subject should charge the American government with a similar claim "so evidently devoid of proof, the Imperial Ministry would certainly have granted it no support."[59]

This was the last official exchange pertaining to the Perkins claim for nearly a decade. In the wake of the Catacazy scandal, Fish debated whether he should continue to press the Perkins claim with the Russian government and ultimately, he decided to let the matter drop.[60] The claim did resurface a number of years later. In a draft of a note to the Russian Legation in the United States sometime in 1881 Secretary of State James Blaine explained the history of the case and the reason for the Department of State's silence about the case over the last decade. First, "Mr. Catacazy's misconduct, much of it having reference to this case, had produced so much irritation that it became Mr. Fish's first duty not to stir the subject again unless absolutely necessary." He also referred to Stoeckl's promise to reexamine the case after the payment for Alaska.[61] Later, in 1886, the case was raised in the Senate once more, but the resolution appears to have had no result. The Perkins claim was never settled and it eventually disappeared, a little known blemish on the famous Alaska purchase and the much-hailed Russian-American friendship.

Despite its ultimate failure, however, the Perkins case had a much larger impact than anyone realized at the time. Throughout his short tenure as Russian minister to the United States, Catacazy was dealing with the Perkins case and it became the basis, in one way or another, for much of the conflict between him and the American government. Catacazy claimed, or actually believed, that the attorneys of the Perkins family were determined to have him removed from his position in an effort to improve their odds in winning the case. He blamed them for creating forgeries, planting news stories, and spreading rumors, all aimed at discrediting him and undermining his relationship with not only the American government but his own government as well. These accusations became the background music of all of Catacazy's interactions with the State Department, so much so that soon after his arrival in Washington, Secretary of State Hamilton Fish began to dread every interaction with the Russian minister.

"Two-Penny Machiavelli": The Early Life and Career of Constantin Catacazy

For all the notoriety that Constantin Catacazy would earn as a result of his time in the United States, we know very little about his life and career before he arrived on American soil. The Catacazy family were Phanariots, Greek nobles from the Phanar region of Constantinople, who served in important positions within the Ottoman Empire. Catacazy's ancestors fled to Russia at the end of the eighteenth century and found a place within the Russian diplomatic service. His father, Gavril Antonovich Catacazy, served at the Russian embassy in Constantinople, first as a lower official during the first years of the Greek War of Independence and later as a diplomatic aide to the commander of the Russian fleet during the famous Battle of Navarino (1827). In 1833, the Russian Foreign Office appointed Gavril as minister to the court of the Sultan. Here he apparently flourished, perhaps a little too much. Catacazy's home was described as one of the most hospitable in Athens, but he also had a reputation as a "born intriguer." According to one historian, "It appears from the material available that he often acted against the spirit of his instructions and gave a false impression of Russian intentions."[1] Consequently, in 1843, the Russian government recalled him after his alleged involvement in the conspiracy to oust the Greek king Otto.[2]

Born in 1830, Constantin followed in his father's footsteps in more ways than one. In 1848, after completing his education, he entered the Ministry of Foreign Affairs to serve in the Asiatic Department. At some point during these first years of service, Catacazy met and married Olga Fitz-James. The details of their early relationship vary and are hard to pin down. Some sources say they met in Rome; others say Brazil, where, in 1851, Catacazy was sent to serve as a secretary in the Russian Legation in Rio de Janeiro for a brief period.[3] At some point during this period, the two met and fell in love, and she either divorced her husband or ran off with Catacazy.[4] At any rate, when the Russian government appointed Catacazy to serve as secretary of the American Legation in Washington, DC, under Russian minister Alexander de Bodisco, he took Olga with him as his wife, though it is unclear when or if they were married. Nonetheless, Catacazy set Olga up in a cottage at Bladensburg, Maryland, about nine miles from Washington, an arrangement that lasted several years.[5] When Bodisco died in January 1854, Catacazy was called upon to serve as interim chargé d'affaires until Bodisco's replacement, Eduard de Stoeckl, arrived. From 1856 to 1859, Catacazy assumed the position of secretary to the Russian Legation in Hanover, but then King George V asked for his replacement for some reason and he was sent to Lisbon.[6] In 1869, Catacazy was appointed as the new minister to the United States. He arrived in Washington in mid-September and soon after met the two men in the American government who would come to play a critical role in his future—Secretary of State Hamilton Fish and President Ulysses S. Grant.[7]

By and large, contemporary accounts of Catacazy are not flattering.[8] In his book *Grant in Peace: From Appomattox to Mount McGregor, A Personal Memoir*, Adam Badeau, a Union Army officer who served with Grant and later as a diplomat in London and Havana, described Catacazy at length. Badeau was serving as secretary of the Legation in London when Catacazy received his appointment and so he had the opportunity to discuss the incoming diplomat with Baron Brunnow, the Russian minister in England. Brunnow painted a negative portrait of Catacazy, and it was clear that he did not like the man. Brunnow described him as "not high-born … but clever, after a fashion" with a "somewhat scandalous life." When Badeau met Catacazy in person, his own opinion of the Russian diplomat was equally low. Though Olga Catacazy was beautiful and graceful, her husband was "short, ugly, and scrubby." But it was Catacazy's insincerity that bothered Badeau most. His description is worth quoting in full:

> He was a man of effusive manners, professing great friendship and admiration for most of those he met, saying the most agreeable things, but without the art to make his hearers believe that his utterances were sincere. His flatteries were too fulsome, his falsehoods too plain. He was easy, but not elegant in behavior, smirked too much to be dignified, and there were few who admired, though many perceived, his phase of cleverness. He tried to make himself acceptable to everybody, entertained liberally, paid all his visits and social duties punctiliously, yet was unmistakably vulgar.[9]

Diplomatic agents like Catacazy were expected to represent their countries in a variety of capacities, but their main duties boiled down to three principal activities: negotiation, observation, and protection. It was the responsibility of the foreign minister to serve as the negotiator between his country and the country to which he was accredited, settling disagreements and pursuing the best arrangements in any matter of significance, financial or otherwise. He was responsible for observing and reporting on anything that might be of interest or importance to his home government, without, however, interfering in the internal matters of the country where he served. It was also his duty to protect citizens of his own nation residing in the host country from "acts of illegality and injustice." In addition to these primary duties, diplomatic representatives like Catacazy also performed other miscellaneous tasks. He could sign various documents on behalf of his country; register the births, deaths, and marriages of his fellow nationals; issue passports; and, in general, serve as a contact person and ombudsman for any and all matters concerning his country and its citizens abroad. He led a small delegation of men, a few secretaries and assistants, and a military attaché; he also maintained an archive of all official correspondence.[10] Though he represented his government and had a great deal of day-to-day autonomy, with the advent of telegraphic communication, regular instructions and feedback from his home government became increasingly important.[11]

Though Catacazy's time as minister in the United States was short, he dealt with a wide variety of matters. His reports to the court covered a broad array of subjects, including American foreign relations and domestic issues. According to American international law, communication from a foreign citizen to the United States government should only be received through their own country's representative; consequently, Catacazy was charged with receiving, assessing, and, if needed, communicating requests or concerns from Russian citizens to the Department of State.[12] Catacazy was also charged with facilitating the establishment of Orthodox churches in the United States and communicating with the church leaders in those establishments.[13] Finally, the Russian minister might also be called upon to see to the needs of its citizens at the end of life. On November 10, 1871, the *New York World* reported that Catacazy had attended and given a short address at the funeral of a Russian naval officer in Brooklyn. The young man had been attached to the Russian corvette *Vzadniff*, but had been forced to stay at the Naval Hospital due to his illness when his ship departed.[14] In the same vein, if a Russian died in the United States, Catacazy might be asked to assist in matters of inheritance.

Catacazy was also the point man for Americans looking to sell something to the Russian government. He received numerous letters from individuals who claimed to have unique or useful products and inventions about which the tsar might wish to know. Rutger B. Miller of Utica, New York, for example, wrote to

Catacazy about his invention that could turn the fibers of the epilobium plant into a substitute for cotton. He included a copy of his patent (No. 46922).[15] Others wrote with their own innovations, such as thicker armor on ironclads or new breech-loading rifles, or offers of other weapons or artificial limbs.[16] John M. Kinney of Columbus, Ohio, wrote to the Russian minister with the following emphatic appeal for consideration: after fifteen years of trial and error, Kinney had succeeded in perfecting a system by which he could "inflate balloons, of immense capacity, in a very few minutes, and at a trifling expense, which makes the process valuable, for Army Reconnoitering purposes" (underline in original source).[17] It was Catacazy's responsibility to receive and respond to all of these letters. He also managed appeals from Americans who declared that the Russian government owed them money. In January 1870, he told Fish that someone named Van Cort from the state of New York had written to him about a claim against Russia in compensation for an invention of some sort, though Fish did not record the nature of the claim.[18]

It was also the minister's job to pursue and defend Russia's best interests in trade and other matters. One of the first issues that Catacazy raised with Fish after his arrival was the duty on Russian hemp, which he deemed unfair, being higher than that levied on Manila hemp. Subsequently, the duty was indeed lowered.[19] The Russian minister was also responsible for protecting the reputation of his country in various ways, such as notifying the American government and the American public when schemers and swindlers pretending to represent Russia or Russian goods were on the make. In October 1869, for example, Catacazy informed Fish that "some shares of the Credit Foncier of Poland, which had been burglariously stolen from the Bank of Warsaw in 1863" (when the Poles unsuccessfully rebelled against Russia) were being sold on the New York Stock Exchange. He urged Fish to warn the American public and "disclaimed in advance all responsibility on the part of the Imperial Government with regard to any claims which might be brought by the holders or purchasers of these shares." Fish had this information published soon after.[20]

Along with all of these responsibilities, foreign ministers had certain rights and privileges. They possessed diplomatic immunity in criminal and civil matters, though if they engaged in private business certain aspects of this immunity could be overridden. If the foreign representative chose to participate in the judiciary process of the host country without invoking his immunity, or "if he himself sets the machinery of justice in motion, … In such cases he must bear the judicial consequences of his action."[21] Their family members and personal effects, and those of their family, were exempt from "seizure, arrest, or molestation," so long as they did not harbor criminals or those fleeing justice. Diplomatic representatives could not be compelled to testify in American courts. They were permitted to import goods without the normal duties, and Catacazy and his wife took advantage of this last guarantee. In July 1871, Catacazy received word that a shipment of silk dresses from Brussels for his wife, as well as "ten cases of champagnes and one case of cigars imported from Havre and Havana" had been received and "in compliance with your [Catacazy's] request the Collector of Customs at New York has been instructed to admit free of duty."[22] Finally, it was understood that foreign ministers should be treated with respect and protected from libel.[23]

There were, however, certain things that a foreign minister was explicitly warned against doing. Representatives of foreign states had the right to appeal to the government to which they were accredited, but it was established as early as 1795 that a foreign minister should never endeavor "by an address to the people, oral or written, to forestall a depending measure, or to defeat one which has been decided." It was also a serious "impropriety" to publish any sort of criticism against the government of the country in which he resided as representative. Diplomatic correspondence was always to be considered confidential, and publication of correspondence between the secretary of state and a foreign minister would be an "improper act." Finally, there was an expectation that foreign ministers would refrain from political interference in the host country.[24] Constantin Catacazy ignored these well-established principles and consequently not long after his arrival found himself at odds with the American government. His tactlessness and refusal to maintain a diplomatic silence in personal and professional disagreements would be his undoing.

3

"The Intermeddling of the Russian Minister"

On July 12, 1869, Hamilton Fish casually recorded in his diary that Waldemar de Bodisco, secretary of the Russian Legation and nephew of the former Russian minister, Alexander de Bodisco, had informed him of the appointment of Constantin Catacazy as Russian minister to the United States. It was an unremarkable entry in a diary filled with the mostly tedious details of a top-level bureaucrat. Fish could never have imagined on that hot summer day that only two years later he would be arguing for the recall and removal of that same minister.[1] The story of how Constantin Catacazy went from sanctioned foreign envoy to despised diplomat is a complicated one and encompasses rumors and gossip, intrigue and self-interest, bruised egos and breaches of protocol.

Constantin Catacazy departed for the United States in late summer 1869. On his way from St. Petersburg, he made a brief stop in Paris where he met with Elihu B. Washburne, the current American minister to France. Catacazy took this opportunity to embark immediately upon one of his assigned tasks as Russian envoy, the settlement of the Perkins claim. Washburne, who had served as the secretary of state immediately before Fish, expressed his disdain for the claim and encouraged the Russian minister to discuss the matter with President Grant in person.[2] Leaving Paris, Catacazy completed his journey, arriving in Washington in mid-September. He took up residence on I Street, and on September 19, 1869, called on Secretary of State Hamilton Fish to present his official papers and arrange a meeting with the president.[3] Neither Fish nor Grant recorded any initial impressions of Catacazy, but Fish did receive correspondence from the American minister at St. Petersburg, Andrew Curtin, that hinted at potential problems. Curtin informed Fish that Catacazy was a close friend of the Russian foreign minister, Prince Alexander Gorchakov, so much so that "he was more with the Prince than any other person in St. Petersburg and not little surprise is expressed here that the Prince should send him abroad." Curtin felt certain that

Gorchakov's choice of Catacazy for the Russian Legation in America had some larger significance, but he could not yet determine what that might be.[4]

By late November, Catacazy was settling into his new life in Washington. He relocated the legation of the Russian government to the lovely mansion on I Street near Fourteenth Street, after having it properly outfitted with decorations imported from Russia.[5] In early February, the *Washington Daily Morning Chronicle* reported that the Catacazys were participating in the social scene of the city, an important aspect of every diplomat's life. Not only had they attended a state dinner given by the president, but Mrs. Catacazy had given an afternoon reception deemed "brilliant in every sense of the word." The Catacazy home was packed with gentlemen and lady callers, including Fish and his wife, and the hostess received her guests with "a grace and hearty cordiality that added greatly to the ease and good feeling of those present."[6] On New Year's Day, 1870, the Russian minister attended the festivities at the White House, "resplendent in garments and decorations."[7]

Beneath the glistening veneer of Washington society, however, Catacazy's approach to fulfilling his diplomatic duties was already causing problems. The Perkins claim was one of these issues, and it was clearly not one that would easily disappear. In January 1870, Curtin relayed to Fish that in a recent meeting with Gorchakov the Prince had raised the subject of the claim, denouncing it strongly and expressing regret that the American government had taken any notice of it. Curtin asked Fish for guidance on how to respond to these comments, adding, however, "in my opinion nothing can change the judgment of the Prince even if a refusal to pay it should disturb the friendship of nations."[8] At the same time, Catacazy asked Fish if he could speak with the secretary of the treasury about the payment of the interest on the Alaska purchase money, though he subsequently made clear that if pursuing payment would be linked to the Perkins claim, then he wished to postpone any discussion of it.[9] In the following month, Catacazy's request became known publicly. An article in the *National Republican* relayed the long history of the Perkins affair and was indignant that Catacazy had inquired about interest on the late payment of the Alaska purchase while his own government had failed to follow through on an examination of the Perkins case. The paper challenged the Russian government that "If there is true friendship … let it be shown in deeds, and not in empty words." The *Republican* did, however, also criticize the Russian minister directly, stating, "It cannot be truthfully said that Mr. Catacazy has at all enhanced the good feeling of the American people towards the Imperial Government since his advent into this country."[10]

In early March, the situation grew worse when J. B. Stewart, one of the attorneys for the widow Perkins, made several scathing accusations against Catacazy. First, he claimed to possess correspondence between Catacazy and his government in which the Russian minister insulted the men involved in the Perkins case. According to Stewart, the letters had been acquired and translated by L. F. Tasistro, the translator for the Department of State, who was reluctant to divulge his sources, but had agreed with the secretary of state forthwith to discuss the origins of the documents. In addition, Stewart claimed that Catacazy had intentionally omitted relevant documents when transmitting information on the claim back to St. Petersburg. Stewart made all of these accusations in writing and gave them to President Grant, who passed them on to Fish.[11] Stewart apologized for bothering Fish, but added that he felt it necessary to take extra precautions, "when dealing with a gentleman like Mr. Catacazy who, respects no rule, or law."[12]

Fish initially doubted that the supposed dispatches could be real, but they were certainly troubling.[13] In this correspondence, Gorchakov had chastised Catacazy for the "uneasiness" that his actions with regard to the Perkins claim had caused the emperor and scolded him for not following instructions or adhering to the "prescribed line of conduct." In his response to this dressing down, Catacazy replied in a sharp and insubordinate tone, insisting that he had done his best to resolve the "Perkins Swindle." But, he declared,

> when I found myself surrounded on every side by robbers, schemers and traitors—when I found the most disreputable men in America, outlaws from society, resorting to bribes of the most daring character in order to command the influence of demoralized members of Congress, and that lacking, even then to inoculate the Minister of State with views of their perfidious ideas, they had recourse to newspaper slanders, vilifying the Government and the character of my most Gracious Sovereign. ... I deemed it my duty, as a faithful servant and subject, to counteract these infamous proceedings by setting a system of investigation on foot, which has enabled me to unmask the would be plunderers of the Imperial Government.

Catacazy also directly attacked the character of the secretary of state; whatever Fish now said, the letter stated, he had earlier given Catacazy reason to believe that he had "no confidence in the validity of the claim" and had even recommended an attorney to assist in defeating "the schemes of these unprincipled speculators." Over many meetings, Catacazy claimed, Fish had given him "indications of unbounded sympathy." He was a "very weak and vacillating man," however, and this explained his recent about-face.[14]

Even as this tempest began brewing, another set of documents appeared that fanned the flames higher. The *Washington Daily Morning Chronicle* published two pieces of correspondence in full between Catacazy and Cassius Clay in which the men discussed the Perkins claim. Clay, who had been the American minister to Russia from 1861 to 1862 and again from 1863 to 1869, stated unequivocally that there was not "a shadow of a legal claim" against the government of Russia. Moreover, Clay believed that the United States should not attempt to link payment of the interest on the Alaska purchase to a reconsideration of the Perkins matter. Catacazy insisted that the Russian government would be sure to pay the claim if it was genuine, but emphasized Russia's desire to take a firm stand against swindlers of all sorts and to avoid setting a dangerous precedent. Catacazy also noted that his government abstained from supporting petitions against the American government, of which there were many. Catacazy also took issue with the news article that had accused him of presenting a claim for the interest on the Alaska purchase. Catacazy denied this, but in what would soon become a familiar pattern, he also admitted he had "called the attention of the Secretary of State to the fact of the non-payment of the money for a period of over two months subsequent to the time stipulated for such payment in the treaty."[15]

Catacazy would later admit to Gorchakov that he had allowed his correspondence with Clay to be published to demonstrate that "we have the most serious and the most valid motives to repel fraudulent pretensions."[16] He admitted his actions to Fish as well, and Fish replied with an admonishment that should have squashed any future attempts by Catacazy at newspaper diplomacy:

> In several instances since the establishment of this government we have felt hurt by similar appeals to the public from diplomatic representatives of foreign powers. We have complained of them accordingly contending that if a foreign government accredit diplomatic agents to the government of the United States it is expected that its business will be transacted by those agents through this Department, and it is hoped that they will abstain from discussion in the newspapers subjects which are under the official consideration of the two Governments.[17]

On March 13, Fish and Catacazy met in person and Catacazy declared the supposed dispatches to be outright forgeries. Fish documented this conversation with a follow-up letter and asked that Catacazy answer for the record whether he (Fish) had ever expressed "a want of confidence in the validity of the Perkins Claim, or … pronounced it unworthy of serious consideration, or have in any way disparaged or questioned the claim."[18] Catacazy responded immediately, repeating his denials, and expressed a "feeling of disgust and indignation" about the "calumnious and gratuitous absurdities" attributed to him. He pointed a finger at the counsel for the widow Perkins, adding, "One is able to judge of the worth of a case by the methods which those who defend it employ."[19] Several days later, Catacazy wrote to Gorchakov about all that had occurred, the alleged dispatches, and his meeting with Fish. He further described how Fish suggested that the Perkins case be examined by a small committee selected by the involved parties. Catacazy saw this as a change in tone, noting that this was "the first time that Mr. H. Fish has shown himself willing to give up arbitration." Catacazy apologized for the prolixity of his letter, but explained that such detail was necessary in conveying "the profane immorality of the American milieu."[20]

Though Catacazy denied the veracity of the alleged dispatches, and Fish seemed to accept his denial, the matter of the slanderous correspondence continued. There were many questions to be answered and a number of names came to the fore as possible participants. Catacazy continued to push for the disclosure of the individual responsible, asking Fish to assist him. The Russian minister was certain that Stewart was behind it all, claiming that the corrupt attorney had boasted publicly in the bar of the Arlington Hotel that he had succeeded "to break the neck of that infernal Russian Minister."[21] Meanwhile, Waldemar de Bodisco was eager to clarify that he had no part in the creation or the conveyance of the dispatches and knew nothing about them, communicating this to Fish in a memorandum of April 1870.[22] The memo recounted an interview at the instigation of Bodisco with Louis Tasistro, an attorney named Frank Turk, and another man. Bodisco confronted Tasistro with the following question: was it true that he (Tasistro) had told Hamilton Fish that he had received the questionable dispatches from Bodisco with a request for translation? (The source of this information was the Russian Minister Catacazy.) Tasistro denied having said this to Fish or anyone else, confirmed that Bodisco had nothing to do with the despatches as far as he knew, and offered to put these statements in writing. He claimed to be at a loss as to how this false premise had been created and expressed his intention to see the secretary of state to discuss it with him.[23] Bodisco's denial of involvement was backed up by other sources as well. Frank Turk also composed a memorandum concerning the matter, relaying his own conversation with J. B. Stewart. The attorney for Mrs. Perkins declared that while the dispatches were certainly genuine, he knew who had furnished them and it was not Bodisco, nor did he have any role in their production whatsoever.[24]

Information about the dispatches came from Russia as well. The American Minister Curtin informed Fish that Gorchakov emphatically declared that the dispatches were forgeries, and Curtin believed him. Curtin also had attempted to discuss Catacazy's other behavior, especially his "indiscreet and violent denunciations of citizens of the United States." He failed in this endeavor, however. Curtin complained of Catacazy's publication of his correspondence with Clay, a sentiment Gorchakov shared, and Curtin confessed he did not share the foreign minister's "warm personal regard" for Catacazy. Curtin noted, moreover, that he had discovered that Catacazy's appointment as minister "was not generally accepted with satisfaction or regarded as proper here." In addition, Curtin accused Catacazy of inaccurately reporting conversations and developments in the Perkins claim to Gorchakov. Echoing a concern already expressed by the Perkins attorneys, Curtin declared, "I am quite sure that the coloring given to that and to the other conversations with you and to the attendant circumstances in Mr. Catacazy's letter to the Prince is quite different from the facts as stated in your confidential letter to me." He added, "I deeply regret that Prince Gorchakov has prejudices as strongly settled against the Perkins claim, and in his friendship and confidence accepts the statements of Mr. Catacazy." Finally, Curtin reported that there was a feeling in both diplomatic and official circles that troubles were beginning to arise between the Russian and American governments.[25]

By the fall of 1870, then, no progress had been made in resolving the Perkins claim and Catacazy held firm that the case had no merit. Meanwhile, another crisis connected to the Crimean War was approaching that would temporarily overshadow all else.

Catacazy and the Black Sea Question

The "Black Sea Question," the debate over control of and passage through the Bosporus and Dardanelles straits that lay within the territory of the Ottoman Empire and determined access to the Black Sea, became part of the tale of Catacazy's missteps in the United States. It was one of the most important issues for Russia and Great Britain in their diplomatic relations in the nineteenth century. Russia had for centuries longed for a southern outlet to the sea and the maintenance of a fleet on its southern shores, yet a fleet on the Black Sea meant nothing without the ability to navigate through the straits to open waters. The British, for their part, needed to protect their traditional route to India and points beyond, and their overall dominance of the seas. During the fifteenth through eighteenth centuries, the Ottoman Empire's policy had been to keep all ships except its own out of the Black Sea. In 1774, it agreed to allow Russian commercial ships through the straits, but the first agreement pertaining to vessels of war was in 1809. This agreement between Great Britain and the Ottoman Empire supported the notion that warships of all nations should be prohibited from passing through the straits in times of peace. Access to the straits subsequently became a central concern in negotiations and treaties on at least three occasions between 1829 and 1841. The Crimean War of 1853–6 between Russia and the Ottoman Empire, backed by Great Britain, France, and Piedmont-Sardinia, made a resolution on the straits necessary yet again.[26]

In 1856, the Crimean War concluded with the Treaty of Paris. Two of the treaty's thirty-four articles would prove to be the source of irritation and debate for the following decade and a half. This first of these clauses specifically stated, "The Black Sea is Neutralised; its Waters and its Ports, thrown to the Mercantile Marine of every Nation, are formally and in perpetuity interdicted to the Flag of War, either of the Powers possessing its Coasts, or of any other Power, with the exceptions mentioned in Articles XIV and XIX of the present Treaty." In essence, the clause prohibited all nations from keeping war vessels in the Black Sea and from maintaining naval vessels on its coasts. A subsequent article in the treaty further elaborated that since the Black Sea was now to be neutralized, "the maintenance or establishment upon its Coast of Military-Maritime Arsenals becomes alike unnecessary and purposeless" for either the Emperor of Russia or the Sultan of the Ottoman Empire.[27] For Russia, who felt it necessary for security reasons to have a southern fleet, these clauses were devastating and perceived as an insult to their honor. Over the next fourteen years, the Black Sea Question became a part of any European conflict, even those seemingly unrelated to that issue.[28]

Never happy about these restrictions, Russia waited for the chance to push for revision, and in the following years, both Austria and France indicated that they would consider abrogating the offensive clauses, but they were also unwilling to alienate England. The British government, of course, was too concerned about the security of its own navy in the region and Russia's interest in the fate of the Ottoman Empire to agree to any changes. There was a moment in the fall of 1866 when Alexander II and Minister of Foreign Affairs Prince Alexander Gorchakov contemplated an open denunciation of the despised Black Sea clauses, but they decided that the timing was not yet right for such a bold move and chose to wait for a better opportunity.[29] That opportunity came in the fall of 1870 when France and Prussia went to war. At that propitious moment, on October 19, Gorchakov issued a circular to Russia's principal ministers abroad, particularly the signatory powers of the treaty, stating that Russia could no longer be bound by the objectionable Black Sea terms. The Russian newspaper *Golos* announced the news with great enthusiasm, declaring that this was "the first step, after many years, of the freeing of Russia from the guardianship of the West." Henceforth, Russia would determine its own fate and would no longer play the role of "the shy student of foreign teachers."[30]

Russia's sudden declaration raised significant concerns in a number of countries, though no one was particularly surprised by its content so much as its timing and manner. The American minister to Greece Charles Tuckerman reported that everyone there assumed that this was a "first step … towards the ultimate absorption by Russia of the European provinces now subject to Turkey."[31] Wayne MacVeagh, the US minister to Turkey, disagreed. He believed that Russia would "have sufficient wisdom to restrain her claims within moderate limits … they well know that time is their most efficient ally."[32] Michael Cramer, the American representative in Denmark, noted a tone of smug satisfaction in the Danish press, where there appeared to be much delight at England's predicament. Quoting from several newspapers, Cramer indicated that Danish public opinion was that England's diplomacy had been short-sighted and it was getting what it deserved. After manifesting so much enthusiasm for the unification of Germany, the island nation would now realize that Germany served as "a bulwark for Russia, and that the great Bismarck, before whom they have prostrated themselves in the dust, participated in plans which threaten England as an Asiatic Power."[33] Moreover, one paper asked, "What would England say, if the United States were to seize this favorable opportunity for the settlement of the Alabama Question and were to signify the same to the English Government in a Note 'a la Gortshakoff?' "[34]

In fact, Great Britain did bristle at Gorchakov's announcement, particularly its tone of fait accompli; in the words of British Foreign Secretary Earl Granville, the problem with Russia's stance was that it was "not a request to those Governments for the consideration of the case, but an announcement to them that it has emancipated itself, or holds itself emancipated, from any stipulations of the treaty." Russia could not, in the view of many British officials, release itself from a treaty on its own, without the agreement of the other signatory powers. It was an offense to a generally recognized rule of international law. British fears about Russian encroachment into India and Afghanistan only intensified the matter. Within a few short days of the announcement, the British press began to declare that the government must not cave in to this obnoxious demand, some even recommending that Great Britain issue an ultimatum to Russia.[35] For a brief period, war between Russia and Britain seemed possible and a split in the British Cabinet over the issue threatened the stability of that government.[36] The British Prime Minister William Gladstone, however, remained cool-headed in the face of this challenge and would not allow his country to be baited into a war.[37]

In Washington, Hamilton Fish recorded in his diary that Catacazy believed that the telegram he had received about the renunciation was in error. He told Fish "that the Black Sea is a secondary consideration with Russia, who does not hesitate to declare that the Treaty of 1856 limiting her Territory &c., is already abrogated by the action of other parties thereto, altering the limits of their territories since 1856." The Russian minister declared that the Treaty of Paris had been designed to protect a balance of power in Europe, but since that time Italy has become a unified nation and the northern German states had joined together as well. Russia had not opposed either of these significant alterations, but "declares that they invalidated the arrangements under the Treaty of 1856 & that whenever in her judgment the proper time shall have arrived, she will openly set aside that Treaty."[38] Three days later, Catacazy called on Fish again and revealed a bit more of his hand. In this meeting, the Russian minister linked the Black Sea Question to the *Alabama* claims and reminded the secretary of state of the long-standing friendship of Russia and the United States. Though he did not say it directly, Catacazy recognized that Russia and the United States could both benefit from the current situation. If the United States pressed the *Alabama* claims now, Britain might feel sufficiently threatened to concede, while also backing down from any possible retaliation to the Russian declaration about the Black Sea. Fish described in his diary that Catacazy "professes not to have any information beyond what is public; dwells upon the intimate relations of Russia & the U. S. & that now is the time for the U. S. to settle the Alabama claims; speaks of co-operation with Russia; the freedom of the Black Sea; our interest in the principle involved therein." Fish added, "The interview impresses me with a conviction of his apprehension of a rupture between Russia & England."[39] Meanwhile, in a draft note to Gorchakov in late November 1870, Catacazy gave a significantly different version of his conversations with Fish: "America would profit from Anglo-Russian conflict to push Alabama claim. Result of talks with Fish: possibility of defensive offensive alliance with us, and sending of squadron in Black Sea. Tomorrow Council of Ministers to decide possible resolutions. Ask for telegraphic instructions."[40] Though Fish's diary mentions no possibility of an alliance emerging from these circumstances, Catacazy clearly believed the moment was right to explore this option, or wanted his superiors to believe that he was making progress in that direction.

There were, indeed, fears that the United States might support Russia's claims, directly or indirectly. In 1867, many in Europe feared that the Alaska purchase and the evolving Russian-American relationship that it foretold was a portent of bad things to come. Edward Joy Morris, the American minister to Constantinople, reported to Seward that the major powers of Europe feared a Russian-American alliance; it was a "spectre that oppresses them & haunts their thoughts by day and their dreams by night."[41] European newspapers had reported on these concerns about what the strengthening of the Russian-American affairs might mean. William Murphy, the American consul at Frankfort on Main, reported that while the liberal press of Europe dispassionately viewed the sale as a mutually beneficial agreement between the two countries, the conservative press felt "very uneasy and vexed." In their eyes, the low selling price hinted that there would be "other compensations … either actual assistance on the part of the United States, in case she might require such for the satisfaction of her ambitions on another scene of action, or passive garantee [sic] upon the demand of some territorial changes on European soil."[42]

Similarly, as the dispute over the Black Sea resurfaced in 1870, there were fears about American involvement. The *National Republican* reported that in the "official circles of Vienna" there was a strong belief that in the event of a war between Russia and Great Britain, "the moral support of the United States will be given Russia."[43] The United States, of course, had no dog in this fight, but that did not prevent the rumor mill from spreading misinformation. The American press hinted that the United States might offer support to Russia. Curtin told Fish that there were "various newspaper reports and communications from Washington circulated here … that the President had written an autograph letter to the Emperor offering the United States fleet to assist in passing the Dardanelles."[44] The American minister assured the secretary of state that he had made every effort to dispel these notions and had "uniformly stated that my Government does not wish to become engaged in European disputes and would always remain neutral in case of a European war."[45] But Curtin was concerned. He reported that he had heard from a variety of reliable sources that Catacazy had telegraphed to the Russian government that "the President told him that in case of a war between England and Russia the US Government would at once send a large fleet into the [sic] sea and to Constantinople." Moreover, Catacazy had reported that there had been a long cabinet meeting to discuss the possibility of a defensive or offensive alliance with Russia.[46] The rumor apparently made its way into the St. Petersburg papers as well.[47] Again, Catacazy seemed to be reporting things that were not true.

In fact, Grant had issued a proclamation of neutrality on August 22, 1870, only a few months earlier at the beginning of the Franco-Prussian War that clearly stated the United States was invoking the "neutrality law" of April 1818, the precursor to the Monroe Doctrine. On October 8, 1870, Grant reiterated these principles in a second proclamation that focused on the use of American waters by armed ships of the warring nations and declared such activity "unfriendly and offensive, and forbidden." The following month, the *New York Evening Post* reported that although Russia hoped that the United States would participate in any peace negotiations that might transpire from the Franco-Prussian War, "There is no doubt that should a European Congress assemble, the Administration will decline to send representatives, in order to avoid placing itself and the United States government into a position so contrary to well-established precedents of American policy."[48]

While publicly the US government declared its intent to remain neutral in European affairs, privately there were many who sympathized with the Russian cause concerning the Black Sea. The *New York World* commented, for example, that Russia's demands were "founded on reason and right."[49] In December 1870, Curtin wrote to Fish, "Apart from the manner in which the Imperial Government abrogated the obnoxious article of the Treaty of Paris, there are sufficient reasons for all that is demanded by Russia, aside from a degradation a great and powerful nation could no longer suffer."[50] In fact, there were those in the Department of State who wondered if the United States should comment on the unfolding situation. A memo that appeared in December 1870 asked, "Is it expedient for the United States directly or indirectly to make known to the proposed conference at London a wish or expectation that no impediment or limitation to the passage of the Dardanelles and the Bosphorus by men of war under their flag will be imposed or continued?" The unknown author of the memo added that American participation in a European conference should only occur if "some great interest or right" was at stake.[51]

In Russia, the general feeling was one of uncertainty. The Russian newspaper *Golos*, for example, criticized the English press for its false bravado, its declarations that its people were ready to shed blood once again.[52] Eugene Schuyler, the secretary of the American Legation in St. Petersburg, disagreed with that view. Writing to his sister, Eva, in mid-November 1870, he acknowledged that many people believed that England and Austria might declare war over the Black Sea debate, but he did not believe it would come to that. "England is not very bellicose," he observed, "and sees how bad a thing a war is just now by the example of France." Still, he warned her that if war occurred, he would not be able to return home in time for her wedding.[53] Just a few weeks later, Schuyler seemed more alarmed: "Here the talk is of nothing but war and how to stop it or prevent it. War with France, war with England, war with America."[54] Curtin echoed his secretary's sense of unease. The people of Russia supported the rejection of the clauses, Gorchakov had told Curtin. Russia's failed efforts in previous years to free itself from the Black Sea clauses had been felt as a "degradation of the national honor" and Russia was now determined to remain firm in its demand, the emperor having "consented to a conference only to preserve peace." Having finally taken such a bold step, Gorchakov reported, the emperor "was like another man … and was perfectly happy and determined to go to any extremity to maintain all he has assumed by his action."[55]

Indeed, more than one diplomat spoke of the possibility of war. In London, the US Minister John Lothrop Motley declared that there was great anxiety about the conflict over the Russian declaration leading to a general European war. Motley added that the British were particularly nervous about "the sentiments of the United States Government at this juncture. … Its attitude will be watched with much interest."[56] Michael Cramer reported from his post in Denmark in November 1870 that the Queen of Denmark herself had expressed to him her apprehensions about the outbreak of a "general war." Both Cramer and the Queen recognized that Russia had strategically selected the crisis between France and Prussia as the moment to renounce the offensive clauses.[57] In early January 1871, Cramer stated that the possibility of war was still being discussed in the political circles of Denmark.[58]

In the end, war was averted and the question was smoothed over by an international conference held in London in early 1871, with representatives from Russia, Great Britain, the Ottoman Empire, Prussia, Austria, Italy, and France. The incident left Russia looking a bit untrustworthy, however. The *London Times*, for example, noted some months later that while Russian newspapers assured the world of the peaceful policies of the current tsar, Alexander II, in truth, "The most powerful of Czars cannot shake himself free from the historical accompaniments of his position, and the Emperors of Russia will for years to come be tempted by offers of hostile combinations for securing whatever they are supposed to covet."[59]

The Alabama Claims

The Russian denunciation of the Black Sea clauses in October 1870 had another result as well; it created yet another opportunity for Catacazy to meddle in the resolution of the *Alabama* claims, a protracted and heated dispute between the United States and Great Britain that had roots in the American Civil War. Though Great Britain had been officially neutral in the conflict, many British merchants did business with the Confederacy, even selling warships to the Confederate government. The most notorious example was the *Alabama*, an ironclad built in Liverpool in 1862. For two years, the warship terrorized the seas, confiscating goods and burning sixty-five ships headed to or from the North, before being sunk off the coast of France. Subsequently, the United States accused Britain of failing to enforce its own laws of neutrality and perhaps even prolonging the war and demanded reparations.[60]

The negotiations to find a settlement for the *Alabama* claims were already underway when Catacazy arrived as minister to the United States in the fall of 1869. Catacazy, like other Russian officials, recognized that a decline in Anglo-American relations could benefit Russia. And indeed, the disagreement over the question of British liability and the reparations that went along with an admission of guilt created enormous tensions between the United States and Great Britain. In the spring of 1869, Senator Zachariah Chandler of Michigan had proposed that Great Britain cede Canada to the United States as payment for the claims, an idea that had growing popular support over the winter of 1869–70.[61] There had been, in fact, annexation movements in various parts of British North America over the previous two decades, so the idea was not entirely without some foundation. British fears about these movements, combined with worries about American expansionism and the weak economy of the Canadian provinces, had encouraged the process of Canadian Confederation. On March 29, 1867, the day before the Alaska treaty was signed, Queen Victoria approved the British North America Act; the Dominion of Canada came into existence on July 1, 1867, comprising four provinces: Ontario, Quebec, New Brunswick, and Nova Scotia. Nonetheless, as the *Alabama* claims conflict intensified, there were those in America who still thought that cession of British North America would be appropriate compensation for Civil War losses. Meanwhile, disagreements over American vessels illegally fishing in Canadian inshore waters or landing for restocking food, ice, and bait complicated British-American relations.[62]

During this period of preliminary negotiations, Catacazy seemed thoroughly to enjoy the discomfort between the two nations. In November 1870, Fish wrote in his diary of Catacazy's interest in the progress of the dispute, specifically his question, "if there be any truth in the telegram from London published this morning of instructions having been sent to Moran to press the Alabama Claims." Fish believed the Russian minister was "on the lookout for complications for Gt. Britain & in his insidious, but most insincere way, endeavors to persuade me that a great opportunity presents for their Adjustment. It is a pity that one can never trust Catacazy or believe a word he says."[63] Soon, however, Catacazy went far beyond insincere conversations with the secretary of state.

On November 29, 1870, an article entitled "Russia and America" appeared in the *World* that announced a rupture in Russian-American relations over the *Alabama* claims, citing its proof as the "cold and distant" attitude of Russia and the complete withdrawal of the Russian representative from official and social visits to both Grant and Fish. In explaining the cause of this rift, the unnamed author assured his readers that his information was unquestionable and came from the most reliable source. The article declared that before renouncing the Black Sea Clause, the Russian Government had asked its representatives to sound out not only the likely reactions of the other European nations but also the attitude of the United States, not because they might offer material support but because their dispute with England would likely prevent the latter from entering into a war with Russia. Catacazy, then, had been instructed to find out if the United States was planning to press the *Alabama* claims or would wait until the Black Sea crisis had passed. The question could not be put directly to Grant or Fish through diplomatic channels, the author claimed, because the Russian government had developed a "great distrust of the present administration on account of its weak foreign policy." As it happened, Grant replied to an inquisitive reporter that he intended to keep the United States out of the affairs of another country according to the Monroe Doctrine, a statement that was subsequently published all over the country. Catacazy, of course, shared this news with his government, which was then inclined to take a "much firmer tone in the exposition of her views" on the Treaty of Paris and redoubling its preparations for war. Soon after, the article explained, Catacazy found out that the United States was postponing its pursuance of the *Alabama* claims, a decision that Russia perceived as sympathy for England and "an uncalled for and unwarrantable violation of the implicit understanding of neutrality … a direct and gratuitous insult [to Russia]." According to the author's unnamed source, "American credit in Russia suffered in an instant a severe if not fatal blow, from the effects of which it will take years of the most conciliatory policy to recover."[64]

The day after the article "Russia and America" appeared, Fish met with Grant and relayed its contents, particularly those parts that claimed to represent his words. Grant confirmed some of the statements, recalling that while on a walk recently he had been approached by a reporter who asked if the rumors were true that the United States might delay the claims against England, but that he had told the reporter that such stories were "pure fiction" and refused to engage in further conversation. Both Fish and Grant suspected that Catacazy was behind the gossip, and the president asked his secretary of state to question the Russian minister on the matter. Fish felt that the effort would be pointless: "The difficulty with this Course is that Catacazy will of course deny. The more he may have had to do with writing or inspiring the letter, the more vehement and profuse will be his protestations to the contrary. He is not to be believed & is tortuous & intriguing & a thorough mischief maker."[65]

Of course, ongoing rumors of American support for Russia concerned Great Britain. On December 14, the British representative in Russia Andrew Buchanan reported to London that various European and American newspapers "have lately contained articles from which it might be inferred that in the event of a war between Gt Britain and Russia, the Govt of the Emperor will find a willing and powerful ally in the Govt of the United States and it is said that the reports of the Russian Minister at Washington encourage such an expectation."[66] A week later, Buchanan again addressed the talk about war, referring to "a letter alleged to have been addressed to the Emperor by President Grant offering to His Majesty the co-operation of the United States in the event of a war between England and Russia." Though he did not consider the report to be credible, he spoke with Curtin nonetheless. The American minister assured him that even if such a letter had been written by the president, it could not have been delivered to the emperor without his knowledge or involvement, and that he considered the report to be "an absurd invention of the Petersburg correspondent of a foreign newspaper." Buchanan concluded his letter with the following assessment: "it appears to be desirable as far as the interests of G Britain are concerned, that the Emperor should no longer be represented at Washington by a minister so entirely discredited and without influence as Mr. Catacazy."[67]

Preliminary negotiations for the *Alabama* claims dragged on until January 1871 when both parties agreed to settle the claims through a representative commission. On February 27, 1871, the members of the Joint High Commission met in the library of the State Department for the first time. At this point, rumors mushroomed that the Russian minister was attempting to derail the settlement. Catacazy denied any meddling, but Fish believed he was guilty of the charge. Only a week earlier, Fish had confronted Catacazy about his loose lips. Referring to the talk of "little birds," Fish told Catacazy, "the little bird says you have been making yourself unnecessarily occupied with the affairs between this country & Great Britain in connection with the Commission about to assemble & the owl says 'that perhaps it may be well to observe a little more caution.'" Catacazy swore that he had only spoken to one or two people about it, but Fish noted in his diary that he had heard from various sources that Catacazy was talking about it all over town.[68]

Fish was not alone in believing that Catacazy was interfering. Buchanan wrote to the British foreign secretary, Lord Granville, concerning the reports that Grant was in touch with Tsar Alexander about "a more intimate alliance with Russia and of sending a fleet to the Mediterranean with a view to its eventually forcing the passage of the Dardanelles." Curtin assured Buchanan that there was no such agreement and attributed the misinformation to Catacazy. To reassure Buchanan, he had shared with him a letter from Fish in which the secretary of state spoke at some length of Catacazy's misdeeds and unreliability. Buchanan explained to Granville that Catacazy had for some time blamed many of his troubles on his enemies, but added that "Mr. Fish remarks that no-one could have injured him more effectually than he has himself by his intrigues, and the conduct and language which have deprived him of the confidence of the American Govt."[69] The American minister also told Buchanan that judging from Gorchakov's statements in a recent meeting, Catacazy was giving a significantly different version of his interactions with Fish than the secretary of state had relayed.[70] Ultimately, however, Buchanan recognized that Catacazy's shenanigans worked to Great Britain's advantage, offering that "I was careful not to tell him [Curtin] that I hardly expected Y. L. wd. take any steps that might lead to the recall of an Agent who perverse activity is apparently so useful in damaging the prestige of Russia in the United States."[71]

On May 8, 1871, the Treaty of Washington was signed and ratified by the US Senate two weeks later. Between June and December, both countries prepared their cases to be presented to the tribunal. American diplomats felt certain that Russia was far from thrilled about the improvement of Anglo-American relations. According to Buchanan, Curtin believed that the conclusion of the Washington Treaty had surprised the Russian government, which had been "led to expect from Mr. Catacazy's correspondence that the negotiations had little chance of a termination acceptable to both parties."[72] In late May, Fish wrote in his diary that Catacazy

> proceeds to congratulate me on the success of the "great treaty" &c. I thank him, & remark that his congratulations are unexpected; that I had been led to believe that he had not entertained the opinion that the Treaty was (as he had just called it) "a great triumph of Diplomatic skill". He professes to have really so regarded it.[73]

Catacazy defended himself against these accusations. In a letter to Fish, he wrote that he had demonstrated his approval of the treaty on three separate and verifiable occasions: "the congratulations addressed by me to the Earl de Grey in presence of General Schenk, the compliments addressed by me to Mr. Bancroft Davis on the day following the publication of the treaty, and finally, my letter to Mr. Cyrus Field."[74] The American press, however, had already tried and convicted the Russian minister as papers across the country—New York, Cleveland, New Orleans—repeated the accusations that he had attempted to derail the treaty negotiations.[75] One paper joked about "That Crazy Russian," stating, "It is calculated that if it hadn't been for his interference these claims would have been all settled up by the year 2171, and now they will have to run at least a thousand years longer."[76] Even members of the commission doubted Catacazy's goodwill. For example, Sir Stafford Northcote, First Earl of Iddesleigh, wrote about the treaty to the future prime minister, Benjamin Disraeli, "I believe every one but the Fenians and Catacazy ... will be very much pleased with the settlement." He added an important comment: "Catacazy tried to make mischief, but I don't think his influence is very great now."[77] In a letter to Lord Granville, however, he was more cynical. Only a few days before the treaty was signed, Northcote wrote to Granville, thanking him for allowing them to stay and see the process through, despite some significant rough spots. As Northcote explained, "I am quite sure that our going away would have been used as an argument against the Treaty, and that 'the author of evil,' Catacazy, would have rejoiced to avail himself of it. He is, I believe, working hard, against us, but we may counteract his influence."[78]

The ratification of the Washington Treaty in May 1871 was only the first step in settling the dispute between the United States and Great Britain. If, in fact, Russia hoped to disrupt Anglo-American relations by means of the *Alabama* claims, there was still time to do so. In November 1871, Fish told General Alexander Gorlov, the military attaché of the Russian Legation, that Catacazy was still interfering in America's affairs, that "even within the last week I heard of his intriguing in order to defeat our negotiations with G. B., & to embarrass our position before the Tribunal at Geneva."[79] An article in the *Russian World*, however, defended Catacazy and decried the notion that he conspired to disrupt the *Alabama* settlement at the instructions of the Russian government. The paper declared, "Such an accusation against our government is in no way proved, it is a mere supposition. So much the more as the cause of the difficulty between Mr. Catacazy and Messr. Grant and Fish, were not so much political as personal."[80] The British press, however, was more convinced of the Russian minister's guilt, declaring that he had tried to influence members of the Senate to reject the treaty when it was presented for ratification.[81]

In December 1871, the American and British representatives submitted their cases to the arbitrators in Geneva. Over the next six months, the two sides went back and forth over the question of what losses—private and/or national—should be included in the reparations amount. Meanwhile, Fish and Grant were keenly aware that the success or failure of these negotiations would seriously impact Grant's upcoming bid for reelection.[82] Catacazy, already dismissed from his position at this point, continued to deny his involvement and was defended by the *Moscow Gazette*. In late January 1872, the paper directly responded to the assumption in the *London Times* that Catacazy was guilty of meddling in the *Alabama* settlement. The Russian paper explained,

> The very fact of such meddling the <u>Times</u> finds perfectly intelligible since during the period of these negotiations a difficulty arose between England and America over the question of the neutrality of the Black Sea; and the Russian minister at Washington might naturally think it profitable to oppose a policy which would strengthen the position of England in a moment so critical for Russia.

The *Gazette* insisted, however, that there was no evidence of Catacazy's interference, nor was he ever in the position to exert that kind of influence.[83] The *London Times* was not the only British paper to believe that Catacazy was involved. The *Spectator* seemed to attribute Catacazy's failure to disrupt the *Alabama* claims, and his overall failure as a diplomat, to his misunderstanding of the "character of the American Government, and … temper of the American people." It suggested that when Catacazy heard grousing about Great Britain from all quarters, he took it as a sign that the American people might be willing to part ways with their one-time adversary. He was mistaken, however, stated the *Spectator*, for "the bonds which bind this country to America are too strong to be severed by any trick of diplomacy."[84]

Catacazy's shenanigans did not pay off; on July 22, 1872, the arbitrators in Geneva decided that Great Britain was responsible for the damages done by three ships, including the *Alabama*, and should pay $15,500,000 (£3,200,000) in damages. Russia's hope of driving a wedge between the two great English-speaking nations came to naught, and Catacazy's reputation as meddlesome became well known in public, as well as in private circles.[85]

4

"Falsehood, Intrigue and Hostility": Catacazy's Breaches of Protocol

While the crisis over the Black Sea clause and the negotiations for the *Alabama* Claims simmered, Grant and Fish attempted to uncover the true source of the article "Russia and America" that had appeared in the *New York World*. Since Fish was certain that Catacazy would lie if questioned, he contacted Colonel H. C. Whitley, chief of the Secret Service, and asked him for assistance. The Secret Service was a new agency, created in 1865 within the Treasury Department to protect the nation's currency from counterfeiters, a problem that had exploded during the Civil War; during its first four years, the Secret Service captured more than two hundred counterfeiters. In 1867, Congress expanded the agency's mission to include investigating fraud against the government in general. This was the situation Fish faced as he approached the six-foot, ten-inch Whitley in November 1870 and asked him to investigate "the extent of Catacazy's connection with the letter."[1]

In the meantime, Fish continued to press Catacazy himself for information and the wily diplomat continued to deny involvement in the *World* article or any others attributed to him. He admitted that he had spoken to one reporter, from the *New York Herald*, but declared that the other articles were written or encouraged by "the Perkins set of fellows." Fish noted that there were numerous articles that had "attracted notice and produced unpleasant impressions," and that they seemed to be appearing frequently and in different papers. He pointed out that Catacazy was "the only one of the Diplomatic Representatives here who is thus in the papers & made to appear in continued intrigue & furnishing information often without any foundation of truth."[2] In response, the Russian minister insisted that these "absurdities" did not emanate from himself or anyone else in his Legation. He reminded the secretary of state that only six months earlier he had been accused of being the author of slanderous dispatches, reiterating a familiar argument: "You know that the authors of these forgeries want to get rid of me at any price because they very erroneously suppose that I am personally opposed to a claim in which they are interested."[3]

Even as Catacazy emphatically denied being the source of the troublesome newspaper stories, new ones appeared. On December 3, Catacazy sent Fish a newsclip from the *National Republican* that contained "fresh calumnies" against him. The article hinted at bad feelings between Fish and Catacazy, noting that the Russian minister and his wife had been excluded from some social gatherings in the capital. The *Republican* claimed that "their absence from the diplomatic dinners at the White House became the subject of public comment," and though they were subsequently reintegrated into Washington social life, there continued to be a "discontented undercurrent of feelings." According to the article, the tension between Catacazy and Fish had increased during the Black Sea crisis. Catacazy, the *Republican* claimed, had been disappointed when the United States refused to give a statement of support to Russia and had made his discontent known by temporarily discontinuing his official calls on Fish; once the crisis had passed and Russia no longer needed the support of the United States, Catacazy resumed his regular visits. Catacazy told Fish, however, that "every line, every word of this article is a lie."[4]

But the articles continued. In late December, Catacazy told Fish that he had been approached by a newspaper reporter who planned to publish an item about a personal clash between the Russian minister and the secretary of state. To prevent this, Catacazy had paid the man fifty dollars not to print it, but he repeated his conviction that all these reports came from the Perkins advocates.[5] Two days later, a new article appeared in the *New York Herald* that seemed to counter the information in the *World* story of the previous month. This article declared there was no unfriendliness between Fish and Catacazy, offering instead that "on the contrary, their relations and those of their families are of the most amicable and cordial character." It also mentioned the forged dispatches and accused individuals interested in the Perkins claim of attempting to get rid of Catacazy to improve their chances of success. The *Herald* article suggested that the forged letter from Grant to the tsar offering the assistance of the American Navy in settling the Eastern Question was also designed to drive a wedge between Russia and the United States. In fact, it stated, "Russia has an abiding confidence in her own ability, unaided, to deal successfully not only with her neighbors, but with England." This article was reprinted in the *Washington Chronicle* the following day.[6] Catacazy seemed to be behind this piece as well, a lame attempt to mitigate the damage done by the previous article while also refining the narrative he wanted others to believe.

The appearance of these suspicious newspaper stories, as well as the forged letter from Grant to the tsar, was something the American government could not ignore, nor take lightly. It was a long-established principle in international law in the United States that a foreign representative had the right to address "the executive" about any concerns on matters relevant to his country. But, as early as 1795, in a statement by Secretary of State Edmund Randolph it was determined that "it will ever be denied as a right of a foreign minister, that he should endeavor, by an address to the people, oral or written, to forestall a depending measure, or to defeat one which has been decided." John Quincy Adams made a similar comment in his memoirs, noting, "it is an impropriety for foreign ministers to publish criticisms on the Government to which they are accredited."[7]

By early 1871, Secretary of State Fish was beginning to receive convincing evidence that Catacazy was involved in the publication of various items in the American press. On February 1, H. C. Whitley of the Secret Service presented his report to Fish. Whitley's lengthy letter, "condensed from voluminous reports," stated that his investigation had determined that the article "Russia and America" had been written by George W. Adams, the Washington editor of the *New York World*. When Adams sent it to the New York editor on the day before its publication, he had enclosed an assurance that the information had been obtained "from the highest and most unquestionable source." Uncovering the identity of that source, Whitley explained, had been a complicated endeavor, and his officers had had to cozy up to a variety of individuals to earn their trust and get them to talk. Of particular interest was a Mr. Diggins, the messenger for the *New York Herald*'s Washington office. Diggins was a "sharp, intelligent young Irishman" who, despite his modest position at the *Herald*, was a close acquaintance of Catacazy and had indicated that the Russian minister had voiced concern about the negative reaction to the *World* article. Diggins told the investigators that "something more would appear in relation to it." Indeed, on December 24, the article had appeared in the *New York Herald* denying any conflict between Fish and Catacazy. Whitley's investigators discovered that the day before this article appeared, someone from the Washington office of the *Herald* had visited the Russian Legation and had met with Catacazy. This indicated to the investigators that Catacazy, "fearing the reactionary effect of the *World* article upon himself, was endeavoring to destroy its influence through the columns of other journals."[8]

Whitley's men still struggled to determine the nature of the relationship between Adams (of the *World*) and Catacazy. During one of numerous interviews,

Adams mentioned a woman named Miss Snead, who wrote Washington gossip for the *World* under the name of "Mrs. Grundy." Adams declared that Snead was frequently at the Russian Legation and "being a sharp and intelligent woman, she heard a great many things outside of mere gossip all of which were woven into letters and dispatches for the World." Subsequently, the investigators confirmed that Snead was an intimate friend of the Russian minister and "evidently the medium of connection between M de Catacazy and the Washington Editor of the World."[9]

The publication of the December 24 article in the *Herald* had unwittingly assisted Whitley's team in that by countering the claims of the *New York World* article, it made Adams feel that his integrity and honesty had been called into question. This prompted Adams to write to the New York editor of the *World*, emphasizing the reliability of his reporting and that he had received his information from a "high functionary—the highest capable of giving the information and that he could make affidavit thereto and bring evidence of another person in support of the fact." In the end, Whitley's men were "fully convinced" that Catacazy was the instigator of the "Russia and America" article and that the negative impression this story generated led Catacazy to subsequently inspire the piece in the *New York Herald* that contradicted the claims of the first article.[10]

The investigation turned up more information about Catacazy's private life as well. According to Whitley's officers, Catacazy was a "frequenter of common saloons and tippling shops" in the neighborhood of the Legation and was known to leave those establishments in a "maudlin condition." Moreover, Catacazy was in a considerable amount of debt to these places. He also exhibited other undignified behavior. The Russian minister apparently had a tendency toward profanity in public, even in front of his wife. The officers reported that casual passersby more than once heard "a torrent of oaths proceeding from him when assisting Madam de Catacazy to alight from her carriage."[11] Whitley received a check in the amount of $816.50 for his detective services.[12]

It is clear that by this point, February 1871, Fish was frustrated with Catacazy and no longer trusted him. A few weeks after receiving Whitley's revealing report, Fish and Catacazy had a meeting during which the Russian minister declared that he was being threatened by a Russian forger and swindler who was now in the United States. Fish's comment on this story in his diary entry for that day was revealing: "It does not trouble C. to state what is not true."[13] Less than a week later, Fish met with Frank Turk, a local attorney who was well acquainted with the Russian minister. Turk inquired if Fish had seen the recent letter in the

Cincinnati Enquirer entitled, "Reported Trouble between President Grant and the Russian Minister." The article, which appeared in late February 1871, claimed that in the midst of the Black Sea crisis Grant privately had expressed sympathy for Great Britain and had stated "that Russia should never be permitted to go to Constantinople." Catacazy, upon hearing this, had shared the information publicly through the American press, and Grant, "upon seeing his anti-Russian views in print, was so annoyed that he employed detectives to ascertain who furnished the material for the garnished stories, the kernel of which was correct and stung him, as he feared the terrible onslaught that would be made upon him by all parties should he show himself unnecessarily overfriendly to England." It was then, the *Enquirer* stated, that Grant had begun seeking evidence to get Catacazy recalled. The article continued with a much more serious allegation, however—that the real reason Grant wanted Catacazy removed had to do with the Russian minister's handling of the Perkins claim, "in which great stake our worthy President is interested." Turk told Fish that Catacazy was behind the article and had admitted as such to him. He further suggested that the Russian minister himself had created the forged dispatches to implicate Waldemar de Bodisco, secretary of the Russian Legation, whom he hated for some reason. Though Turk was enthusiastic about sharing this intelligence with Fish, he was less eager to testify to any of this openly for fear of retaliation by the Russian minister. Armed with this new information, Fish confronted Catacazy with these accusations, without referring to Turk. Catacazy, not surprisingly, denied any knowledge of the article or any association with Adams or Diggins.[14]

At this juncture, a definite sharpness can be detected in the communications between Fish and Catacazy. On March 12, 1871, Catacazy wrote to Fish about stories appearing about him in the press, citing one that linked him with Senator Charles Sumner and his opposition to the American acquisition of Santo Domingo and his disapproval of the administration. Catacazy blamed the "Perkins men" and added, "knowing by experience that these rumors are but too easily accredited in high quarters I am placed in the painful necessity of denying again these falsehoods and of requesting you to do it in my name in case of need."[15] Fish responded two days later, clearly incensed at Catacazy's suggestion that he and the president were quick to believe gossip. Fish answered, "your allusion to your experience with rumors … could not be tolerated, but finding it possible to give it a different construction I desire to do so, and remark that no mere rumors which may have been in circulation have been 'accredited in high quarters.'"[16] A few days later, Fish had reason to chastise Catacazy again after he admitted that he had allowed his correspondence to be published in the newspaper. Fish took him to task, stating, "if a foreign government accredit diplomatic agents to the government of the United States it is expected that its business will be transacted by those agents through this Department, and it is hoped they will abstain from discussion in the newspapers subject [*sic*] which are under the official consideration of the two Governments."[17] Some weeks later, Catacazy told Fish that yet another man affiliated with a newspaper had approached him asking for comment on the connection between the Perkins claim and members of the Grant administration. Fish understood that Catacazy wanted him to believe that Stewart and Tasistro were behind this encounter, but he no longer trusted the Russian minister. He wrote in his diary, "This looks to me like a very shallow cover of another of Catacazy's movements."[18]

Catacazy was becoming a nuisance to Fish in other ways as well. In late March, Fish requested that Catacazy stop using the diplomatic mail pouch for large parcels, as that service was intended for small items only. The language of the letter gives the impression that this was not the first time that Fish had reminded the Russian minister of this rule.[19] Then, in early May, a woman named Mrs. A. Andrews paid a call on Fish to ask his intervention to get Catacazy to pay money he owed her. Fish forcefully replied that he had no intention of getting involved in the matter.[20]

* * *

Catacazy's decision to take his personal and diplomatic battles to the court of public opinion via the American press may not have been a wise one, but it was certainly an intentional one. Catacazy clearly understood the reach and power of the written word in American politics and society. Even as the earliest newspapers appeared with the birth of the new nation, their place was firmly staked out as central observers and players in the world of politics. In the first half of the nineteenth century, editors took clear sides in politics, overtly backing political parties and individual politicians, many of whom owned or provided financial backing for those papers. The intrusion of the press into American political matters was commonplace. In the presidential elections of 1828 and 1832, Andrew Jackson had accused his rivals of using the editors of certain newspapers to advance their campaigns. Once he had won, however, he became a friend of the press, appointing more newspaper editors to important posts than any president before him.[21]

Over the course of the nineteenth century, the perceived role of newspapers would shift away from being primarily political organs. They would still take political stances and endorse candidates, but they increasingly strove for independence from politics and focused on producing something that would appeal to the broader interests of society and to readers of various walks of life. Articles about sports, entertainment, books, and fashion became more prominent as the circulation grew and advertisers rather than politicians began to provide the bulk of the revenue for these publications. Women became an important demographic target, as well. Some newspapers began to articulate a notion of "public community," a recognition of the unavoidable interdependence in modern urban life, and discussed the obligations of the city to its people through public works. But even with these noticeable changes, politics would always remain a central focus of newspaper headlines.[22] Catacazy recognized the power of the press in the United States and used it to muddy the waters of the Perkins claim and other matters pertaining to Russian-American relations. His involvement with the publication of articles critical of the Grant administration and containing misleading and false information would ultimately be his undoing, however.

* * *

It is almost possible to pinpoint the day that Fish ran out of patience with the troublesome Russian minister. In late May 1871, Catacazy showed Fish a letter and a newspaper article, both highly abusive of him (Catacazy). When the Russian diplomat once again blamed the men associated with the Perkins claim, Fish asked for proof. In a display of circular logic, Catacazy declared that the fact that the article mentioned the Perkins claim was evidence that the Perkins men were behind it. At this point, Fish seemed to have reached the end of his rope and confronted the Russian minister with "a very common rumor that he himself writes, or procures the publication of this class of articles."[23] Fish further criticized Catacazy's attempts at interference in the *Alabama* claims. Catacazy initially admitted to have only spoken to one person about the claim, but over the course of the conversation, that number grew to three or four people. Catacazy then apparently took the conversation in an entirely different direction and complained about Fish not inviting him to dinner. Hinting at another possible source of enmity, Fish replied that Catacazy could rest assured that "the fact of his not being thus invited will not be the subject of any boasting letter from me or from my wife." Fish's veiled accusation was clear, and Catacazy inquired if Fish had heard of such a letter emanating from his house. Fish replied that indeed he had, and had heard that the letter had been "exhibited in New York." Fish's diary entry of this encounter also mentions that the letter in question was rumored to have been written by Catacazy's wife, but it is not clear if Fish confronted Catacazy with this information. The meeting concluded on an icy note. Catacazy stated that clearly he no longer had the confidence or respect of the secretary of state. When Fish did not reply, Catacazy remarked that Fish maintained "a very diplomatic silence."[24]

Catacazy, unfortunately, did not maintain a diplomatic silence. Not long after this confrontational encounter, Catacazy resurrected the subject of the forged dispatches that had appeared over a year earlier. He claimed that Fish had never responded to one of his notes about those documents. Though he had not complained earlier out of a sense of courtesy, now, Catacazy stated, "the impunity which has been enjoyed for more than a year by the fabricators of these false dispatches, seems to have encouraged them to renew these guilty devices." The Russian minister was specifically referring to a recent article from the *New York Evening Post* that once again raised the topic of the mysterious dispatches. The title of the article was "A Diplomatic Feud—The Estrangement between Secretary Fish and the Russian Minister—A Disputed Letter," and it revived the accusation against Catacazy regarding the dispatches and their harsh words pertaining to those associated with the Perkins claim and the secretary of state. Catacazy declared that he had remained silent, "knowing what unlimited liberty the press enjoys in the United States, and being unable to deviate from diplomatic propriety." Now, however, Catacazy felt he would be derelict in his duties if he allowed his silence to be construed as an admission of guilt and he therefore firmly reiterated to Fish that "this pretended dispatch was never written by me, that it is absolutely false from beginning to end, and that I could, in no case, have expressed myself with regard to you in the unworthy terms which are calumniously attributed to me."[25] The Russian minister was hoping Fish would publicly declare his belief that the dispatches were false, and that Catacazy was not involved in their creation.

The following day, Catacazy sent a lengthy addendum to his previous appeal. In this letter, the Russian minister confronted Fish directly: "You have expressed to me, sir, faintly disguised doubts as to the veracity of my assertions, by saying that you could not assume the responsibility of their corrections … I must hence conclude that the persons interested in prejudicing you against me have succeeded completely in doing so." Catacazy attempted to persuade Fish that the published dispatches and various articles revealed a plan to have him removed from his post and ruin the friendly relations between Russia and the United States. Catacazy denied any connection to an article from the Cincinnati newspaper published under the name Don Liatt but attributed to him. He asked Fish to reveal the source of his information, reminding the secretary, "I have begged you to confront me with this calumniator, or at least to name him to me." He requested that Fish put an end to the rumors by publicly contradicting them, adding in a threatening tone, "it would be much to be regretted if things were allowed to go so far as to put the Imperial Cabinet under the necessity of showing, by the official publication of the documents, that the legitimate demands of the Emperor have been met with persistent refusal."[26]

In the midst of these exchanges, Fish realized that he needed to persuade Frank Turk to reveal himself as his source. After some discussion, Turk agreed that he would reply to a written request, but he would only permit the use of his name if Catacazy denied authorship of the *Cincinnati Enquirer* article and it became necessary. Fish reassured Turk that his identity would be kept secret as long as possible, but his reflection in his diary was much less optimistic—"I tell him that I may have to use, [sic] and wish to use the information, & probably will do so, but that I will not give his name, if it can well be avoided, though possibly it may have to be used."[27] The conditional nature of Fish's promise worried Turk, however, and only a few days after their meeting he sent a letter explaining that in all of his conversations with Catacazy there was an implied confidence that he could not ignore. He therefore did not feel he could give Fish the statement he wanted.[28] Turk had confided to the Assistant Secretary of State Bancroft Davis, however, that if Fish asked again, he would comply.[29] Unsurprisingly, Fish did ask again, and this time Turk gave Fish a full statement that cautiously specified that while he had never accused Catacazy of the authorship of the *Cincinnati Enquirer* article, Catacazy had told him he had written it. Turk added that, while he would hate to damage his friendly relationship with the Russian minister, he was not "willing that Mr. C should contradict a fact which I have asserted and he most certainly knows is true."[30]

As Fish had waited for Turk's statement, he had begun to lay the foundation for a possible dismissal of the Russian minister. On June 1, 1871, Fish wrote in his diary that he had told Grant that he would soon have sufficient evidence to request a recall, observing that the president "would be glad to be rid of C. for whom he entertains a thorough mistrust."[31] Fish had apparently mentioned the possibility to Curtin as well, since on June 2, 1871, the American minister wrote to Fish, "Prince Gorchakov is so fond of the minister that you are quite right in not intimating that his presence is not agreeable until you have evidence which you can use."[32] Once Fish had Turk's letter in hand, he drafted a letter to Curtin requesting Catacazy's recall and presented it to Grant for his approval. The president wholeheartedly approved and even suggested immediate dismissal, but Fish advised that it was "more courteous to the Russian Government to ask for his recall."[33]

While Fish gathered evidence and reached out to various individuals, the American public was aware that something was afoot in the capital. Though many of the details of the Catacazy case were not yet disclosed, the American press commented on what was known. The *New York Post* attributed the rift between Fish and Catacazy to the dispatches the Russian minister had supposedly sent to his government, quoting the letters at length, but acknowledging that Catacazy declared the dispatches to be forgeries.[34] Some papers were very vocal about who they thought was to blame. The *Philadelphia Inquirer* believed that the dispute was more personal, specifically, because Fish had "absolutely snubbed" Catacazy. The paper added, "we cannot afford to quarrel with one of our best foreign friends, and, to placate the Muscovite, Mr. Fish must retire."[35] The *New York World*, on the other hand, stood firmly behind the president and secretary of state. It challenged the tsar to recall the Russian minister, stating, "Russia can afford, as she have often proved, to send a gentleman, a man of honor and man of veracity, to represent her in the United States." The *World* subsequently declared, "there need be no extraordinary delay in ridding the imperial legation of a minister in whom neither gods, nor men, nor President Grant himself can take the least delight."[36] Getting rid of the troublesome minister would be far more difficult than the journalists of the *World* could imagine.

5

"She Had a Story and a Past": Olga Catacazy and the Washington Wives

A lesser-known dimension of Constantin Catacazy's recall involves Catacazy's wife, Olga, and how her scandalous past denied her entry into Washington society and possibly negatively affected her husband's career as well. The Catacazy Affair demonstrates the power of women in American politics before they obtained the right to vote and highlights the intertwining of social and political life in the halls of power.[1]

Olga Fitz-James was born in France in 1828 into a noble family. At the age of nineteen, she was married to Nicola Greuther, an Italian duke who would serve as minister plenipotentiary of the King of Two Sicilies in Brazil and later (beginning in 1853), as secretary of the Italian Legation in Berlin. (He died in 1854.) During their short time together, Olga bore Nicola two children, a daughter and a son.[2] While she was married to Greuther, however, Olga met Catacazy and they fell in love. Some sources say they met in Rome; others say Brazil, where Catacazy served as a secretary in the Russian Legation in Rio de Janeiro.[3] Whatever the case may be, at some point during this period, she either divorced her husband or ran off with Catacazy.[4] When Catacazy came to the United States as minister in 1869 he brought Olga with him.

The role as a minister's wife was a very important one, "a full-time position made up of responsibilities, restrictions, and privileges." She served as an assistant to her husband but dealt primarily with the unofficial, symbolic aspects of diplomatic life, though her actions even in seemingly private places could have diplomatic significance. Her world was also governed by social rules, and deviations from them, that could be used to communicate "indirect or covert diplomatic messages," such as "the intentional breaking of protocol in assigning seats at a diplomatic party" or "omissions from and additions to guest lists." Though this definition was from 1969, it could easily have been describing the life of a diplomatic wife a century earlier.[5]

Diplomatic wives, in fact, were very busy women who had many responsibilities. They "organized and managed social functions, packed and unpacked households, hired and fired servants, met new people, threw lavish dinner parties, volunteered in the local community, and learned new languages, customs, and rules of protocol all over the world." They facilitated their husbands' careers in other ways as well. As they formed relationships with local women and other diplomatic wives, they participated in the exchange of information and the building of friendly relations. They viewed their husbands' profession as their own and took that responsibility very seriously. These wives understood that they were representing their husbands and their countries in all they did.[6] Their receptions and parties brought men and women of importance together. Though diplomacy became more formalized in the nineteenth century, ladies' salons were still important as places "where elites would regularly gather, collude and conspire, although as much in personal matters as in the great issues of high politics." In this world, the ambassador's wife was the hostess for diplomatic and social gatherings, and served as "a symbol of the national culture."[7] The *New York World* observed, "It has been dictated by social critics that the merits of a candidate for a place in the Cabinet go for nothing unless his wife is an agreeable woman, and likely to contribute to the pleasures of the capital."[8]

Several sources say that Madame Catacazy was accepted at the time of their arrival in the American capital.[9] As far as can be determined, she attempted to fulfill her role as the Russian minister's wife, hosting regular receptions and appearing beside her husband when appropriate. The *Washington Daily Morning Chronicle* attributed a "brilliant reception" to her in January 1870, and she also attended a ball given by the British minister and was praised for her white silk dress and overall magnificent costume.[10] She hosted another reception in February, attended by "distinguished gentleman, and the beauty and fashion of the city."[11] These gatherings were attended by cabinet members and their wives, including the Fishes.[12] That same month, February, both the Catacazys attended a state dinner given by the president.[13]

The American press raved about the beauty of the Russian minister's wife. Olga was described as a "woman of remarkable beauty," with a clear complexion, a lovely figure, and "a wealth of golden hair which all admit to be natural in color and quantity … of that rare shade about which poets and painters rave."[14] Her eyes were "full, lustrous, and of a dark blue" and her beauty was enhanced by "the tastes of a Parisian and the instincts of an artist … She gets herself up wondrously well."[15] According to the *Cincinnati Daily Enquirer*, she took coconut baths for her skin, while the *Wheeling Daily Intelligencer* declared that her "beauty is so wonderful that she always attracts very special attention."[16] Her demeanor was also the subject of praise. One paper described her manners as "very fascinating," adding, "she knows how to pay dainty little compliments, though her vocabulary of English words is not large."[17] The *Memphis Public Ledger* pronounced her "the handsomest woman in Washington," the only lady in that city "who depends wholly upon Europe for the details of her apparel."[18] The women of Washington elite society assessed one another critically, tallying points for beauty, fashion, manners, and polish, so such lavish compliments in the American press carried more weight than one might imagine.[19] Adam Badeau, Grant's associate and chronicler, noted of Mrs. Catacazy that she was fascinating to men, "dressed with gorgeous taste, and her superb neck and arms, long, golden hair, and melting eyes made many think that Catacazy's sin had not been without its provocation."[20]

Olga's beauty undoubtedly made some women jealous, but it was the stories of her past that made her presence objectionable. According to Badeau, when she arrived in Washington, she and her husband may have hoped that her previous indiscretion had been forgotten, but "the ladies remembered it, and those who were in power held a consultation as to whether the envoy's wife should be received." Though she would not have been received in private life under these circumstances, Badeau declared, "in public life things are different, and it was decided to ignore her past, lest to notice it might complicate international relations."[21] At some point, however, this decision to turn a blind eye shifted.

Many sources hint that the ostracization of Madame Catacazy began with Julia Kean Fish, the wife of Secretary of State Hamilton Fish. Mrs. Fish was, according to one newspaper, "the leading representative of officialdom in society" and the "embodiment of womanly grace and dignity." Another paper described her as "dignified and reserved, but never haughty … quietly attentive to all her guests, makes each feel at ease without making the slightest parade about it."[22] One of her contemporaries described her as "a fine, queenly looking woman, of middle age. Time has gently touched her, for her figure is as erect, her complexion as faultless, and her eyes as bright as in the days of her girlhood."[23] Hamilton Fish had served as governor of New York from 1849 to 1850 and as the senator from New York from 1851 to 1857, so his wife fully understood her role when he became secretary of state in 1869. During the Grant administration, Julia Kean Fish set many of the precedents for social calls and invitations. She was often the first official wife to visit new congressional wives and invite them to tea. The Fishes were wealthy and did a great deal of entertaining. During the social season, they had two formal dinners a week, in addition to Julia's weekly reception and other gatherings. Some estimated that the Fishes spent $75,000 a year on entertaining. Given these many years as a "first lady," Julia was well experienced in the etiquette of entertaining and the politics of the parlor—too experienced, in fact, not to foresee the ramifications of excluding a prominent couple from an important social event.[24]

In November 1870, Julia Kean Fish hosted a grand diplomatic dinner in honor of the Joint High Commission for the settlement of the *Alabama* claims. Every foreign minister or ambassador was invited except Constantin Catacazy. Such a slight, in the words of the *Milwaukee Sentinel*, "sent the poisoned arrow through the quivering heart of one woman superior to them all in breeding, accomplishments and beauty."[25] The *Sentinel* was critical of Mrs. Fish's behavior, noting that while she was entitled to her own opinions as a private citizen, in her capacity as wife of the secretary of state, she violated diplomatic courtesy.[26] Another newspaper declared that Mrs. Fish had "opened the barrel of powder, which may yet blow up a war between Russia and America."[27] The Russian minister, of course, was angered by the exclusion of himself and his wife from a dinner of such significance, and it became one more irritant between him and the secretary of state.[28] In December 1870, a month after the alleged snubbing by Mrs. Fish, Catacazy raised the issue with Fish in one of his frequent meetings. Fish recorded that Catacazy stated that "an article which lately appeared in some papers reflecting on his wife, had been sent to him, the address being in Tasistro's handwriting."[29] Fish made no further comment on the matter in his diary, but the article in question was likely one that appeared in the *Daily National Republican* in early December 1870. It stated that the relationship between Fish and Catacazy was less than cordial, attributing it to the fact that the Catacazys had been "partly ignored last winter in the social relations required by the conventionalities of diplomacy" and "their absence from the diplomatic dinners at the White House finally became the subject of public comment."[30]

Even had the dinner in question not been such a high-profile affair, the blow would have been a sharp one. Receptions and dinners were central to the fabric of proper society and the bar was set extremely high. Memoirs and letters from the period attest to the demands, both physical and material, of polite society. The Washington correspondent for the Russian newspaper, *Golos*, described the hectic pace of the "gay season" in the city, a period of several months, consisting of "an endless line of day and evening receptions."[31] Harriet Blaine, wife of Senator James G. Blaine of Maine, wrote to her son in October 1871, "As to my custom, I dread to take up the gay life in Washington. Shall like it no doubt when my dresses are made and I am well initiated." In subsequent letters, she described the exhausting pace of her social life of receptions, dinners, and parties and expressed relief as the season drew to a close.[32] Women especially worried about being judged by their peers. Blaine confessed to her daughter that she had been concerned about her wardrobe, which consisted of many refurbished dresses. But once she realized that the other ladies were similarly attired with their own minor shortcomings—"the skirt of her [Mrs. Boutwell] black silk dress had evidently felt the deadly pressure of an iron"—she was relieved.[33] This demand to fit in was no small matter. Marian Adams, a descendent of Boston nobility and wife to historian Henry Adams, described a situation in which she was asked to visit a neighbor woman who was not accepted in polite circles, a form of social suicide she was unwilling to commit. Adams likened Washington society to the dangerous waters of a speeding river: "To steer one's small cock-boat in these rapids is as difficult in the season as shooting 'El Bab' at the First Cataract of the Nile."[34]

Society life in the second half of the nineteenth century followed certain rules of etiquette regarding invitations and attendance. This was even more true in Washington where social networks were so intertwined with politics. At the beginning of a new administration, the protocol of party-giving dictated that the president should give a dinner for the cabinet members and their wives; then, beginning with the secretary of state, all the cabinet members took their turns as host.[35] Other dinners in Washington involving members of the government would have had similar expectations. Foreign diplomats followed the rules of the society in which they found themselves and recognized that it behooved them to be on the good side of the secretary of state.[36] At the same time, the rules of etiquette also suggested that foreign diplomats be given extra courtesy as representatives of other sovereign states. One guide book advised, "we would grant a Foreign Minister precedence, wherever it can at all be given."[37]

Washington society blossomed in the years after the Civil War as the capital became one of the most fashionable cities in the country. The bar was set high for spending on clothing and entertainment, and all of this was reported in the press by society reporters, a new phenomenon that appeared in Washington during the Grant administration. In a similar vein, a variety of etiquette books became available for those needing clarification of the rules and protocols.[38] The composition of high society changed after the war as well, as the southern elites disappeared and were replaced by more congressmen in residence in the capital. The diplomatic community grew also, as more legations were established, bringing both foreign ministers and their staffs. These men increasingly brought their wives with them, swelling the ranks of high society to nearly twice its size, and adding "precisely those individuals with the leisure, the inclination, and the training to pursue and perpetrate its intricate rituals and protocol."[39]

Prominent women in society typically held weekly open receptions of several hours, and visits by and to other ladies also required adherence to certain guidelines. In an 1873 guide to social life in Washington, the female author specified that a calling card should be left at the home of the person one visits, whether or not the person being visited was at home, but especially if they were not. A folded right corner indicated that the card had been delivered in person. How one responded to a visit, or missed visitor, also had its rules and subtle meanings—"An intervening period of three days marks high breeding, as it evinces your pleasure at forming the acquaintance, so that a return visit, within a day or so, is therefore a delicate compliment."[40] When Johan de Hegermann-Lindencrone, the Danish minister to the United States, arrived with his wife Lillie in 1875, she wrote, "There seems to be no end of card-leaving and card-receiving, and a list of rules on etiquette … as long as your arm. I never knew of anything so confusing … I am knee-deep in engagements, actually wading in them."[41]

As the arbiters of etiquette and the ringmasters of the social world, women were keenly aware of the unwritten rules and corresponding slights and nods. It was well known that omitting someone from a dinner or party was perceived as an insult, an intentional snub that communicated the hostess's opinion of the excluded party. Likewise, failure to attend was also interpreted as an insult. Julia Fish certainly knew these rules, and her choice to exclude the Russian minister and his wife communicated a message to other women in Washington society that Madame Catacazy was no longer to be accepted. Tolerated perhaps, but not accepted.[42]

Despite Julia Fish's sharp snubbing, a scan of the newspapers of the period indicates that the Catacazys continued to engage in the social scene of the capital. In January of 1871, Mrs. Catacazy was holding her regular Tuesday afternoon receptions at their home.[43] That same month they also attended a reception at the White House during which Mrs. Fish played assistant hostess to Mrs. Grant and the president.[44] The following month, the Catacazys hosted several dinners, including one that earned the praise of the *New York World* as "one of the most elegant dinners recently given." The dinner welcomed eighteen guests, including the Fishes.[45] In March, the Catacazys attended a dinner hosted by Don Manuel Freyre, the Peruvian minister to the United States; they also hosted a banquet for the High Commission, "among the most brilliant of entertainments yet given" for that body. The Fishes, however, were not listed as attendees and it is not known if they were invited.[46] In April, the Catacazys attended a dinner for the members of the Joint High Commission by the Post-Master General John Creswell and his wife, and hosted yet another dinner for the Commission which, it appears, the Fishes did attend.[47] That same month, the Russian minister and his wife gave a dinner party in honor of Simon Cameron with fourteen guests, to which the Fishes were not invited.[48] The *New York World* also reported, however, that both Mrs. Fish and Mrs. Grant held several dinners and receptions in April and May, but in none of these instances were the Catacazys listed as attendees.[49]

It is certain that the inclusion or exclusion of the Catacazys had become a point of contention between the Russian minister and the secretary of state, as well as a matter of public attention and speculation. In May, Catacazy complained to Fish once again about the social exclusion of his wife. Fish recorded in his diary:

> Refers to not having been invited to dine with me, to which I reply that he may be assured that the fact of his not being thus invited will not be the subject of any boasting letter from me or from my wife; to the enquiry if I had heard that he had written any similar letter, he is told that I have been informed that such a letter written from his house, (it is said to have been written by his wife), is said to have been exhibited in New York. He denies &c.[50]

Following this meeting, Fish dedicated an entire letter to Andrew Curtin in St. Petersburg to this social aspect of the Catacazy Affair. The secretary of state had recently given a dinner in honor of Baron Friedrich von Gerolt, the German minister to the United States, who was retiring after more than twenty years of service, and someone Fish considered a personal friend. The Catacazys were not on the guest list, and Fish was not surprised that the Russian minister confronted him about it. Nor was he surprised to see something about it appear in the press. As Fish told Curtin, "As I anticipated when he spoke of the subject it has since become a matter of newspaper comment—Mr. Catacazy has a peculiar infelicity, of getting all his troubles real, imagined, or entirely figured and without foundation into the public prints." Fish underscored that despite Catacazy's poor behavior, he and his wife had been invited to all official dinners and receptions "as his rank entitled him." Catacazy, however, had excluded Fish from a dinner for the Joint High Commission earlier that spring. Fish claimed to have taken no notice of the omission until friends of his in New York told him that a letter "written from Mr. Catacazy's house" had been shown around town boasting, "'you see we did not invite Mrs. Fish.'" For this reason, Fish felt no obligation to invite the Catacazys to his home. Since Catacazy would likely report this to his government, he instructed Curtin to use his letter as needed to counter any misinformation caused by the Russian minister's version of events.[51]

By this point, the American press was keenly interested in the unofficial aspects of the Catacazy quagmire. Only days after Fish had this exchange with Catacazy, an article appeared in the *New York World* that declared that the secretary of state did not want to invite the Russian minister to dinner, adding, "The Minister resents this disinclination; and … insists upon having it published to the universe … That he was not permitted to stomach the Secretary's banquets he considers to be an insult which he will not stomach."[52] Later, in July, the *New York World* hinted at the scandal in the Russian minister's life, commenting that he was officially and socially regarded as "a tainted sheep" in the diplomatic flock: "Everybody in such circles who are believed to be informed upon the under current shake their heads solemnly when M. Catacazy's name is mentioned, and assert that they could tell if they would why that Minister will not long remain here as Russian envoy."[53] Many articles referred to the questions about Olga Catacazy's past.[54]

There were also rumors that Catacazy had insulted Julia Fish. In early October 1871, the *New York Herald* reported that at a dinner at the Russian minister's home he declared that he could bribe the secretary of state, and that "Mrs. Fish was also purchasable." Catacazy furiously denied that he had, or would, say such a thing about the secretary or "his most amiable, honorable and respectable lady," but the story seemed to many just one more example of the Russian's lack of tact and decorum.[55] Still, some sources offered a degree of sympathy to the minister. The *New York Times* declared that the social wounds suffered by the Catacazys at the hands of the diplomatic ladies of Washington had caused the Russian minister to lash out: "Smarting under this alleged unkind treatment … he expressed his opinions, both by spoken and written words, in such decided terms that the President and his cabinet took up the gauntlet."[56]

Even after Catacazy's recall was decided, the subject of Olga's social rejection continued to be raised in official conversation. Fish wrote in a diary entry of November 17, 1871, that he had a meeting with General Gorlov and during the conversation, the men discussed Catacazy's "attempt to make it appear that a social question was connected with his trouble." Fish denied that the recall involved such matters, describing Catacazy's "personal reception, & of the respect & treatment of Mrs. C."[57] Even British diplomats were aware of the rumors about Madame Catacazy. On September 20, 1871, Buchanan wrote to Granville, "I understand also that alleged failings since her arrival in the U.S. on the part of

Mrs. Catacazy who did not leave Russia with an unblemished reputation, have complicated the question and that Mrs. Fish has ceased to receive her."[58]

The American press joked and sneered about the possibility that a disagreement between women had contributed to the Russian minister's downfall and delighted in the scandal's more salacious possibilities. The *Chicago Times* admitted, "What is known as the spicy and personal part of the Catacazy controversy will probably never be made public."[59] Referring to the history of the Catacazys' relationship, the *Buffalo Commercial Advertiser* argued that the tsar should never have sent "the meddlesome Mr. Catacazy" to Washington, given his personal situation.[60] The entire episode, however, had seriously impacted the flow of Washington social entertainment, since Fish "gave up his house, and took board at a hotel, that he might not be obliged to exchange courtesies with the obnoxious Russian: and [since] it is too late to set up an establishment for the present season … it has fallen out that Fish must be omitted from the social bill of fare."[61]

There was also serious criticism. The *New York Times*, for example, published an article on the scandal in the fall of 1871 and chastised the Russian minister for using his wife as an excuse for his recall. According to the *Times*, "One's opinion of the real character of this man can be safely based on this effort … to bring his wife before the world, to shield himself from the just consequences of his own intrigues, falsehoods, and even worse things, in his intercourse with this Government."[62] The judgmentalism of female society was also held to account. The *New York Sun* observed,

> It seems rather late for the Administration to set up this last reason for a recall. Mme. Catacazy had been received in an official way by the very ladies who are said to be shocked and embarrassed, and the moment had been permitted to pass when such objection to her presence could have been urged with propriety, or, to say the least of it, in good taste.[63]

The *Chicago Times* defended Mrs. Catacazy, stating that even if the worst rumors about her past were true, she excelled in the virtues demanded of Washington society, and in "education and manners, and personal presence, she is far superior to them all."[64]

American journalists also deliberated the true cause of this "tea-party intrigue."[65] Many believed that it boiled down to simple jealousy. The *Detroit Free Press* said that the ladies of the Grant administration were jealous of Madame Catacazy "on account of her superior intelligence, brilliancy and great beauty," and the only way to get rid of her was to get rid of her husband.[66] In fact, many newspapers believed that the potential rift in the Russian-American relationship "all started about a woman."[67] The *Kansas City Times* humorously chided Madame Catacazy for her "singular superiority" that offended the "female department of the Government at Washington," adding, "If she had had the inaneness (sic) to disguise her beauty and appear always as an ugly woman, her unhappy husband might have stayed there as the representative of the Russian Government the rest of his life."[68] The *Milwaukee Sentinel*, remarking on an engraving of Madame Catacazy in the publication *Every Saturday*, wrote that she had a beautiful face, "lovely enough to rouse all the envy and jealousy" of the ladies of the city. The *Sentinel* claimed to be ashamed of the women of Washington and lamented the Russian lady's shabby treatment, explaining, "Upon her arrival in this country, every newspaper reporter went mad over her beauty, and every woman near enough to her to feel its blaze went to work with all the venom which women are capable of under such circumstances, to defame and injure her."[69] After Catacazy announced that General Gorlov would be his successor (prematurely, as it turned out), one newspaper declared that Gorlov was entirely acceptable because "Doubtless his wife is old and ugly."[70] The *Cleveland Daily Leader* joked that the Russian minister was sure to write a book about the whole incident and suggested he might call it "Hoop-Skirt Diplomacy"; subsequently, it declared that this kind of imbroglio would mean that diplomacy would fall "into the hands of bachelors."[71]

As the supposed instigator of the rift, Julia Fish featured in the center of more than one article. The *Brooklyn Eagle* referred to Mrs. Fish and Ms. Catacazy each as "a querelous queen of a court circle in the Republican Capital." The competition between two women for social preeminence was at the root of all the trouble; according to the *Eagle*, Fish disliked Catacazy because "the wife of the Plenipotentiary successfully rivalled the wife of the Secretary of State in the contest for social laurels in Washington last Winter and Winter before last."[72] The *Cleveland Daily Plain Dealer* observed, "It was a big day in Secretary Fish's domestic circle when Catacazy *and wife* were dragged in the dust. Mrs. Fish looks ten years younger since that event."[73] In the meantime, the Grant administration had agreed to tolerate the Russian minister until the end of the Grand Duke's visit. The *Cleveland Daily Plain Dealer* found humor in the fact that "Mrs. Fish, too, will have to suffer the torture of seeing that beautiful but 'disreputable' Mrs. Catacazy the most favored woman at the capital all the time his lovely highness is there."[74]

The press of other countries chimed in as well. The *Montreal Gazette* dismissed the rumors that a snubbing of Madame Catacazy had caused all the trouble, citing instead the Russian minister's penchant for airing dirty laundry in the American press. The London *Daily News* agreed.[75] The *Freeman's Journal and Daily Commercial Advertiser* in Dublin accepted the likelihood that the entire brouhaha boiled down to the competition between Mrs. Fish and Mrs. Catacazy.[76] The *Toronto Globe*, reflecting on the questionable nature of Catacazy's marriage, supported Fish and criticized Russia for sending such a man as its representative, observing, "There is not a court in Europe where M. Catacazy and his mistress would be received, *and there is not one to which they would have been sent.*" The *Globe* sympathized with the United States, stating, "We suppose the Emperor thinks it is a matter of no consequence what sort of persons he sends as his accredited representatives to the Great Republic." Finally, in a wholly moralistic tone, the paper concluded with, "Perhaps there is a large amount of relationship in Washington equally 'naughty,' but they are not so ostentatiously flaunted in the faces of people who are old-fashioned enough not to believe that it is quite the thing, to covet other men's wives and run off with them, without even saying, 'by your leave.'"[77]

Not all sources believed that the disapproval of Washington society had caused the rift. The *New York Times* wrote on the eve of the Grand Duke Alexis's visit that Catacazy's claim that his fall from favor was linked to his wife's exclusion by some of the diplomatic wives was ridiculous and not to be trusted since he had also loudly proclaimed to be the victim of the Perkins attorneys.[78]

* * *

The Catacazy Affair is reminiscent of an episode that occurred forty years earlier during the administration of Andrew Jackson. In 1829, Jackson selected John Henry Eaton to be his secretary of war. Eaton was married to Margaret Timberlake Eaton, a widow with two children. Her family had for many years owned a boarding house and hotel where many Washington officials, including both Jackson and Eaton, stayed when Congress was in session or when other duties called them to the Capitol. As a frequent resident Andrew Jackson had come to know and grow fond of Margaret. Eaton was a close friend and confidante of Jackson, so his selection of Eaton as secretary of war was not a surprise to anyone. Yet the social and political ramifications of that choice were more than Jackson or Eaton could have anticipated.[79]

Margaret came from a working-class family that ran a boarding house. She married and was widowed, and remarried to John Eaton less than a year after her first husband's death. There were also rumors that she and Eaton had begun their affair before she became a widow, while her husband was away at sea. Beautiful, feisty, and outspoken, nothing about Margaret Eaton fit into the rules of elite proper society, and the Washington wives made this abundantly clear. Though Margaret attempted to enter the capital's world of polite society, making the appropriate visits and leaving calling cards as required by contemporary etiquette, the wives of Jackson's cabinet members refused to return her visits. Moreover, they snubbed her at dinners, receptions, and parties, thereby taking a private affair to the public and into politics. Jackson spent two years defending John and Margaret Eaton, even threatening to fire cabinet members if they refused to persuade their wives and daughters to cease their ostracization of the controversial woman. It was a losing battle, and even Jackson's own relatives refused to associate with Margaret. Jackson took this defiance personally. His deceased wife, his beloved Rachel, had also been the subject of rumors and gossip, and Jackson believed it had contributed to her death in 1828, just days after his election as president. Jackson came to view opposition to Margaret as tantamount to a rejection and betrayal of him. As one historian described it, "Jackson had made the social matter of the ladies into a litmus test of political loyalty." In the end, the Washington wives were victorious—all but one of Jackson's cabinet members resigned rather than interfere in the politics of female society.[80]

There are some strong similarities between the Eaton Affair and the Catacazy Affair, though the role of women was much larger and more public and pronounced in the former. Both Margaret Eaton and Olga Catacazy were described by contemporaries as exceptional women. Margaret was both pretty and outspoken and, because of her family's business, had a comfortable rapport with men unusual in that era for women of the upper class. She was "a vivacious beauty who radiated sexuality in a manner that was deemed highly improper."[81] Olga was also described as exceptionally beautiful and the press made much of her grace and charm, declaring that the withdrawal of the Catacazys represented "the triumph of Mrs. Fish and her following of the plain but proper Washington matrons."[82] Another paper, however, felt that the departure of the Russian couple still failed to settle the question, "Which is the handsomest woman—Mrs. Secretary Fish or Mrs. Catacazy?"[83] In both the Eaton Affair and the Catacazy Affair, the women at the center of the scandal challenged the expectations of refined society, daring to attempt an entrée with no regard to their unconventional or scandalous pasts. And in both cases, it was the world of women and their rules for societal acceptance and interaction that determined the fates of men. The similarities between the two cases were so strong that even the *Cincinnati Daily Enquirer* noticed them: "Yes, woman were at the bottom of it, just as they have been at the bottom of more than one White House squabble, from Mrs. Eaton down to Kate Sprague and Mrs. Lincoln."[84]

The rules of society, and the determination of women to uphold them, should not be underestimated. The wives in Washington could be vicious and ruthless in their attempts to exercise control in one of the few domains that was entirely theirs. Andrew Jackson once told Margaret Eaton, "I had rather have live vermin on my back than the tongue of one of the Washington women on my reputation."[85] Jackson eventually understood the power of women in this particular arena. During the Eaton Affair, he tried to convince several of his cabinet members, the husbands of these social tyrants, to order their wives to receive Margaret Eaton. The men would not. Even under the threat of termination, at least three of Jackson's cabinet members insisted that it was the right and duty of the women to dictate the rules of social intercourse and the job of their husbands to support their decisions. None of them dared to intervene in the strict and vicious world of women and social etiquette.[86] In 1871, the *Boston Herald* acknowledged the role women could play in politics and diplomacy, assessing the Catacazy imbroglio as "entirely personal … entirely out of an unseemly squabble between those members of the social circle not necessarily recognized in diplomatic relations … female jealousy of a pretty woman lying at the bottom of it."[87]

The Eaton Affair and the Catacazy Affair both underscore the fact that women, though still excluded from the suffrage, could exert a great deal of influence in the world of politics. It is well understood that American women had long played an influential role in society in its more general definition thanks to the antebellum belief that women were morally superior. Therefore, benevolence in its various manifestations was necessarily the work of women. The causes that women often embraced included the betterment of the poor, prison reform, abolitionism, temperance, and the elimination of prostitution. After the Civil War, benevolent activism became more engaged in pushing for changes that required government action, thus leading to a greater intersection of charity work and politics. This kind of activism could, and did, result in policy changes. Thus, women were not entirely outside the world of politics just because they could not vote.[88]

Another example of women's influence, though in a more indirect way, was their ability to participate in political gatherings and campaigns. As voting became a rite of passage to manhood in the second half of the nineteenth century, women found other ways to exercise their political views via the men in their lives—brothers, beaux, and husbands. Some women used romance to express and assert their opinions and advocate for certain candidates. It was not unheard of for a woman to turn down a marriage proposal because the young man's political views were unacceptable to her. Once married, women continued to exert influence on their husbands regarding politics or, at the very least, they tried.[89]

In the cases of Margaret Eaton and Olga Catacazy, the "Washington wives" were displaying a different kind of power—one exercised in "polite society," the world of parties and dinners and social visits, where etiquette dictated certain behaviors and courtesies, and the failure to observe these expectations would be interpreted as an insult or extremely poor manners. This arena of polite society seems superficial and perhaps even silly to modern, democratic readers, but it was anything but insignificant in the period we are examining. In a world where women were known only by their husbands' names and titles, it should be no surprise that women fiercely defended the rules and protocols of society and were "ever vigilant against the slightest encroachment upon their place in the social pecking order."[90] This was particularly true in Washington, where the interactions and alliances in private society often intersected with politics. Moreover, American women exercised virtually unchallenged dominance in this arena. This "queen bee" status distinguished American women from their European counterparts where men dictated the rules of social life and even in many cases authored the books of good manners. By the end of the nineteenth century, "ambition and social drive were ... the outstanding characteristics of the American woman," as French visitors to the United States observed.[91] Jackson, the victor at New Orleans and the slayer of the Bank of the United States, proved unable to coerce even members of his own family to accept Peggy Eaton. As Henry Adams wrote in March 1872 of his soon-to-be wife, "She rules me as only American women rule men."[92]

* * *

Not everyone believed that Olga Catacazy's place in Washington society had contributed to her husband's recall. Harriet Blaine wrote to her son Walker in October 19, 1871, "I suppose you see by the American papers all the Catacazy gossip. I don't think his wife has anything to do with the trouble, as it is really all diplomatic, but it seems very hard on her."[93] In the end, how much the drama surrounding Olga Catacazy contributed to the downfall of her husband is impossible to determine. The Russian minister had certainly alienated and angered several important people in the administration, and his intrigues and breaches of protocol were the primary cause of his dismissal. His personal life played a role also, however. In a personal and unofficial letter to Elihu Washburne, the American minister to France, Fish sketched out Catacazy's various offenses, but added, "the scandal of his private & domestic life, is terrible—but with that we cannot officially concern ourselves."[94]

One cannot ignore the importance of the social crisis created by the disapproval, and perhaps jealousy, of the Washington wives. Women could not vote or participate in politics officially, but they could influence certain situations and exercised a specific power in "society" that men dare not challenge. John W. Foster, in his *Diplomatic Memoirs*, implied that the Russian couple should have known better. He observed that scandals among diplomats in Europe were so common that they were hardly noticed, but in America diplomats found "the standard of social life very different, and some of them are inclined to look upon it as prudish and puritanic." The Russian minister would have also known this, but "Catacazy and others of his day lived quite in disregard of the ideas prevailing in Washington."[95] Perhaps the meddlesome diplomat would have fared better had he conformed a bit more to the expectations of American society.

6

"A Thorough Mischief Maker": The Recall of Catacazy

The recall of a foreign representative was no small affair. It had, however, been necessary on more than one occasion. The first time the US government had to dismiss a foreign minister occurred when the nation was still in its infancy, and coincided with the first time the United States had issued a declaration of neutrality. Both of these actions were precipitated by the French Revolution. The storming of the Bastille on July 14, 1789, initiated a revolution that became increasingly radical and violent with each passing year, sending shock waves through the other monarchies of Europe, and setting France at war with much of Europe by late 1792. In America, the Washington administration was split over the question of America's obligation to intervene. France had assisted the American revolutionaries during their war of independence, making some Americans, like Thomas Jefferson, believe that a debt was owed. Alexander Hamilton and his supporters, however, argued that the French Revolution had drifted far from its Enlightenment roots and should not receive American support. Ultimately, President George Washington agreed with Hamilton and issued a Proclamation of Neutrality in late April 1793.

Edmond-Charles Genêt, popularly referred to as Citizen Genêt, arrived as French minister to the United States in the midst of this debate, however. The thirty-year-old Frenchman spoke seven languages and had already served in diplomatic posts in St. Petersburg and London. Despite these credentials, Genêt lacked the tact and finesse required of a successful diplomat and displayed these shortcomings fully during his short term as minister. Genêt hoped to get material assistance for France's wars in Europe and intended to encourage attacks against British and Spanish possessions in North America as well. He also began to facilitate the creation of privateers to seize British merchant ships and recruited a small army to attack St. Augustine, Florida, then under Spanish control.[1]

As Genêt traveled from Charleston, South Carolina, to Philadelphia to present his letter of introduction to Washington, he was celebrated and fêted as a celebrity. Citizens who feared that the failure of the French Revolution might lead to the collapse of the American experiment formed societies and advocated sympathy for the French. Genêt welcomed and encouraged these public displays of Francophilia, particularly in Philadelphia where republican sentiment was strong. For Hamilton and others, these were potentially dangerous developments. Meanwhile, Genêt also continued to convert private vessels into pro-French privateers, even after Secretary of State Thomas Jefferson told him to stop doing so. Genêt's final misstep was challenging the constitutional legitimacy of Washington's statement of neutrality while simultaneously declaring that he would appeal directly to the American people for support for France. This alienated even Jefferson, and in mid-July, he and Hamilton agreed that it was time to ask the French government to recall Genêt; a month later, Jefferson sent the request to France. By this time, however, the situation had grown so dangerous for Genêt in France that the American government granted him asylum to remain in the United States.[2] Nonetheless, the episode with Genêt established the beginning of a precedent, as defined by Jefferson, that "It is a general rule that no nation has a right to keep an agent within the limits of another without the consent of that other."[3]

During roughly the same period of time, the United States had trouble with its Spanish minister as well, Don Carlos Martinez de Irujo. Soon after arriving in the United States in 1796, Irujo became embroiled in an argument with Secretary of State Thomas Pickering that turned into a battle in the American press, expressed in a series of letters written under pseudonyms (Irujo was one of the participants). Irujo claimed that he had been libeled personally, as had the reputations of the Spanish monarch and the Spanish nation, and filed charges against one of the authors of these articles.[4] Henry Adams, in his *History of the United States during the First Administration of Thomas Jefferson*, described Irujo in a manner that suggests a much more charming and capable version of Catacazy: "irascible, headstrong, indiscreet as was possible for a diplomatist and afraid of no prince or president, young, able, quick, aggressive, devoted to his king and country, a flighty and dangerous friend but a most troublesome enemy; always in difficulties, but in spite of fantastic outbursts always respectable."[5] For his part, Irujo did not like President John Adams, whom he called Machiavellianist, nor Thomas Pickering, declaring him "a violent man, of very little culture, without morals or civility."[6] Needless to say, Irujo's actions tested the patience of the president and the secretary of state as well.

Unable to tolerate the abrasive minister any longer, the Adams administration asked for Irujo's replacement, and the Spanish government agreed. But Irujo insisted that he should wait until his successor arrived, a tactic that paid off, because when Jefferson took office, the new president asked the Spanish government to keep Irujo in his post. Jefferson later changed his mind. In April 1805, Secretary of State James Madison requested the removal of Irujo, due to his

> very disrespectful conduct & expressions … towards the Government of the United States, on different occasions; his attempt to suborn a Citizen of the said States, in violation of an Act of Congress, into a combination with him to attack the measures of their Government; his own direct attacks on the same, by the publication of papers in the Gazettes, which were the no less obnoxious, by being addressed to the Secretary of State himself, in which he attempts to make an appeal to the people against their own Government; as well as the whole tenor of his conduct for a considerable time past.[7]

The Spanish government responded that Irujo had asked to leave, so the change could take place without an official recall. Irujo, however, lingered, forcing Madison to address him in a letter of January 1806: "It is seen therefore not without Surprize [sic], that at this late Day, you should have repaired to the Seat of Government, as if nothing had occurred rendering such a step improper." Madison made clear that Jefferson wanted Irujo to leave, though he would not "insist on your Departure from the U. States during an inclement Season, he expects it will not be unnecessarily postponed, after this Obstacle sh⟨all⟩ have ceased."[8] Irujo still did not leave, however, and finally, John Quincy Adams, who was then serving in the Senate, put forth a bill that allowed the president to arrest and transport out of the country any minister who had been recalled and refused to leave within an appropriate amount of time. This was finally the end of Irujo in Washington. The Spanish government demanded that he leave and Irujo finally obeyed, if reluctantly.[9]

These early cases established a precedent that the recall of a diplomatic representative from another nation could be requested when necessary. Moreover, it was assumed that the nation that diplomat represented would cooperate. In 1847, the future president James Buchanan, who was then serving as secretary of state, wrote, "In the intercourse between friendly nations, when the diplomatic representative of the one has rendered himself as so unacceptable to the authorities of the other as to impair or destroy his usefulness, it has ever been the custom, unless under extraordinary circumstances, to yield to such a request when made in respectful and friendly terms."[10] Accordingly, President Grant and Secretary of State Fish were well within their rights to ask for Catacazy's removal and Russia should have agreed without challenge. The rules of diplomacy, however, are never as straightforward and transparent as they seem.

* * *

The mechanics of Catacazy's recall are complicated and involve many pieces of correspondence. The primary persons engaged in these exchanges were Fish, Curtin, Catacazy, and Gorchakov, though their letters, telegrams, and dispatches refer to conversations and consultations with many others. Fish first discussed Catacazy's recall with Grant on June 16, 1871, submitting for his approval a letter to the American minister in St. Petersburg. Having secured Grant's approval, Fish sent the letter to Curtin later that same day. The letter stated that both Catacazy's official and personal conduct had been "such as materially to impair his usefulness to his own government and to render intercourse with him for either business or social purposes highly disagreeable." Consequently, Grant believed it was in the best interest of the friendly relations between Russia and the United States for the Russian representative in Washington to be changed.[11] That same day, Fish and Catacazy met and once again Catacazy attempted to persuade Fish that agents of the Perkins claims were behind the mysterious dispatches of the previous year. Fish declared that though he never believed that the dispatches were genuine, he also did not accept the notion that they came from the Perkins men who were smart enough to recognize that provoking a controversy with the person who might determine the fate of their case would be a bad strategy.[12] Catacazy believed, or claimed to believe, otherwise. Only a few days after this meeting with Fish, he wrote to Vladimir de Westmann, undersecretary at the Russian Foreign Ministry, that he hoped the Perkins case was drawing to a close, despite "foreign intrigues and Mr. Fish's unspeakable volte face."[13]

In mid-July, Fish received a most unwelcome reply to his request for Catacazy's recall. Because the Russian Foreign Minister Gorchakov was in Germany for health reasons, Curtin had to discuss the matter with Vladimir de Westmann. Westmann was apparently unaware of Catacazy's conduct and only knew there had been some difficulties with individuals involved in the Perkins case. He argued that there was no proof against Catacazy to warrant his dismissal and expressed regret that this issue should arrive on the eve of the Grand Duke Alexis's departure for the United States. Curtin found himself in a difficult position. Westmann did not dare act on such a delicate matter without Gorchakov's express direction, asking that it wait until October, when the foreign minister returned, but neither could Curtin present it to the tsar directly. Curtin disliked the delay necessitated by the foreign minister's absence, especially because he believed Gorchakov to be a man of common sense who desired good relations with the United States. Moreover, Curtin observed, "Mr. Catacazy is emphatically his man, and it is said here, the Emperor yielded reluctantly to his repeated requests to give him a diplomatic place, and I believe he would be glad to make the change at Washington without giving the Emperor the reasons for it."[14]

Two days later, Westmann asked to meet with Curtin again so that they could both clarify the content of their exchange on the subject of Catacazy's recall. As they discussed the situation, Westmann noted that the recall of a foreign minister was a serious matter and, therefore, rarely requested. He expressed his opinion that foreign representatives in the United States had greater difficulty than those elsewhere because of the American policies of free speech and freedom of the press, and "of everybody being permitted to write or say what he pleased, and what he thinks most necessary for the purpose of advancing—openly or underhand—his private interests." Westmann suggested that in addition to the Perkins men there were others who might benefit from animosity between Fish and Catacazy—the British, who were always jealous of the Russian-American friendship. He also pointed out that the Russian government had, in the past, tolerated a problematic American minister, referring to Cassius Clay, and "although the authorities prohibited any mention in the daily papers," the Russian government "never thought of demanding his sudden recall, simply for the reason, that it was anxious to spare the feelings of the American Government and people."[15]

* * *

Westmann may have had a point. The United States was not beyond reproach with regard to misbehaving ministers. Contemporaries made comparisons between the Catacazy Affair and similar scandals involving American ministers to other countries. The *Buffalo Commercial Advertiser* questioned the stories about Mrs. Catacazy's past, but added, "it does not behoove a Government that sent General Sickles to represent the American people at the court of Madrid, to be over-squeamish about the proprieties."[16] Dan Sickles, a Civil War general, was a man with an interesting and shockingly checkered past. Sickles became secretary to the American Legation in London in 1853 and, leaving his wife and very young daughter behind, invited his mistress, a prostitute named Fanny White, to join him; he subsequently took Fanny with him to a reception hosted by Queen Victoria at Buckingham Palace. Six years later, Sickles became the center of an enormous scandal when he murdered his wife's lover, the son of Francis Scott Key (author of "The Star-Spangled Banner"), and then became the first man to successfully use the plea of temporary insanity in his defense. Despite these considerable blemishes on his reputation, Sickles was appointed minister to Spain in 1869. The *Buffalo Commercial Advertiser* recognized the irony that anyone should criticize Catacazy and his wife while Sickles sat in Madrid as the American representative.[17]

The other scandal involving an American minister was that of the Kentucky abolitionist, Cassius Marcellus Clay, who served as American ambassador to Russia from 1863 to 1869. During his time as ambassador, he became acquainted with a Swiss-Irish couple, Jean and Elisa Chautems. The details of the relationship are unclear. Mrs. Chautems declared that when she and her husband faced financial ruin and the confiscation of their belongings, Clay took it upon himself to assist them, engaging several other Americans to contribute money for their aid as well. He then became a regular fixture at their home and took a keen interest in their fourteen-year-old daughter, attempting to get her alone to molest her. Mrs. Chautems also declared that Clay attempted to assault her. In his memoirs, Clay later declared that all of these accusations were false, and that Chautems herself was guilty of trying to "sell her daughter's chastity." As to the claim that he had attacked the mother, Clay's defense was that Chautems was too repulsive for him to have taken a sexual interest in her: "She was over forty years old, with chronic bronchitis all the time I knew her, confining her for weeks to bed; with a most offensive breath; and even had she been virtuous, she was decidedly *passee!*" He admitted that he gave them money, but insisted they took advantage of him, selling the furniture he had just reclaimed for them and never repaying him any of the money.[18] Leaving this particular scandal aside, Clay also had a reputation for his liaisons in the Russian capital, and even fathered a child with a Russian ballerina.[19] The *Cleveland Daily Plain Dealer* noted with irony that in light of the "bad habits … and shocking company" of Clay, perhaps Gorchakov's slow action in removing Catacazy was "paying us back in our own coin."[20] Comparing this to the Catacazy scandal, the American linguist and translator Jeremiah Curtin wrote in his memoirs, "If Grant had been aware of all Russia condoned during Clay's stay in St. Petersburg, he would have probably been wise enough, not to have been influenced by women and Bancroft Davis" in the removal of Catacazy.[21] Fish and Curtin did not think it was an accurate comparison. In a letter to Fish, Curtin wrote,

You are perfectly correct when you say that the toleration of the presence of my predecessor at St. Petersburg offers no parallel to the case of Mr. Catacazy as presented to that Government and at all times when that consideration was presented to me I answered that without they could convince me that he had maligned the Emperor on the Chancellor of the Empire or indeed any of the Official Dignitaries who surround the Emperor I would accept it as a reason for the retention of Mr. Catacazy to be seriously considered.[22]

In mid-August 1871, Fish asked his assistant Bancroft Davis to send a letter and telegram to Curtin stressing the necessity of an early recall. The letter expressed frustration at the suggestion that any action could not be considered until the return of Gorchakov, noting that telegraphic communication allowed consultation with him. Davis warned, "If, however, the decision should be indefinitely postponed or if the request should be refused, the most disagreeable results may follow from such a course, results which might even tend to impair the good understanding between the two governments."[23] At this time, Fish also informed Catacazy of the request for his recall.

Before receiving these communications, Curtin had already sent Fish another telegram (in late August) describing yet another meeting with Westmann in which the latter expressed frustration that the matter of Catacazy was still not settled, with the Grand Duke set to sail within the week. Curtin declared,

I begged him to consider that it was the desire of the President to extend to the Grand Duke such amenities as would be most agreeable to him and acceptable to the Emperor and people of Russia, but that he desired that the representative of Russia should not be a person obnoxious to him and one who has been in the habit of defaming him; I insisted that the change was asked now so as to be relieved of the presence of a man who is odious and disagreeable.[24]

Westmann insisted that there was no time to change the Russian minister and Alexis could not visit if there was no representative present. He declared that this entire episode was "a political intrigue, in which there are many actively participating, to prevent the visit of the son of the Emperor and to break the friendship of the Governments and peoples of Russia and the United States." Moreover, he was certain that if the United States demanded the immediate recall of the Russian minister, the tsar would order the Russian fleet to return and cancel the visit of the Grand Duke. Westmann once again referred to Clay's questionable behavior and the Russian government's tolerance of him.[25]

Curtin was very concerned about the intensifying conflict and its potential ramifications, noting, "the Russian people have really such exaggerated ideas of our country, that they look with large expectations to the reception the Grand Duke will meet there." Both the tsar and his wife had expressed great enthusiasm about their son's departure for America. The visit of a member of the Imperial family to the United States was "an event of great political significance," Curtin pled: "Pardon me, my dear Governor, if I exceed the proprieties of my place when I suggest, that if it is at all possible to tolerate the presence of Mr. Catacazy, the visit of the Grand Duke had better not be interfered with by the demand for the recall of the Minister."[26] A few days later, when he finally received the letter and telegram from Davis (approximately two weeks after Davis had written them), he immediately responded, repeating his tense and unpleasant conversations with Westmann. Curtin requested a quick reply, adding that he awaited Fish's response with "great anxiety, as this affair becomes very grave and [may] indeed lead to unpleasant differences."[27] Curtin was also worried about the speed and security of his dispatches; he began to send some of them via General Schenk in London, noting, "If sent from Petersburg I might just as well had the foreign office a copy, and the cipher used by our Government is not a secret here."[28]

Fish was very unhappy with the pace and direction of the conversation about Catacazy's recall, and he was quick to let Curtin know. In the first week of September, Fish sent an angry telegram to Curtin, reprimanding him for his poor handling of his meetings with Westmann and declaring, "the suggestion of an intrigue is unworthy and should have been repelled." It was Catacazy who had encouraged this notion when, in fact, he had "made himself personally offensive in conversation and by publications abusive of the President and it is for this cause that his recall is asked" (underline in original source). Fish's frustration is apparent in this brief, yet significant, telegram, and it is safe to assume that Curtin was beginning to dread receiving communication from the secretary.[29]

Fish's anger may have been further provoked by the publication on September 5 in the *New York Herald* of an article with the byline "St. Petersburg, August 12, 1871" that claimed that reliable sources in the Russian capital revealed that the stories about Catacazy's recall were false and that the minister was, in fact, fully supported by his government. The unknown author of this report declared, "I have very high authority for the statement that M. Westmann has forwarded to M. Catacazy an official approval of his conduct in the Perkins claim … this approval is at the special request of the Czar." The anonymous informant also claimed that when Fish had told Catacazy about the request for his recall, Catacazy had been delighted to hear it and had replied, "that it would please him very much to be summoned back to his native land." The story was printed in other newspapers as well.[30] Subsequently, several papers noted a discrepancy that revealed the author of the mysterious report to be the Russian minister. The conversation alluded to in the unsigned article, during which Fish informed Catacazy about the request for his recall, took place on August 16; yet, the report that claimed to have come from St. Petersburg was dated August 12, four days prior to the meeting. Even the Russian newspaper *Golos* noticed the inconsistency with the dates of these events, though it did not accuse Catacazy.[31] Though there was no absolute proof, the most likely culprit for this unidentified report was the Russian minister, particularly given his penchant for using the American press to mislead and misrepresent.

Curtin did his best to fulfill the American government's wishes and consequently he met frequently with Westmann during this period. Westmann continued to mention "intrigues" designed to prevent Alexis's visit, and Curtin countered these arguments with assertions about Catacazy's poor conduct. Westmann repeated that there was no evidence, and Curtin declared that "as the President believed he had been abusing him in conversation and through the press, no proof should be asked." Westmann read Curtin a letter from Catacazy to the tsar in which he described a visit to President Grant at Long Branch, his seaside retreat in New Jersey; Catacazy declared that Grant had treated him with great kindness, courtesy, and respect. Curtin was surprised by the story of this encounter as it was inconsistent with his understanding of the state of affairs, but Westmann took it as confirmation that Catacazy was still well received at Washington.[32] Curtin was surprised by another bit of news as well. Westmann announced that the tsar was now aware of the conflict and, speaking on behalf of the tsar, he requested that the president "tolerate" the Russian minister until after the royal visit.[33] The two-hour meeting was at times "unpleasant and much excited," and Curtin feared that the Russian-American friendship was on the verge of collapse. He hoped that he would receive a quick reply from Fish with a conciliatory solution, adding, "and then this vexatious affair will be off my hands."[34]

Curtin understood the significance of the Grand Duke's visit. He observed with cynicism, "there is in the United States an impression there is great sympathy between the people of the two countries which is a delusion," but the American press had "magnified into ridiculous and absurd extravagance … excited expectations in our people that to disappoint would require explanation." Nonetheless, he felt that if Catacazy was recalled before the visit, the tsar would order his son home and "it would lead to very unpleasant comments in Europe.[35] George Pomutz, secretary to the Russian Legation in St. Petersburg, concurred and reported that the press in Russia was enthusiastic about the Grand Duke's journey and complimentary to the people and government of the United States. No Russian newspaper, so far as he had seen, had mentioned the Catacazy difficulty, which indicated to Pomutz that the Russian Imperial Foreign Office had done a good job of keeping it a secret.[36]

By this point in the process, Catacazy had been aware that Fish and Grant had asked for his recall for almost a month (August 16, to be exact). In a letter of September 13, Catacazy wrote to Westmann about the situation, referring to "gratuitous acts of hostility" and suggesting that Fish was hoping to ruin the Grand Duke's visit by attempting to quarantine the Russian squadron under the pretense of cholera. While there was, in fact, a significant concern about that dreaded disease at the time, Catacazy's accusation regarding cholera was entirely unfounded. The United States had been hit by cholera in 1866, beginning in New York and affecting twenty-four other cities.[37] The *New York World* reported in late August 1871 on the path of cholera "from the Ganges to the Hudson" and asked, "Has it arrived in the city?"[38] Fear undoubtedly intensified when the *World* reported only days before the Grand Duke's arrival that a German steamer had arrived at Staten Island with cholera on board. Forty-one people had died at sea and another nineteen were admitted to the hospital when the passengers disembarked.[39] Catacazy, somewhat presumptuously, proposed to Westmann that in the event of his recall at the time of Alexis's visit, the Grand Duke should abstain from going to Washington to see the president and should travel incognito as a simple tourist; actually, Catacazy countered, even if they did not recall him but simply continued in their "hostile manifestations," Alexis should circumvent the capital and travel independently.[40]

* * *

While Curtin anxiously awaited a reply to his latest dispatch and further instructions, Fish discussed Catacazy's recall with Grant and expressed his expectation that all would soon be settled. The secretary of state understood that there would certainly be some disappointment should the royal visit be cancelled, but, like Curtin, he viewed it all with some cynicism:

> Our people have an exaggerated idea of the friendship of Russia for this Government—like all international friendships, this one is of interest rather than of sentiment or sympathy but the popular belief that it is real cannot be mistaken. Russia has used it (as we have also done) as an element to operate upon other Powers in negotiating with them. It may still be of some avail to us, while the Arbitrations of the Alabama question or the San Juan boundary are pending.[41]

He suggested that they telegraph Curtin that the president would "endure the continuance of a very obnoxious minister" for the duration of the Grand Duke's visit, but would not receive him unless in the company of the royal guest and would hold no conversation with him. Moreover, if the Russian minister was not summoned at the conclusion of Alexis's trip, he would be immediately dismissed.[42] Asking Bancroft Davis and two others to review the proposed telegram, Fish stated that the threat of immediate dismissal was the only part that might upset the Russian government, but he believed it was necessary and would only leave it out if they believed it to be too potentially offensive. Fish observed, "an Envoy Extraordinary has not the <u>right</u> to claim to be personally received i.e. after his official presentation, by the President" (underline in original source).[43] Grant was highly irritated by the matter, stating to Fish, "The course you recommend is no doubt right, but I feel very much like sending Mr. C out of the country verry [sic] summarily … No Minister of any pride of character would concent [sic] to remain at a Capital after just such an interview as Mr. C. had with me."[44] Ultimately, Grant approved Fish's proposal and the offer was sent to St. Petersburg. Though they did not know it, both governments had arrived at the same compromise, but the slow speed of overseas communication hampered their ability to resolve the crisis, further exacerbating tensions.

Meanwhile, Catacazy was losing ground in his efforts to gain, or retain, allies within the ranks of his diplomatic colleagues back home. Even as Westmann awaited a response from the US government, it is apparent from his correspondence with Catacazy that Westmann began to doubt parts of the Russian representative's story. In particular, he questioned Catacazy's account of the alleged friendly meeting with Grant, wondering why the recall continued if he had been so well received. "You see, my dear Catacazy," Westmann wrote, "how serious the matter is, … To appreciate exactly the character and scope of it we would have to be enlightened on its true motives. At the distance we are, we can only make assumptions based on your reports. The Perkins affair is obviously not sufficient to justify an irritation." Westmann continued that the Russian government understood that a foreign representative had a difficult position that required a certain amount of involvement in American affairs, "but this interest has its limits." A minister should not cast his lot with one political party, particularly the party in opposition to the president. Westmann believed that this was at the heart of the matter. Catacazy had been accused of stating that Grant had a monetary interest in the Perkins claim. Westmann stated, "If you have let this conviction out, the irritation of the President would be conceivable to a certain extent." Above all, the tsar wanted to be sure that this difficulty did not affect the success of the Grand Duke's visit. Westmann recommended circumspection and tact, emphasizing, "be reserved, do not put yourself too much forward personally." Finally, he suggested, if Catacazy could successfully navigate the Grand Duke's visit, it could "reflect favorably" on his personal situation.[45]

By this point in the scandal the Russian press had become aware of the unfolding drama and began to comment. In mid-August, the Russian newspaper *Golos* emphasized that the clash between the US government and the Russian minister was of a "totally personal character" and would not affect the Russian-American friendship which was, at that moment, experiencing a renewed pledge with the impending visit of Grand Duke Alexis.[46] Many of these articles were complete reprints or quotes from news sources abroad, often citing newspapers from the United States.[47] They primarily relayed the basic outline of the case, occasionally commenting on certain points of conflict. *Golos*, for example, justified its government's delay in July and August in addressing the American government's request, explaining that it was not immediately clear that Catacazy had done anything wrong and no clear evidence had been presented. Moreover, the timing was problematic, with the departure of the tsar's son on the immediate horizon. Finally, the paper added, the Foreign Office also had hoped that the conflict might be solved by some mutual agreement.[48] More than once the Russian papers challenged the haughty tone of American papers, for example, criticizing the way in which they reported on the American government's threat to deliver Catacazy's passports to him. *Golos* declared that this was "neither in agreement with diplomatic habits or propriety, nor the friendly relationship of the two countries." It was unfortunate, the paper suggested, that the American press had been unable to report this without "passion and prejudice, as it should have."[49]

Over the next several months, Catacazy made every effort to defend himself and to garner sympathy in Russia. In early October, he wrote to Westmann concerning a letter he received from Fish, declaring, "Every line, every word of this communication contains an insult and denotes a provocative bias."[50] Catacazy also reported that Fish had told him that he was being asked to leave, and that he was only being "tolerated" until the end of the Grand Duke's visit. Catacazy pled his innocence to Westmann and blamed his situation on outside forces, concluding, "At the height of six months any successor would see himself struggling with the same difficulties."[51] Subsequently, Catacazy wrote to Westmann and appended several articles from the *Herald*, the *World*, the *Sun*, the *Times*, and the *Evening Post*, in an attempt to convince Westmann that these articles were intentional provocations: "The obvious goal … to exasperate me into some act of imprudence which would prompt a return of passports."[52] Meanwhile, Catacazy appealed to others as well. In a letter to Peter Stremoukov, head of the Asiatic Department, Catacazy claimed, "It is not only from Washington, it is from St. Petersburg in particular that the most treacherous and dangerous attacks are composed against me."[53]

Catacazy also appealed to Gorchakov, of course, touching on a number of points in a long letter to the foreign minister. He insisted that the accusations against him were connected to the Perkins claim and declared that Grant and his entourage had a stake in the claim for $100,000. Catacazy stated, "It is clear that the money-makers who make up the present administration are meditating on hostile projects and that they are seeking a pretext for quarreling for this purpose."[54] He also intimated, however, that the affair was intended as a distraction to ensure the conclusion of the *Alabama* claims. According to Catacazy, Grant, Fish, and Davis "foresaw that the Congress would oppose the enactment of the onerous clauses of the Washington Treaty, and they would like to turn the difficulty by a diversion which absorbed public attention."[55] Ultimately, however, Catacazy believed that the United States was looking for an excuse to break with Russia. "If that were not the case," Catacazy argued, "if the incident was only personal, they would be satisfied with the promise of my recall … and Mr. Fish would not go boast to all the diplomats to have tamed and humiliated the Imperial Government."[56] Catacazy boldly suggested that the Russian government fight back by appealing to the "common sense of the American people" and expose these projects of President Grant, whose "administration is already very discredited … and acts of audacious corruption … notorious." Catacazy proposed that Russia should "note the inanity of the arbitrary charges … and declare that as long as the current administration is in power the Imperial Government can not have a minister in Washington." Catacazy believed that taking such action would demonstrate to the American government that "while being very well disposed to them we do not fear them and we do not intend to be treated by them lightly." Catacazy was aware that not everyone in St. Petersburg had faith in him; he complained that Westmann had insinuated that he had engaged in too much "feverish activity" in the United States, as well as altered his reports to the Russian Court, provoking the trouble he now faced.[57]

Catacazy apparently had supporters, however, both in the United States and at home. In a letter of early October, Catacazy thanked George B. Cowlan, a messenger for the postmaster of the House of Representatives, for his kind words and his offer to defend him publicly in the press. Explaining, with no apparent sense of irony, that his official position did not allow him to take such action, Catacazy added, "Dishonesty and cowardice do never prevail at length on justice and manliness. Sooner or later truth will be known and the slanderers and their abettors will receive their well deserved punishment."[58] Catacazy told Simon Cameron, a senator from Harrisburg, Pennsylvania, a similar thing. Citing his inability to defend himself, he suggested, "If you should feel inclined to … secure a proper treatment I think you would … render an eminent service to your country and to the President himself who I am firmly convinced has only been misled by intentional misrepresentations."[59] Catacazy's tone in these letters was dignified, yet heavy with martyrdom. In correspondence with another supporter, he wrote, "Whatever a ring of unscrupulous men could do for attaining their sordid end, I am fully convinced that the great majority of the American people will not approve their mischiefs and their outrages against the Representative of Russia."[60] The Russian paper *Golos*, meanwhile, defended Catacazy's official honor, taking issue with the notion that the president of the United States would not speak to him. The paper stated, "until such time as the representative has been presented his papers, he is expected to fulfill his obligations and, it follows, has the right to respect."[61]

Overall, however, the Russian minister had more detractors than sympathizers. Many newspapers supported Fish and Grant in their decision regarding Catacazy. The *New York World* humorously noted, "We so rarely have an opportunity of approving the conduct of President Grant."[62] At this point, however, so little of the truth was known publicly that it must have been difficult for the average American citizen to untangle the various threads of the scandal. There are always those who are willing to take a strong stance, however. In early October, Catacazy received an anonymous death threat. Written on a blue piece of paper, with no date or signature, the note said: "You damned lying, thieving son of a whore! Considering the contempt in which you are held in the country, you would no doubt like to get out of it safely, - but you never shall; your scattered brains will surely disgrace an American cesspool, so be prepared, you hound!! I will have a chance at your thick head soon" (underline in original source). The threat was postmarked "October 7th, Washington, D. C."[63]

The fact that Catacazy had Greek ancestry led some people to blame his questionable behavior on his ethnic heritage, resulting in some unfortunate racial stereotyping. As far back as Virgil's *Aeneid*, one can find characterizations of Greeks as dishonest and duplicitous. More than one newspaper saw fit to use the adjective "Greek" in a pejorative manner. The *New York Times* called Catacazy a "Greek intriguer" and the "remarkable Greek" and commented that his "Greek curiosity … cannot refrain from dabbling in newspapers."[64] The *Leavenworth Daily Commercial* called him "that meddlesome Greek."[65] The *Brooklyn Eagle* was more explicit: "Catacazy's policy of back stairs diplomacy, correspondent retaining and colossal lying was thoroughly consistent with his education as a Russian Ambassador with a Greek cross in his pedigree."[66] This characterization was not limited to the American press. In describing Catacazy's interference in the *Alabama* claims settlement, the *Aberdeen Journal* in Scotland noted, "that person, who is Greek, exercised all the cunning of his race."[67] Similarly, the London *Daily News* snidely observed, "he has all the Greek fondness for petty intrigue, without the necessary adroitness to conceal his manoeuvres."[68] Even Blaque Bey, the Turkish minister to the United States, slurred the Russian minister, commenting on the current situation: "He is a Greek, that accounts for it … he is a Greek <u>doubled</u> upon a Russian" (underline in original source).[69]

∗ ∗ ∗

Throughout this period, Catacazy continued to appeal to Fish for reconsideration. In late October, he once again declared,

> The people who have sworn for a long time to make me leave America have been redoubled in recent days by publishing articles in the newspapers of New York all the more treacherous, that have the appearance of having been inspired by me; whoever does not know me or has been warned against me, might believe that I inspired these articles.

Addressing Fish not in his capacity as the Russian minister but as a private man, Catacazy asked for the secretary's help in clearing his name. He acknowledged their tense relationship but felt he could rely on Fish's integrity, suggesting, "one never addresses in vain an adversary gentleman to ask for his assistance against intrigue and cowardice."[70]

Fish, however, felt no compulsion to help Catacazy, nor to change his mind about the Russian minister. In fact, he continued to receive information that incriminated the problematic foreign diplomat. In one of Curtin's long missives, the ambassador informed the secretary of state that Catacazy was not in good standing in Russia, his character "quite as well understood there as it is in Washington." Moreover, though Gorchakov had some affection for Catacazy, he could not secure him a promotion or even an official position equal to his current rank. Curtin observed, "It is unfortunate for Mr. Catacazy that the Emperor now understands him fully." Curtin had other things to say about Catacazy, as well. He now understood Westmann's comments about Grant receiving Catacazy with respect and kindness; Catacazy had lied about this encounter. Curtin commented that he would take "great pleasure" in setting the matter straight and would insist "that the Emperor be informed that Mr. Catacazy asked for an interview directly and without passing his request through your hands as is the etiquette of diplomacy."[71] It was, indeed, a well-established principle in American international law that foreign ministers were to recognize and communicate with the secretary of state as the "sole organ of the executive," the representative of the president.[72] The breach of protocol and Catacazy's dishonest representation of that meeting had infuriated Fish and Grant both. When Fish told Grant what Catacazy had been saying, the president had interrupted, "'that is a lie from beginning to end, every word of it.'" It made Grant wish he had dismissed Catacazy immediately without asking for his recall, but Fish believed a sudden dismissal would have insulted the Russian government.[73]

Other information was coming to light as well. On Fish's instruction, Bancroft Davis met with a man named Adolphe de Chambrun, legal attaché for the French Legation in Washington. De Chambrun declared that the mysterious dispatches of the previous year had been prepared by Catacazy, then given to a Russian named Dolgoriuki, who passed them on through several other individuals until they landed in the hands of Stewart, the attorney for Anna Perkins. This confirmed what Fish had believed to be true—"that Catacazy was the originator of the fraud"—but he needed proof. Davis asked de Chambrun if he could procure such proof, adding that Fish was willing to spend $500. De Chambrun agreed and said that "he felt confident that he would be able to furnish the desired proof."[74] (In the end, Chambrun was paid $600.)[75]

The Russian government continued to be uncooperative, or so it appeared. On November 1, the *Journal de St. Petersbourg*, an official or semi-official organ of the Russian Foreign Ministry, published a statement that Catacazy had not been told he had to leave after the Grand Duke's visit, nor had Curtin ever told the Russian government that the American government had threatened to send him his passports.[76] Over the next two days, the statement was widely printed in American and European papers.[77] The *New York Times* declared that if the *Journal* had indeed made the statements attributed to it, there was a likely explanation—"the only way for accounting for the inexactness of the journal referred to is that Mr. Catacazy has misled it, as he did so many newspapers in this country before his intrigues were discovered." The *Times* added with the ring of indignation, "Mr. Catacazy will not, unscrupulous as he is, dare assert that he has not had official reason to know that his passports will be sent to him if he is not then recalled."[78]

On November 16, the secretary of state sent a lengthy description of all of Catacazy's missteps to the Russian Foreign Office. Fish's note began with a statement that would later be quoted in subsequent cases involving the recall of ministers:

> The official or authorised statement that a Minister has made himself unacceptable or even that he has ceased to be persona grata to the Government to which he is accredited is sufficient to invoke the deference to a friendly power and the observance of the courtesy and the practice regulating the Diplomatic Intercourse of the Powers of Christendom for the recall of an objectionable minister.

In addition to describing Catacazy's clumsy handling of the Perkins claim, his alleged interference with American foreign affairs, and his use of the American press for sowing rumors and dissent, Fish also specifically addressed the Russian minister's complete misrepresentation of his meeting with Grant. Fish wrote, "I am directed by the President to say that this extract conveys an utterly inexact account of his interview with Mr. Catacazy." Moreover, Catacazy's mendacity concerning this meeting

> made it necessary that the President protect himself during the time that he might consent to tolerate the minister against the possibility of further obtrusion or misapprehension. He was therefore constrained to accompany his assent to the Emperor's request that Mr. Catacazy be tolerated with the announcement, that thereafter Mr. Catacazy would only be received when he might accompany His Imperial Highness, the Grand Duke and that on no occasion would the President hold any conversation with him.

Thus, the restriction on Catacazy that otherwise might have seemed excessive and intentionally insulting was, according to Fish, necessary to protect the president and his integrity.[79]

Fish also sent an abbreviated description of the reasons for Catacazy's recall to the American ambassadors stationed in other countries in order that they could answer questions and minimize gossip and speculation. In a private and unofficial letter, Fish wrote to Elihu B. Washburne, the American representative in Paris, "I enclose an article on Catacazy … his conduct has been atrocious—continual low intrigue, & resort to the newspapers, with calumnious insinuations against the President." In Fish's words, Catacazy was "a first-class scamp, & his reputation with his Diplomatic Colleagues is infamous—I believe, that without a solitary exception, they detest & despise him." He also relayed the story of Catacazy's breach of protocol in barging in on Grant at his retreat in Long Branch. Fish described how the president had treated Catacazy with "the greatest possible coldness," yet the Russian minister had telegraphed to his own government that he had received "the greatest cordiality & friendship."[80] Washburne was shocked by Catacazy's behavior and surprised that he had been tolerated as long as he had, referring to the Russian minister as "an unprincipled and unscrupulous man."[81]

It would seem that most diplomats understood that it was Catacazy himself who had caused his rapid fall from grace. Michael Cramer, the US ambassador to Denmark, thanked Fish for the explanatory dispatch, understanding that it would allow him to "correct any erroneous representations of the circumstances."[82] He also reassured Fish with more information about the general perception among the diplomatic corps. According to the German minister to Denmark, Gorchakov had put Catacazy up for the post in Washington three times and each time the tsar refused to appoint him; it was only at Gorchakov's "urgent fourth request" that the tsar reluctantly consented to make the appointment, confirming what Curtin had told Fish some months earlier.[83] Cramer also spoke to the English minister in Copenhagen who confirmed that Catacazy was "known to be an intriguer" and expressed surprise that the American government did not request his recall sooner.[84] George Marsh, the American minister to Italy, informed the secretary of state that he had heard talk of the Catacazy affair by just one other diplomat, and this unnamed individual, already familiar with the facts of the case, had said that the American government's reaction was "abundantly warranted by the circumstances."[85] Fish similarly received a very reassuring dispatch from George Bancroft, US minister to Germany, who stated that among the diplomats there, Catacazy's character was so well known that no one was surprised by the announcement of his recall. "The only astonishment expressed," Bancroft noted, "is that the Emperor of Russia should consent that a person known to be justly unacceptable to our Government should be allowed to remain to present his own son."[86] Charles T. Gorham, the American representative in the Netherlands, reported that "Even the Russian Minister worries that his friend should have so forgotten the proprieties of his position."[87] The Spanish minister in Washington, Lopez Roberts, told Fish that he was "glad to get rid of him."[88] Finally, Curtin assured Fish that Catacazy was "well understood" in St. Petersburg and had "little if any sympathy." Though the Russian Foreign Office was eager to "smooth the whole matter down," Curtin had been told that Gorchakov understood that Catacazy was "unfavorably known" in St. Petersburg and to try and maintain him in his post would have required going against public sentiment.[89]

Fish also continued to seek information about the origin of the November 1870 news article, "Russia and America." In a meeting with Fish, George Adams, correspondent for the *New York World*, declared that the article was written by one of his journalists, a man named Harrington, whom he had sent to interview Catacazy about the "condition of the Eastern question." Harrington based the article on notes written during that interview at Catacazy's house and had submitted it to Catacazy for revision. This version, revised by the Russian minister's own hand, was sent by Adams to New York, where it was published without alteration. Adams put this description in writing for the secretary of state, stressing that although he would not normally disclose the identity of a source, he had to consider whether the same rules applied

> when fictions have been given to him as facts, when a base coinage of falsehoods has been passed off upon him for his utterance and circulated as truth, when he has been dealt with in bad faith, when the privity of his office has been abused with intent to make him and his journal the tool of an unpatriotic intrigue.

Ultimately, he believed that professional integrity and a duty to his country dictated complete transparency. Citing fifteen years of experience in the field of journalism, Adams was eager to defend his honor. Summarizing the information in the *World* article, he stated,

> It should be obvious that no journalist of experience would transmit and no journal of high repute would publish these two dozen averments upon any authentication inferior to that of a member of the Russian Cabinet or that of the Russian Envoy to the United States, for no other personage in this country not even the Secretary of State could be aware of all the occurrences they note, or guarantee their truth.[90]

While Fish continued to investigate Catacazy's role in the mysterious dispatches and the various newspaper articles that had appeared over the past year, another point of contention arose. In early November, Catacazy wrote to Fish, informing him that the tsar had granted him "permission to go, on leave of absence to St. Petersburg," as soon as Alexis concluded his travels in the United States. This letter became the beginning of a debate over the precise and accurate terminology for Catacazy's departure.[91] Only a few days later, Fish received a dispatch from Eugene Schuyler, secretary of the American Legation in Russia, that also referred to Catacazy's "leave of absence."[92] Fish perceived this choice of words to be intentionally misleading, Catacazy's attempt to save face, and he would not allow it to go unchallenged. Catacazy, in fact, had told others this version of events. For example, he told Simon Cameron that he had "asked from His Majesty the Emperor to be relieved from the irksome duty of remaining at Washington."[93] Fish thus told Catacazy that the announcement of his leave was "at variance with the understanding which had been supposed to exist with your government as to the manner of terminating your official residence here."[94] Gorlov, the military attaché at the Russian Legation, tried to explain away this discrepancy, claiming that the "granting of leave" was only "a different mode of recalling him," and that Catacazy would not be returning to the United States. Fish rejected Gorlov's explanation and chastised the Russian government for allowing Catacazy to announce publicly, including in the press, that he was leaving America at his own request instead of that of the US government.[95] Gorlov held out hope that Catacazy could be allowed to stay, but Fish was adamant and told him, "we will not consent to let him remain in charge of the Legation and travel through the Country."[96]

Fish's objection to Catacazy's self-proclaimed "leave" was not the only squabble over word choices. There was also a quite lengthy quarrel over the American government's use of the word "tolerate." It appears that the word was first used in a meeting between Curtin and Westmann, who was acting as foreign minister while Gorchakov was convalescing in Germany. On September 9, in a telegram from Curtin to Fish, the American minister relayed what had transpired in that meeting and stated that Westmann had affirmed that he was speaking for Alexander II when he stated, "The Emperor requests the President to tolerate the presence of Mr. Catacazy until after the visit of the Grand Duke, and then will be recalled."[97] From this point forward, the word "tolerate" appears in many letters, telegrams, and dispatches. Curtin, of course, used the word repeatedly in correspondence with Fish, and Fish used it in his responses as well.[98] Catacazy used it as well in a letter to Westmann and one to Simon Cameron, both written in October.[99] Not surprisingly, Fish used it in his diary multiple times.[100]

At some point during the fall of 1871, however, Westmann began to protest this characterization. In a meeting with Schuyler in early November, Westmann declared that he did not use and could not use the word "tolerate," remarking that whatever the word might mean in English, it had a "disagreeable signification" in French and could not be used in speaking of His Majesty's minister. Westmann insisted, "I know I used no such word, and must protest against it being put into my mouth."[101] Schuyler referred to Curtin's written account of their meeting and the correspondence that subsequently took place between Curtin and Fish, and

Fish and Catacazy, pointing out that all three men used the word repeatedly. Westmann repeated "very firmly" that he had not used that word. Schuyler concluded from this encounter that Westmann had been "personally involved in some unpleasantness or difficulty with the Imperial Cabinet on account of the use made of the word 'tolerate' and would feel very glad if you [Fish] could devise some means of relieving him."[102] Several days later, Schuyler informed Fish again, "The Imperial Cabinet protests against language of your note to Russian Minister of September twenty-second."[103] Curtin, meanwhile, was emphatic: "That Mr. Westmann repeatedly used the word 'tolerate' there can be no doubt or misapprehension. The words 'accept, continue, retain' or 'induce (the word you used in your telegram of 18th Sept.) would have answered quite as well but as he said 'tolerate' to me and to General Pomutz separately and together we cannot be mistaken."[104] He suggested to Gorchakov that if Westmann continued to insist that he "did not intend to use the word 'tolerate' or that he was not authorized by the Emperor to use the word," he would be happy to make such a modification as would relieve him.[105]

As the Russian and American governments wrestled over the specific words used to explain Catacazy's continued presence and eventual departure, the American press reported on the twists and turns of this very public diplomatic brawl. Not everyone approved of the American administration's handling of the situation. In early October the *New York Herald* remarked that "Mr. Fish, or whoever else inspired the highly-flavored despatches that have come to us from Washington recently, might well have postponed them until after the reception and departure of the Grand Duke Alexis. Whatever peccadilloes Catacazy may have committed, surely our Premier could have screened them from the public for a few weeks."[106] The *Philadelphia Inquirer* was even more critical. Referring to Catacazy's unpleasant position as one who would only be "tolerated," the paper observed, "There are many persons holding as high a position as he, and who instead of waiting until their passports are sent them … would have indignantly demanded their passports and sought to return to their own governments as fast as steam transportation could carry them."[107] The *Brooklyn Eagle* was similarly critical of Fish's rough handling of Catacazy, declaring that the entire affair reflected as poorly on the secretary as it did on the Russian minister, and adding, "There will be laughter in Europe over this expose—but not at the expense of Mr. Catacazy." The *Eagle* viewed the entire episode with a cynical eye, declaring, "Diplomacy is deception."[108] The *Eagle* labeled Fish's accusations as "querulous allegations" and called the whole disagreement "essentially petty," while the request for recall was "trivial and almost contemptible."[109] The *New York Sun* remarked with disdain of Fish's engagement of various individuals in the "dishonorable capacity of spies."[110] Other papers took aim at the president. The *Cincinnati Daily Enquirer*, for example, declared, "Grant's way of cultivating friendly relations with Russia is to maliciously denounce the late Russian Minister."[111] There was even a rumor that in order to avoid having to entertain and invite Catacazy to his home, Fish had taken temporary residence in a hotel.[112]

Other papers defended the actions of the Grant administration. On November 13, the *New York Times* weighed in with a lengthy commentary that occupied the equivalent of a full column of the paper. The *Times* asserted with some passion that a foreign minister should not under any circumstances "promote his objects, no matter how worthy, through the newspapers, or by public speeches," and, most of all, he must "treat the officers and people of the Government to which he is accredited with respect, and ever avoid outside participation in their internal affairs." Accepting as true the various accusations against the Russian minister, particularly his meddling in the *Alabama* claims, the *Times* concluded, "It is to be hoped he will have the decency to withdraw before he has succeeded in lowering himself further in public opinion."[113] Two weeks later, the *Times* added that when the full history of "this annoying case" appeared, it would be clear that Grant and Fish handled this matter "not only with a due regard for the dignity of the offices they hold, but with a determination to vindicate the dignity of the Government."[114]

Many papers focused criticism on the Russian minister, of course. The *New York World* published a lengthy column on "The Immunities and Obligations of a Foreign Minister," declaring that Catacazy had violated the basic rules of diplomacy and asserting that the tsar should "instantly burn into the forehead of his intriguing representative a mark of disgrace which will testify what value he places upon the good will of the United States."[115] The *New York Times* was also harsh in its assessment of the "obnoxious" minister and the "gross impropriety" and "insolence" of his conduct. In a humorous comment on the American right of free speech, the *Times* stated, "It may be that our own people inflict unreasoning abuse on our elected agents in public affairs, but that is a luxury of our own not permitted to diplomatic representatives of foreign nations."[116] In a later issue, the paper remarked that Catacazy loved to get stories about himself into the paper. Quoting a flattering portrayal of the diplomat and his wife in another paper, the *Times* suggested that the article was likely written by the man himself.[117]

Fortunately for Catacazy, the approaching visit of the tsar's son diverted public interest away from him, and though various disagreements continued on an official level, the press soon shifted its attention to the handsome young Russian visitor being welcomed to the United States instead of the problematic diplomat being told to leave.

7

The "Industrious Flea": Catacazy and the Visit of Grand Duke Alexis

The visit of Grand Duke Alexis from late November 1871 through mid-February 1872 was deeply interconnected with Catacazy's missteps with the American government and his ultimate recall. Secretary of State Hamilton Fish was already irritated with Catacazy when the first discussion about the visit of the Grand Duke began, and his impatience with him increased over the coming months. Though Catacazy was ultimately expelled for other reasons, he did himself no favors before and during the royal visit, only exacerbating the already existing tensions.[1]

Alexis's arrival in late November 1871 had actually been several years in the making. In the 1860s there had been several conversations about the possibility of one of the tsar's sons coming to visit, but none of these plans ever came to fruition. Only in early 1870 did the United States receive some promising indications that a visit might actually occur, and by March 1870, it seemed that Alexis would be that person. In early 1871, Catacazy began to receive and reply to letters inviting the Grand Duke to various places and events.[2] He also began to make plans for the royal trip. With his characteristic zeal and presumptuousness, Catacazy sent a report to the Russian court with a proposed itinerary in late March, suggesting visits to New York, Hartford, Annapolis, Washington, Boston, Niagara Falls, Chicago, Cleveland, Detroit, and San Francisco, a journey of a minimum of forty-eight days.[3] Gorchakov replied from the Foreign Office on April 5, informing Catacazy that Alexis would depart Russia no earlier than August and encouraging him to allow the Grand Duke's reception to come together organically. Gorchakov stated, "The Emperor desires that you be satisfied with the simple announcements of the arrival of His Imperial Highness, that you do not make any preparations, do not provoke any demonstration." Convinced that the tsar's son would receive a friendly welcome, Gorchakov added, "Anything that would diminish its spontaneity should be displaced." While the Foreign Office appreciated Catacazy's proposed itinerary and expected the traveling party would want to consider his advice, it also reminded the Russian minister that Alexis, with the assistance of his guardian and senior officer, Admiral Constantin Possiet, would make the final decisions about which cities and sites they would visit.[4]

These admonishments from his superior did not dissuade Catacazy from engaging in, and undoubtedly encouraging, correspondence with the emerging reception committee in New York City. In late April, Catacazy received several letters from Silvanus Macy, a wealthy New York businessman, regarding plans to extend to Alexis a "warm and heartfelt welcome" and show "appreciation of the form and sincere friendship that has ever existed between your nation and our own." Citing a reception committee of "one hundred of our most prominent citizens," Macy laid out a plan that would begin with "the grandest spectacle ever witnessed in New York Harbor," followed by dinners, visits to local sites, and a ball.[5] Catacazy replied to these letters and others, updating the men on the latest information about the Grand Duke's departure and addressing various suggestions made by the eager New Yorkers. The Russian minister thanked them for their kind expressions and promised to communicate any new information he might receive.[6]

Planning for the Grand Duke's visit gave the Russian minister yet another opportunity to make a nuisance of himself, however. As early as April 1871, Catacazy began to prod Fish about the protocol of the royal visit. In one of the many tense conversations between the Russian minister and the secretary of state, Catacazy observed that the habit in Russia and in Europe was for an officer to be appointed as a representative of the receiving government to attend the Grand Duke. Catacazy suggested that the same honor should be accorded to the young Russian duke. Catacazy also noted that when the Prince of Wales came to visit in 1860, he was received and stayed at the White House. Fish replied that the Prince of Wales was the heir to the throne and, since the Grand Duke was not, he could not be treated in the same manner. Fish similarly rejected Catacazy's suggestion of an appointed officer. In fact, a similar issue of protocol had arisen the year before when Prince Arthur of England, the son of Queen Victoria, had visited the United States. President Grant did not understand why he should be expected to pay respect to a child, particularly one who was not heir to the throne, and there had been much debate and discussion about how the prince should be received. Eventually, a compromise had been reached whereby Grant and Fish received Prince Arthur on their own terms at the White House and the Grants attended the ball for the prince only after the prince had greeted them outside their carriage. After this wrangling over the reception of Prince Arthur, it should have come as no surprise to anyone that President Grant would be no more inclined to pay homage to the Grand Duke Alexis than to any other royal child. Fish summed it up rather succinctly: "while we have adopted many European conventionalities, we have not adopted all, & especially not those which are mere deference to birth, or rank."[7] Interestingly, some in the press anticipated that the Russian minister was likely to encourage lavish displays of adoration and toadyism to the Grand Duke. The *New York World* declared that Russia had earlier been represented by wise diplomats: "Neither M. de Bodisco nor Mr. Stoeckl would have suffered committees to be organized for the purpose of dancing and dining a boy of twenty until the advent of the said boy had at least been officially notified to the government of the United States." Clearly, the paper did not trust Catacazy to use such sage judgment.[8]

* * *

By early summer 1871, Fish so thoroughly distrusted the Russian minister that on June 9, 1871, he wrote to Curtin, "Is there reason to expect that the Grand Duke is coming to this country[?] We cannot believe what the Minister [Catacazy] says." Curtin confirmed that the Russian fleet would depart in August, and over the following months, more information about the Grand Duke and his entourage passed through diplomatic channels to American officials. In late August, rumor had it that Catacazy was preparing his mansion in Washington for a royal visit; the impressive team of upholsterers, gilders, paperhangers, and painters seemed positive proof that Alexis would indeed come to America.[9]

It is at this point, however, in the summer of 1871, that Fish and Grant had asked Curtin to request that the Russian government recall its problematic minister. The proposal to recall the Russian minister on the eve of the visit of the tsar's son generated a great deal of concern and anxiety in Russia and much speculation elsewhere. Alvey Adee, secretary to the American Legation in Spain, wrote to Bancroft Davis that the new Russian minister of Spain, Mr. de Kondriaffsky, had approached him "in a state of much inquietude" after reading an excerpt from the *New York World*. The article had described the poor relations between Fish and Catacazy and Kondriaffsky feared that this would make the Grand Duke's stay in Washington unpleasant. Adee had assured his colleague that whatever was occurring between the secretary of state and the Russian minister, it would not be allowed to affect the diplomatic affairs of the two countries. Adee then shared with Kondriaffsky some of the reports about Catacazy's activities, one of which he commented on directly. Adee reported to Davis, "A passage in the *London Times*, speaking of Mr. Catacazy's rumored opposition to the *Alabama* settlement, attracted Mr. Kondriaffsky's attention and he said it confirmed what he had heard about Mr. Catacazy's disposition to meddle in what didn't concern him."[10]

Once Fish and Grant recognized that the best course of action was to tolerate Catacazy until the end of the Grand Duke's visit, they needed to establish the proper protocol for this unusual situation. On September 22, 1871, Fish wrote to Catacazy,

> The Imperial government has set forth that during the contemplated visit of the Grand Duke to this country it will be indispensable for it to have a Minister here, and that there will not be time to appoint and despatch a new Minister before the arrival of the Grand Duke. The weight of this reason for allowing you temporarily to remain as the Minister of Russia here has been acknowledged, and Mr. Curtin has been instructed to inform your government to that effect, and that if when the visit of the Grand Duke shall have been concluded, you should not be recalled, your passport would be sent to you; and that until the conclusion of the visit of the Grand Duke, the President will not receive you unless when you may accompany that Prince and will at no time hold any conversation with you. It has been deemed advisable to give you this information in order that there may be no misunderstanding on the subject.[11]

A few days later, Fish communicated with his assistant, Davis, regarding how the Grand Duke should be received and clearly wanted to minimize the fanfare. He acknowledged that a reception was necessary but added, "the danger is that our people may 'over do' it … we should not do more for the Russian than for the English prince and must not form a precedent that will be troublesome in the future." Some sort of naval demonstrations would be expected, particularly since Alexis was an officer in the Russian Navy, but "Catacazy and Admiral Porter had put their heads together to have Porter specially detailed or on duty to receive or escort the Prince—this would highly inappropriate." Fish wanted to be sure that everyone involved in the Grand Duke's welcome, especially the naval officers, understood the position of the Russian minister: that his recall was requested, that by the special request of the emperor he would be tolerated during the royal visit, but that the president would hold no conversation with him. Fish added that the American naval officers should be instructed "to hold as little official [?] … with him as possible—in fact I see no reason for <u>any</u>" (underline in original source).[12]

The American government tried, at the same time, to assure the Russian government that the Catacazy Affair was in no way an indication of disrespect or disregard for the long friendship the two countries had shared. It is for this reason that Curtin worked so hard to assure Russian officials that Fish's language on various issues was harmless and misconstrued. Curtin also suggested to Fish that he might on his part smooth over any hard feelings by speaking directly with Admiral Possiet, the senior naval official and longtime guardian of the Grand Duke who would be traveling with him. Curtin proposed, "You will I am quite sure find in Admiral Poseata … a very sensible man and you can without hesitation talk to him freely if in your judgement it should be necessary to explain to him the coolness of the President and yourself towards Mr. Catacazy," and that it "must not be regarded as want of respect for the Emperor an opportunity would be afforded to give him the true character of the Minister."[13]

There was, however, another potential problem with the Grand Duke's pending visit, one that fell under the Russian minister's purview: a reported assassination plot by Polish nationals in New York. At some point in the summer of 1871 Catacazy received information that a Russian man had met with Father Nikolai Bjerring at the newly established Russian Orthodox Church in New York City and told him that he considered it his "sacred duty" to report that a man he knew, a Pole, had told him of a plot to murder Alexis. Catacazy also received several letters attesting to the same thing and contacted the head of the New York Secret Police. Catacazy interviewed the author of one of these letters, a Mr. Krzheminsky, who gave the names and addresses of several individuals who had formed a committee to kill the Grand Duke. The police agent confirmed that the names given by Krzheminsky were real individuals residing in the city, including one man described as "a dangerous person recently out of prison." The conspirators had contacted an international society and arranged for the travel of a hired assassin. The head of the Secret Police doubted this last bit of information, stating, "There is no reason to bring a killer from abroad when you could find an evil-doer in New York who for $1000 would kill his own father."[14] Nonetheless, the threat of an assassination plot to kill the tsar's son had to be taken seriously.

In the 1840s, many Poles had fled Europe, and by 1860, there were about 25,000 Poles in the United States.[15] By 1870, that number had grown to about 50,000 with over 2,000 living in New York City alone.[16] The Polish community had many reasons to be disdainful of the hype surrounding the visit of the Russian duke, a member of the dynasty that participated in the partition of Poland and then subsequently crushed two attempts at regaining independence, most recently in 1863. During that uprising, a group of Poles in New York had formed a Polish Central Committee, and though it had done nothing actively to assist its struggling brethren, Russian officials in the United States had watched the group closely.[17] Under such circumstances, and given the persistence abroad of Polish nationalism, it should have come as no surprise that Polish nationals might take offense at the enthusiastic welcome of the tsar's son.

The reality of assassination was still very much within the recent memory of citizens and officials in both the United States and Russia. The murder of Abraham Lincoln at Ford's Theatre in April 1865 was an alarming event, both at home and abroad. The shock of it was amplified when it became clear that there was a larger plot in play, one that included eight conspirators and plans to murder not only Lincoln but also Vice President Andrew Johnson, General Ulysses Grant, and Secretary of State William Seward. Though only Lincoln was killed, Seward suffered serious injuries from the attack against him, as did his son. One year later, Dmitrii Karakozov attempted to assassinate Tsar Alexander II in St. Petersburg. Though Karakozov acted alone, his violent attack was still unnerving and disturbing. In both the United States and Russia, the threat of assassination became part of the public consciousness and could not be treated cavalierly.[18]

In late September 1871, Catacazy informed Westmann that the New York Secret Police had determined that the Polish committee had indeed sent a ticket to a man by the name of Pezhanovskii for him to travel from Europe. Once in the United States, he had been set up with an apartment and a job. The potential assassin was described as about thirty years old, with dark skin and a thin face. Catacazy hired Pinkerton's Detective Agency and they confirmed that the names and addresses provided by Krzheminsky were accurate and that some of the men named were indeed dangerous or questionable characters. Pinkerton's could not prove an actual assassination plot, but did recommend that the individuals named be closely watched.[19] Meanwhile, Catacazy had informed Fish of this threat and asked him to notify the district attorney for the Southern District of New York to investigate the supposed plot. On October 3, Fish wrote to Catacazy that the information had been transmitted and that he should feel free to get in touch with the district attorney to convey any names or information of further use.[20] Two weeks later, the *New York Tribune* reported that a secret meeting of the prominent Poles of New York and surrounding areas had met and "steps were taken to avert a danger said to threaten the Grand Duke Alexis on his arrival in New York."[21]

Whatever the truth, the threat of an assassination plot was serious enough to warrant the assignment of two detectives who stayed with Alexis constantly in New York and Washington.[22] Moreover, the press subsequently wondered if any of the mishaps later in Alexis's trip, such as the derailment of a passenger train only hours before the ducal train was due to pass on the same track, had any connection to the Polish plot.[23] Some papers resorted to gallows humor as well. The *Cleveland Daily Leader* reported that at Mathew Brady's photographic gallery in New York, Alexis had signed his name "G. D. Alexis," adding, however, that if any "unfortunate Polander" had written the same thing, "there would have been a Coroner's inquest."[24] The *Cincinnati Daily Enquirer* wondered if the rumor about the Polish plot had been invented by relatives of the Pinkerton's detectives to create a lucrative opportunity for the men.[25]

* * *

By early November, with the Grand Duke's arrival imminent, the American press, American citizens, and government officials at various levels across the country, but especially in New York City, anxiously awaited news that the royal visitor had completed his transoceanic journey. The ladies of New York were said to be particularly excited and eagerly purchased exquisite dresses of silk, satin, and velvet, to be worn by "courtly dames and scheming mammas, who hope to catch the possible heir to an Empire."[26] By early November, all of the preparations for the Grand Duke's reception in New York were in place, and the city's newspapers expressed the public's impatience with columns entitled, "Why Don't He Come?" and "Has He Come?" The *New York Times* reported that "There is no doubt that the reception programme has been much detracted from in public interest by the great delay," and, "the bright eyes of the New-York belles have become dim and weary watching for his arrival."[27] There were also concerns for his safety. On November 5, the *New York Times* declared that "the anxious elite of New-York are now conjuring at visions of shipwreck and death by flood and fire."[28]

Meanwhile, people of means were eager to secure tickets to the various planned events, which would not be open to the general public. For the ball at the Academy of Music, for example, the reception committee resolved to distribute three thousand tickets to "none but persons who they, after due inquiry, find to be thoroughly respectable." In particular, the committee wanted to prevent the appearance of "shoddy aspirants for good society, Ring politicians and corner liquor-store millionaires."[29] Indeed, some people were willing to go to great lengths to meet the young Russian. Cyrus McCormick, the inventor of the mechanical reaper, had sent Catacazy $5000 to procure him a ticket to dine with Alexis in New York, but the Russian minister had returned the check.[30]

Catacazy's role in the Grand Duke's visit, though relatively small, was still galling to some. The *New York Times* hoped that the Russian minister would not "dampen or mar" the reception of the Grand Duke "by his officious and offensive inspirations against those who this nation honors."[31] The *New York World* was relieved that Catacazy would only be the "bear-leader to the young Russian bear," adding, "in no other circumstances would he or ought he to be suffered to stay an hour after his passports could be made out."[32]

It was, in fact, the question of when and how Catacazy's passports would be delivered to him that caused another stir, offending the Russian government, and not only Westmann but Gorchakov and the tsar as well. Once again, the debate came down to the meaning of a particular phrase, the words that threatened a return of Catacazy's passports if he engaged in any further mischief while escorting the Grand Duke around the United States. On November 10, in his letter to Catacazy regarding the Russian minister's representation of his departure as his own request, the secretary of state had stated, "your passports … will be transmitted when this government shall consider the visit of his Imperial Highness the Grand Duke Alexis has concluded."[33] At a moment in time when nerves were frayed and national pride was already a bit bruised, this phrase did not sit well with the Russian Legation and led to another debate on verbiage. Several days after his letter to Catacazy, Fish met with Gorlov, who questioned the meaning of Fish's words. The secretary explained that the United States in no way intended to imply that it would determine the length of the Grand Duke's visit. Catacazy's own "intrigues and interference," however, would likely lead to the delivery of his credentials immediately after Alexis's visit to the president. Referring back to the disagreement about Catacazy's declaration of a "leave of absence" versus a recall, Fish pointed out that a "leave of absence" left Catacazy "still accredited as a Minister with liberty to return." He added that Catacazy had boasted that he would go on leave and return "when a different or better Administration should be in power here." Fish clearly believed that Catacazy had the potential to be dangerous. He emphasized to Gorlov that the Grant administration did not want Catacazy "travelling through the Country in his official capacity, intriguing against the interests and policy of the Country, in its relations with other Powers."[34] The following day, Fish wrote to Curtin a lengthy set of instructions that reiterated much of the intelligence he had already shared, but also addressing this newest point of contention. Fish explained that Catacazy's ongoing improprieties left the president "no alternative but to immediately deliver passports to Mr. Catacazy" after the Grand Duke Alexis visited the president. Removing "this light and transient" obstacle, the friendship of Russia and the United States could be protected.[35]

Fish realized that Russian officials might, on their own or through Catacazy's influence, interpret the acceleration of Catacazy's demotion as an offense. To prevent that, he clarified his purpose. On November 16, 1871, he specified in a letter to Catacazy that "The President ... requests that this change may not be construed as indicating the period, when this government will consider the visit of His Imperial Highness the Grand Duke Alexis as concluded, that it will not abridge that visit or interfere with any movements which he may contemplate in this country."[36] Fish addressed the matter in greater detail the following day with Gorlov.[37] Subsequent to these conversations, however, Fish and Grant were forced to ease off their plans to oust the Russian minister as soon as possible. Two days after Alexis's arrival, Fish discovered that Catacazy had received orders to accompany the Grand Duke throughout his American travels until the conclusion of the trip. Moreover, Catacazy had informed the secretary of state that he was transferring the Russian Legation to General Gorlov. Fish informed Catacazy that they would suspend the delivery of his passports for the time being, but they could, and would, be transmitted to him at any time in the event of "a recurrence of the causes which had determined him to send them at this time."[38] In fact, Fish was so prepared to eject the Russian minister that he had completed a passport document dated "November --, 1871," accompanied by a similarly undated letter that insisted that the action "should not in any way lead to an interruption of diplomatic relations."[39]

Once again, Fish discussed this threat of immediate dismissal with Gorlov who, unwittingly, put his foot in his mouth. In protesting the idea of Catacazy inspiring news articles, Gorlov exclaimed that Catacazy could not help talking to reporters; they pursued him constantly. Just recently, Gorlov confessed, he was with Catacazy when he was approached by a reporter from the *New York Sun*. When Catacazy refused to engage with him, the reporter said to him, " 'We have done so much for you, and written so much, that you ought not to refuse us.' " Fish recorded all of this in his diary, adding, "It did seem to occur to Gorloff that this was an admission of one of the charges against Catacazy and that it connected him directly with the most malignant and abusive of the newspaper attacks on the President and other Officials."[40]

Still, the misinterpretation of Fish's words about the delivery of passports continued to be a problem. On December 1, Fish wrote to Gorlov once again about the timing and logistics of Catacazy's departure, clearly concerned that Catacazy would attempt to linger after his termination. While acknowledging the need for a certain amount of time for the departing representative to settle his affairs, he pointed out that if "the privilege shall be abused by an undue lingering in the country by such agent after his official functions are at end, the government of the country is justified in regarding the immunities as forfeited."[41] In the second week in December, Fish received a letter from Curtin that indicated that not only was the Russian Foreign Office offended by his choice of words but the Tsar was as well. Curtin specified that "the tone of the letter they say strikes them as if you meant that the Grand Duke could make his visit if he wished, but that Mr. Catacazy must leave even if it should prevent the visit."[42] Fish also received a telegram from Curtin that said that Gorchakov had summoned him in order to express great dissatisfaction at the threat that the American government would send Catacazy his passport.[43]

Even late into December, the meaning of Fish's words was still debated. On December 22, Curtin again wrote to Fish and described his conversations with Gorchakov over the previous few weeks. Among other items discussed was Fish's threat to return Catacazy's passport. According to Curtin, the emperor and members of the Russian Foreign Office interpreted it "as if the American Government wished to express its power of preventing or abridging the visit of the Grand Duke, but kindly permitted him to make it." Curtin added, "Exception is also taken that the President says nothing of his own regret if the visit should not be made, but speaks only of disappointment to others, as if the Grand Duke were a show and were on exhibition."[44]

* * *

On the evening of November 11, a Russian ship finally appeared on the horizon at New York's harbor. It was the corvette, *Abreck*, part of the Grand Duke's fleet, at sea for thirty-two days. After the requisite exchange of gun salutes and the presentation of colors, Vice Admiral Stephen Clegg Rowan boarded the *Abreck* briefly to extend an invitation to the chief Russian officers to dine aboard the *U.S. Congress*. Lunch took place the following day in the early afternoon and included the Russian Minister Catacazy. Only a few days later, a second Russian corvette, the *Bogatyr*, arrived. In subsequent days, officers from both fleets dined with Catacazy at the Clarendon Hotel and they waited for the third, and final, ship of the Russian fleet—the one carrying the Grand Duke Alexis—to arrive.[45]

With the appearance of the Russian fleet, Grant discussed preparations for the royal visit with members of his cabinet. Grant emphasized that Catacazy was only "tolerated" for the purpose of attending the Grand Duke; consequently, he was "not to receive honours due to a Minister fully accredited." Moreover, Grant instructed his secretary of war and secretary of the navy to inform their officers in New York that the Russian minister should be given "no salutes or honours … unless he accompanies the Grand Duke."[46]

In spite of all the tensions and misunderstandings between the American government and the Russian minister, the visit of the Grand Duke Alexis would be a grand event. Alexis arrived on November 22, 1871, and over the next three months traveled throughout the United States, visiting America's major cities—New York, Boston, Philadelphia, Washington, St. Louis, Denver, Louisville, Memphis, and New Orleans. He was in Chicago only weeks after the Great Fire, hunted bison with Buffalo Bill Cody and General George Armstrong Custer, and was present for the first daytime Mardi Celebration in New Orleans. He saw the spectacular natural wonders of Niagara Falls and Mammoth Cave. In every city, except Washington, there were parades, balls, and dinners. The press followed his every move and reported on his dancing partners and the food he ate. Catacazy was present and participated in many of the activities in the first half of the visit, but did not travel west with the Russian party. When the Grand Duke's visit concluded, it was declared an enormous success, but behind it all lurked the unpleasantness of the Russian minister's recall.

On November 22, 1871, the day that Alexis came ashore in New York, Catacazy visited Fish to make arrangements for the Grand Duke's trip to Washington. Fish recorded the exchange in his diary, and his version of the meeting leaves the impression of a terse and uncomfortable interaction. After establishing the time for the meeting with Grant, Fish inquired about the order and manner of introductions. Catacazy replied that "the Prince will introduce himself, insomuch as he (C) has been informed that the President will hold no conversation with him." Fish corrected Catacazy, undoubtedly with some irritation. He told the Russian minister,

> it is true the President will hold no conversation with you, but he does not prohibit your doing what is appropriate to your official position; it will be better to observe the same course pursued when Prince Arthur was here; he and his suite, & the British Minister 7c., at the appointed hour, attended at the White House, were shown into the Blue Room; the President & Cabinet then entered, Mr. Thornton introduced the Prince &c. I told him he had better pursue the same course & introduce the Prince & confine himself to the simple introduction.[47]

Later that same day, the Grand Duke's train made its way to Washington. The Russian guests were greeted by some four hundred to five hundred people at the depot and then transferred to waiting carriages. The carriage containing the Grand Duke and Minister Catacazy proceeded directly to the minister's home on I Street, near Fourteenth, where a special reception awaited, as well as another eager group of spectators. After welcoming Alexis to his home, Catacazy then departed to make arrangements with Hamilton Fish for the official visit with the president the following day. That night, following the reception at Catacazy's home, Alexis retired to the Arlington House, a lovely hotel at Vermont Avenue that had been built only a few years earlier. There, the Grand Duke and his retinue occupied the north wing, known as the Johnson House, a separate section of the hotel that contained eighteen rooms, including several elegant parlors and a large dining room.[48]

On Thursday, November 23, Grand Duke Alexis finally met with President Ulysses Grant in the Executive Mansion. Members of the Cabinet began to arrive shortly after noon, including Secretary of the Interior Columbus Delano, Attorney General Amos Akerman, Secretary of the Treasury George Boutwell, and Secretary of the Navy George Robeson, as well as a number of other political and military figures. At 1 o'clock, the Russian visitors arrived and proceeded through the entrance hall to the Blue Room, where the American party waited. The ceremony was short and there were no formal speeches, but despite the brevity and unspoken tension, the meeting created an impressive picture. There, under a sparkling crystal chandelier, Catacazy presented the son of Tsar Alexander II to the president of the United States. Alexis cut a dashing figure in a blue uniform with gold epaulets and a light blue sash. The president and the Grand Duke shook hands, and Alexis expressed his pleasure at meeting the head of the country with whom Russia had such good relations; Grant responded with his hope that Alexis would have a good journey through the United States. The president then introduced the members of his Cabinet, who also shook hands and exchanged greetings with the members of the Russian party.[49]

Having completed these formalities, the men all moved to the Red Room, where the Washington wives eagerly awaited their turn to meet the special guest. The Grand Duke spoke briefly with Mrs. Grant, but the reception was very short, and soon the Russians boarded their carriage for the minister's home, where they spent much of the remaining day and evening. Mrs. Grant later wrote in her memoir that "we ladies were greatly disappointed" by the brevity and stiffness of the Grand Duke's visit. While she claimed not to remember the details of the Catacazy imbroglio, Mrs. Grant did recall that it had made the Grand Duke's reception awkward since "in order to entertain the handsome young Duke, the offending Minister had also to be received, and their presence together at this time was very embarrassing." The sad result was that Alexis was received in an official capacity only, with no social entertainment, and the ladies of Washington were deprived of an evening of dancing with the dashing young Russian.[50] It is unlikely, however, that Julia Dent Grant, an integral part of Washington society during her husband's time in office, would have actually forgotten the particulars of the Catacazy scandal.

Despite the brief visit, Alexis had made a favorable impression on Hamilton Fish, who recorded in his diary that the Grand Duke was "very affable, speaks English fluently, as does also Admiral Possiet." About the odious Russian minister, however, Fish wrote, "Catacazy is limping, walking with a cane (I think) for the purpose of exciting sympathy & inducing questions to him to enable him to be in conversation with some persons at the reception." Fish worried that the request for Catacazy's recall might jeopardize the success of the Grand Duke's visit. While at the Executive Mansion, Alexis had expressed doubts about traveling to San Francisco, and Fish worried that this was a response to the recent difficulties over the Russian minister. Fears about the Russian-American friendship increased when Alexis politely declined repeated invitations to return for a second visit to Washington. In fact, the secretary of state had reason to be concerned. In letters to Catacazy and to the tsar, Admiral Possiet confessed that even before arriving in the United States he had been opposed to a second trip to Washington, but then, after the "inhospitable welcome that Alexis received from the President," he was definitely against it. In fact, Possiet was repeatedly approached with the request for a second visit, even in the last leg of the trip, but since the circumstances that had caused Possiet to refuse the first time had not changed, he had to decline.[51]

The American press took note of the discomfort of the reception at the White House, and many recognized the cause of that awkwardness. *The Nation*, for example, blamed the Russian government for keeping Catacazy in the country to serve as the Grand Duke's escort, bluntly stating, "His presence was a source of embarrassment to everybody. He was not only of no service to the Grand Duke, but a serious hindrance."[52] The *Washington Daily Morning Chronicle* agreed and also addressed the question of Grant visiting the Grand Duke. According to the *Chronicle*, "the President is never expected to call on any one."[53] The *Cheyenne Daily Leader* remarked that although Uncle Sam was not usually as particular in matters of international etiquette as other European nations, occasionally, "the old fellow's forbearance and good nature may sometime give unexpectedly, and then look out."[54] The St. Petersburg correspondent for the *New York Herald* observed that the perceived slight to the Grand Duke by the president had upset many in Russia and led to curiosity in diplomatic circles as to what the tsar would say to Minister Curtin at the exchange of New Year's greetings. Specifically, they wondered whether he would thank the American people or the American government. The *Herald* journalist reported with some amusement that the tsar had circumvented the problem by thanking the American "nation" for the reception of his son.[55]

The day after his meeting with Grant, Alexis went to Annapolis for a tour of the Naval Academy. The Russian party, accompanied by a group of naval officers, arrived amidst a cold, steady rain at the Naval Academy, where a battalion of marines in full dress welcomed the visitors, accompanied by the Russian national hymn and a twenty-one-gun salute. The Russian party also observed a military drill and parade, as well as the various facilities of the academy, followed by a light lunch. Here, the Russian and American officers toasted one another with smiles and good wishes, but it was Catacazy's words that drew the greatest applause. In a toast that would have special meaning for some of those present, the Russian minister lifted his glass to the most powerful members of the American government, "their fairnesses the women of America" (underline in original source)[56] One wonders if Catacazy's tribute was, in fact, meant to be a barb.

Catacazy's toasts would not always be so well-received. After visiting the famous Smith and Wesson factory in Springfield, Massachusetts, the Grand Duke and his party along with several dozen guests sat down to a short, but elegant, dinner at the Massasoit House, a fine hotel that could boast of such guests as Abraham Lincoln, the Prince of Wales, Charles Dickens, Daniel Webster, and the Hungarian revolutionary and exile Louis Kossuth. There, amidst glasses of champagne and the sweet perfume of fresh flowers, the men enjoyed a delicious meal and, as always, exchanged a series of toasts. A number of glasses were raised to the prosperity of Springfield and the health of the royal visitor, followed by one particularly maladroit toast by the Russian minister. In the midst of this jovial atmosphere, Catacazy declared, "We have found here a city with remarkable facilities for preparing to kill people and we have also found a very fine city whose people know how to receive and entertain visitors very agreeably." There followed an awkward silence, broken only by "the cracking of almonds and a whispering around the table." Soon after Catacazy's peculiar compliment, the Russian guests departed for the train depot, leaving the station at about 7 o'clock for a week in Boston.[57]

In Boston, Catacazy stumbled over his own tongue yet again while attending a private banquet at the Revere House hotel. Two hundred of the leading citizens of Cambridge and Boston organized the banquet, and the guest list was impressive and included many prominent politicians and businessmen, as well as luminaries such as Henry Wadsworth Longfellow and Oliver Wendell Holmes. There were many long, enthusiastic speeches that evening, welcoming

Alexis with sentiments that would be repeated many times during the Grand Duke's excursion—enthusiasm for the Russian-American friendship and praise for Alexander as the liberator-tsar. Catacazy spoke last, and once again his words were clumsy and inappropriate. Referring to his own recent troubles, he began by declaring that, were he to sculpt the goddess of diplomacy, he would portray her "in a dark cloak with a finger on her lips." Catacazy continued that he, more than anyone, should hold his finger to his lips as closely as possible, but that evening, he would instead place it over his heart in order to celebrate the friendship between Russia and America. Longfellow later wrote to a friend that several of the speeches that evening were "amazingly funny"; one wonders if he included the Russian minister's speech among that number.[58]

One might imagine that the presence of the Grand Duke and Catacazy's own predicament might encourage the Russian minister to use more discretion and maintain a low profile. But such was not the nature of the stubborn diplomat. On December 5, the *New York Times* called Catacazy a "low schemer" and reported that he had published a new article accusing Bancroft Davis of "making war upon him."[59] Moreover, while in New York, the Grand Duke's party had visited Bryant's Minstrels, a blackface troupe, and on December 8, a newspaper claimed that Catacazy had remarked, "this is but a side-show compared to the Congressional circus."[60]

Still, the American government worried about how the Russian government was interpreting the Grand Duke's reception. In early December 1871, Curtin wrote to Fish that most people in Russia, including the Imperial family, were pleased by the way in which the young duke had been received thus far, and it was reported upon favorably in the Russian press. On the other hand, "much complaint is made in the Foreign Office … There the reception is pronounced cool and they allege that no invitation to dine or other evidence of hospitality was offered to the Grand Duke by the President. I find the impression prevalent in society here." Curtin also warned that Gorchakov had expressed doubts that Alexis would return to Washington; though he tried to explain "that it was proper and expected that he should make another visit to the Capital … This matter is still in doubt."[61] Still, Curtin believed that most people in St. Petersburg took a sensible view of the Catacazy imbroglio. In mid-December, he sent Fish an article from the *Russkii Mir* that said, "The unpleasantness arising between him and President Grant and the Minister of Foreign Affairs, Mr. Fish related to our Minister personally, and therefore ought to have no influence on the international relations of Russia to the great American republic. The glad reception shown in the United States to the Grand Duke Alexis serves as confirmation of this."

The article concluded, "this circumstance does not define the friendly relations between Russia and the American Republic. This friendship has existed for nearly a century on such solid foundations that, as the Grand Duke Alexis said to the Americans, 'nothing can break it.'"[62]

Despite these positive assurances from Curtin, Fish felt it necessary to reassure the Russian government. Almost immediately after the Grand Duke's arrival, Catacazy had informed Fish that he had been ordered to accompany the royal visitor on his journey and then sail for Russia, so he was transferring the business of the Russian Legation to General Gorlov.[63] Fish was relieved and told Grant that they could consider this action "as a practical compliance" with their request for Catacazy's recall. He viewed Gorlov as a gentleman and assumed that he would eventually become Charge d'Affaires, though no such order had yet been sent.[64] On December 19, Fish wrote to the acting Russian minister, "You are probably aware that unavoidable circumstances much to be regretted may have contributed to make the recent visit of His Imperial Highness the Grand Duke Alexis to this city very brief"; however, the manner of the meeting was not to be misinterpreted. During that brief encounter, Grant had invited Alexis back to Washington, but Fish was concerned that "the informal character" of the invitation may have led Alexis to view it as "an act of ordinary courtesy merely, and as such to have implied more or less indifference as to its acceptance." Nothing was farther from the truth, Fish explained, adding that the president very much desired that the Grand Duke would return for a second visit during which they might extend their acquaintance further.[65]

The American press, of course, had much to say about the Russian minister's role in the Grand Duke's visit. The *New York World* commented that Catacazy had avoided "the toe of the Executive boot" by handing over the Russian Legation to Gorlov; however, his statements that he would defend himself before the tsar in St. Petersburg and return to the United States were clearly "the dying spasms of the Russo-Greek." When all was said and done, the paper declared, "This Catacazy business will not be without good if it teaches *us* something about the obligations of a diplomatic agent."[66] The *Buffalo Commercial Advertiser* regretted that the Russian minister's disgrace should happen to coincide with Alexis's visit, but noted that if the young duke had "the good sense that is attributed to him, he must be aware that Catacazy's conduct has been that of which no gentleman would be guilty, and to which a Government with any sense of pride would never submit."[67] The *Cleveland Daily Leader* was weary of the Russian minister, however, and sighed, "Why don't he go? If he has got any defence [sic] to make, let him make it when he gets to St. Petersburg. We have had quite enough of Catacazy."[68]

* * *

On December 4, 1871, President Grant gave his third annual State of the Union address to Congress. In it, he mentioned the Franco-Prussian War, the annexation of Rome to the Kingdom of Italy, the reduction of the national debt, and the growth and significance of the Post-Office Department. One whole paragraph was dedicated to the "intimate friendly relations" between America and Russia. Grant cited the visit and reception of Grand Duke Alexis as proof of the continued "cordiality" of that relationship, yet approximately three-fourths of this discussion of Russia focused on the "inexcusable course" of the Russian minister and his recall. Grant stated flatly, "It was impossible, with self-respect or with a just regard to the dignity of the country, to permit Mr. Catacazy, to continue to hold intercourse with this Government after his personal abuse of Government officials, and during his persistent interferences, through various means, with the relations between the United States and other powers." He concluded his discussion of the Catacazy Affair by noting that the Russian Legation had been handed over to "a gentleman entirely unobjectionable."[69]

There were criticisms of Grant's decision to discuss the thorny matter of the Russian minister in his annual speech. Andrew Curtin wrote from St. Petersburg that

> exception was taken to the fact that the President mentioned the recall of Mr. Catacazy in his message. Here the duty and the usage of the President of giving to Congress and thus to the people a clear and truthful statement of all of importance that has occurred at home and abroad during the recess are not understood and it is made the subject of serious comment in official and social circles, and to me of complaint.[70]

Subsequently, he reiterated several times that both Gorchakov and the tsar were unhappy that Grant had mentioned the Catacazy situation in his statement to Congress.[71]

Though the Russian government may have disapproved of Grant's address, it was really not its place to criticize. The President's State of the Union Address was a message from the executive branch to the legislative branch in the American government, an entirely internal communication. According to a statement of US Secretary of State William Marcy in 1856, it was not "proper or respectful" for a foreign government or its representative to comment on the president's annual message "or even to resort to it as the basis of a diplomatic correspondence." Marcy flatly stated, "It is not a document addressed to foreign Governments."[72]

All in all, however, Curtin believed that many Russians understood the American response:

> There is unquestionably a large measure of political sentiment here which is in harmony with your action. Catacazy is not regarded by those who know him as a reliable man, and is unpopular. Many of these defenses and explanations are intended to relieve the Government of censure which relates back to his appointment as Minister to the United States, which it now seems was received with distrust and surprise at the time.[73]

By this point, even Gorchakov had admitted to Curtin that although the full story was still not known, it was clear that Catacazy had acted "most improperly."[74]

In response to Grant's address, Senator Simon Cameron proposed a resolution requesting access to all the official correspondence related to the Catacazy case.[75] Fish submitted the documents as requested and two days later, the *Washington Daily Morning Chronicle* dedicated three whole columns to reprinting a number of the letters exchanged between the secretary of state and the Russian minister; soon, other papers followed suit.[76] The *Chicago Republican* quoted several letters at length and called the correspondence "quite spicy."[77] The release of these documents provided the American press more information with which to pass judgment.

For many journalists, the evidence showed that Fish and Grant were right to ask for Catacazy's removal. *The Cleveland Leader* was convinced that "The correspondence contains proofs showing the truth of the statement of the Secretary."[78] Similarly, the *Washington Daily Morning Chronicle* declared, "Mr. Fish has conducted this whole business with more than usual propriety and ability," and the only possible criticism of Catacazy's dismissal is that it should have occurred earlier.[79] The *Philadelphia Inquirer* called Catacazy a "busy-body" and declared that he belonged to "the old-fashioned school of diplomacy" and his assets were "of dissimulation and intrigue" and did not suit the character of the American people.[80] The *New Orleans Republican* declared that Fish and Grant had acted with great leniency as long as possible, but at some point, Catacazy's behavior made his recall necessary. As for Catacazy, the paper hoped, "We shall hear nothing more from the dismissed minister, unless he recovers his senses and makes an apology."[81] Anyone acquainted with the Russian minister would have found this comment highly amusing. Constantin Catacazy had no intention of apologizing.

Once the Catacazy correspondence became public, Fish presumably saw no reason to keep quiet about his troubles and sent copies of the letters to several friends. These men responded with colorful language about the Russian minister and his character. John H. Clifford, ex-governor of Massachusetts, had met the Russian minister during the Grand Duke's tour. Clifford told Fish that he wished he had read the documents before he saw Catacazy in person, stating that it affirmed his impression of him as "a poor scrub who, like most of his race, believes that the world is governed only by craft, and that he who can exercise that bad quality most adroitly, attains the highest degree of success in affairs." Clifford had sat next to Catacazy at one of the dinners in Boston and detected in the Russian minister a "malignant intent" and an eagerness to criticize the American government. At the banquet in Boston, he saw Catacazy manifest "the same spirit … in the adroit and cunning speech which he volunteered, it not having been included in the programme, at a late hour of the festivities." Overall, Clifford sensed in the other Russians "a decided lack of appreciation of Catacazy's merits."[82]

Another sympathizer felt that the correspondence completely vindicated the American government's actions and revealed the Russian minister to be "more of a scamp than I had thought he was."[83] William W. Campbell, a lawyer and politician from New York who claimed to have only a slight acquaintance with Catacazy, declared, "There is a little household instrument called an extinguisher; you have placed it upon his head, and his fire has literally gone out. How a man of his presumed intelligence and sagacity could have put himself in so exposed a situation is certainly a mystery" (underline in the original source).[84] Benjamin Haight, another New York attorney, expressed a similar thought, saying, "What an impudent, lying rascal he is! I marvel that you endured him so long."[85]

Another recipient of the correspondence was Francis Lieber, the jurist and political philosopher whose Lieber Code on the rules of the conduct of war became the basis of the Geneva Conventions. Lieber also thanked Fish for the correspondence, adding, "but, with all due deference to your judgement, it does not seem to me to be fitting to call him a wild cat. Wild cats are malignant indeed, but there is a certain feline respectability in them which appears to be wanting in the Greco-Russian diplomat."[86] Robert C. Winthrop, the Boston lawyer and philanthropist, told Fish that he was glad he had not read the Catacazy documents before the banquet for the Grand Duke. He recalled, "It was awkward enough, as it was, to deal with a guest who had incurred such serious displeasure from the Government. I must say, however, that Mr. C. behaved with great propriety here, and that his little speech was one of the cleverest and most adroit utterances, under the circumstances, which I ever heard."[87] Secretary of the Interior Jacob Cox, however, read something more into the correspondence. He confided in Fish that as he read the documents, he could not

> avoid feeling that the tone of Catacazy's last letters + his persistent refusal to recognize the fact that he was dismissed, naturally implies a confidence of <u>backing at home</u>. Keeping in mind the despotic character of the Czar's government, I could not help feeling that no subordinate, with his fortune in his career as diplomat yet to make, would ever hold such a tone unless he had assurance that he would be <u>secretly</u> sustained, even if sacrificed publicly for the moment. (underline in the original source)[88]

The Russian press also weighed in on the matter as more information became available. The newspaper *Golos* continued to portray the United States in a negative light, reporting—erroneously—that the American government had demanded that Gorchakov's office pass judgment and impose punishment on the dismissed minister.[89] The *Russkii Mir*, on the other hand, declared, "Such an accusation against our government is in no way proved, it is a mere supposition. So much the more as the cause of the difficulty between Mr. Catacazy and Messr. Grant and Fish, was not so much political as personal."[90] Curtin labeled the opinion of the *Russkii Mir* "a very sensible view of the subject—a view, I am glad to say, shared by most people at St. Petersburg."[91] Curtin would soon be sending Fish more bad news, however. The bounds of Catacazy's presumptuousness apparently knew no limits.

On December 13, Curtin informed Fish that Catacazy had not been given the authority to pass the legation off to anyone. Indeed, when Gorchakov found out, he called a cabinet meeting on the subject, and Catacazy's action was "disapproved" and the first secretary of the Russian Legation in Washington, Boris Danzas, was ordered to take charge.[92] On December 17, the *New York Herald* reported on Danzas's new role, underscoring that Catacazy's initial transfer to Gorlov "of his own motion" was another breach of protocol and a diplomatic faux pas. "The appointment of a simple Military Attaché without orders that could have been applied for and received in a day," the paper argued, was a serious offense, made clear by the Russian government's immediate change of the transfer from Gorlov to Danzas.[93] This too, however, turned out to be a temporary situation. The day after this article appeared, Fish received a visit from Gorlov who apologized for the "unauthorized" article of the previous day and informed him that Danzas would not be placed in charge of the legation after all. Apparently, when Grand Duke Alexis and Admiral Possiet were in Washington, they learned that Danzas "had subjected himself to disfavor" and in consultation with Catacazy concluded that Gorlov should temporarily head the Russian Legation. Fish was aware that Danzas had done "some things which were objectionable," but had assumed he had acted under orders from his superiors; other accusations against him were unproven. Fish assured Gorlov that they would have had no objection to him as chargé.[94] Catacazy, however, had told Gorchakov that Danzas was too closely associated with the Perkins case to be acceptable.[95]

This was not the end of the matter. Less than a week after the appointment and unappointment of Danzas, Curtin reported that the new Chargé d'Affaires appointed to the Russian Legation in Washington was Baron Henri d'Offenberg, "the present political agent at Bucharest, who is said to be a man of ability and character."[96] Until Offenberg's arrival, however, the second secretary of the legation, Valerien Schirkov, would take over.[97] In the meantime, Fish must have felt that he could not rid himself of his diplomatic nemesis. In early January 1872, he complained to Shirkov that the Catacazys were still on the list of members of the Russian Legation delivered to the Department of State. Fish warned, however, that he would not be including those names in the department's annual published register of individuals associated with the diplomatic service. He had, after all, been assured by Catacazy himself that "he had been definitively called to Russia."[98] Schirkov replied with the requisite politeness of diplomatic correspondence, though it did little to hide his irritation. He informed Fish that "according to the only official information which I possess, Mr. Catacazy has only been <u>summoned</u> to return to St. Petersburg" (underline in the original source). Schirkov added,

> Having no official information of the <u>recall</u> of Mr. Catacazy, and the ulterior intentions of the Imperial Cabinet being entirely unknown to me, I have placed the name of His Excellency the Minister of the Emperor at the head of the list of persons forming the Imperial Legation and I sincerely desire, Mr. Secretary of State, that it be allowed to remain there.[99]

It is unclear how the standoff over this particular document ended, but the *Biographic Register* published by the Department of State later that year listed Catacazy's term as minister as having ended on November 24, 1871.[100]

As Fish wrestled with Schirkov over the definitive membership of the Russian Legation, a new tempest had emerged. On January 4, Curtin received a note from Prince Gorchakov that was a reply to Fish's note of November 16, in which the secretary of state had described the Russian minister's crimes. The following day, Gorchakov's note was widely published in the Russian press, as were articles discussing the exchange. Curtin reported all of this to Fish, enclosing translations of Gorchakov's letter. The Russian foreign minister declared that when the American government had agreed to allow Catacazy to fulfill his duties regarding the Grand Duke Alexis, he believed that the matter was settled. The note sent by Fish on November 16, then, seemed to Gorchakov "objectless and in which the respect due to the Minister of Russia, still in the exercise of his function was not sufficiently consulted." Gorchakov suggested that several of the charges against Catacazy had already been refuted by the accused; he also stated unequivocally that the Russian government could not judge Catacazy until he was able to produce whatever evidence he could to defend himself. His exact words contained a hint of sarcasm: "the feeling of justice is too developed in the United States for the Secretary of State to admit that we could deviate from an elementary principle of justice in pronouncing judgment before having heard the party interested." The Russian foreign minister expressed certainty, however, that the painful incident would "alter in no way the feelings of old and sincere friendship which quite recently have received a striking evidence by the cordial reception that the American nation has made to the son of my August Master."[101]

Curtin's dispatch also included a translation of an article from the *Moskovskie Vedomosti*. This article took a less generous interpretation of the Grant administration's handling of the situation, casting doubt on the evidence against Catacazy and raising questions about details that were missing. The *Gazette* disapproved of Grant's discussion of the matter in his annual address and criticized Fish for inflating and publicizing the disagreement. It believed that England had influenced the scandal in some way, noting, "it would be very convenient that such relations should arise between Russia and America." The article insisted, however, that these shenanigans had not and would not destroy the Russian-American relationship, which remained strong, as evidenced by the warm and enthusiastic reception of Grand Duke Alexis. Curtin believed that this article could be interpreted as what Gorchakov himself would have said had he been allowed to speak freely. Specifically, he observed, "The article bears many evidences of being inspired and there is one passage (which I have marked) which refers to Prince Gortchacoff's note … which at the date of the article … I had not yet received. This would point to the Foreign Office as its source."[102]

The publication of Gorchakov's note attracted attention in the American press, as well, and several papers published full translations.[103] The *New York Herald* pronounced the tone of the note to be "one of studied insolence and of resentment," and other papers agreed that the Russian correspondence was insulting to Fish and President Grant.[104] There were also hints that perhaps

Gorchakov's anger and sensitivity indicated that Catacazy had indeed been acting on his government's orders, thus making a criticism of his actions a criticism of his superior as well.[105] A rumor arose that the American government might break ties with Russia and recall its own representative from St. Petersburg.[106] The *Chicago Times* was more alarmist, with a headline that shouted, "On the Brink of War—Russia and the United States Brought Face to Face." Giving credence to the rumors about Mrs. Catacazy, the *Times* further explained that the dangerous conflict had been created by "two rash men who have become personal enemies over a social matter, and about an old claim." Ten days later, the paper was still warning of hard feelings and high tensions, stating, "There is said to be very savage feeling at Washington over the tone of Prince Gortschakoff's letter."[107] The *Cleveland Daily Leader* humorously proclaimed that "the Russian bear growls a little over the treatment of Minister Catacazy by President Grant and Secretary Fish at Washington."[108] The *Cleveland Daily Plain Dealer* joked about the impertinence of Gorchakov's letter and declared, "Well, if war breaks out, we can clap hands on Alexis and hold him as a hostage."[109]

Some sources viewed this as the last gasp of the Catacazy Affair, however. The *Washington Daily Morning Chronicle* believed that "the Russian complication is daily losing its magnificent proportions." The paper argued that the physical distance between Russia and the United States made any sort of significant clash unlikely, but acknowledged "a degree of coolness" emerging in relations between the two countries. Nonetheless, the *Chronicle* concluded, "When the late unpleasant incidents have faded from public notice the former status of our cordial relations may be restored."[110] In general, it would seem that most news outlets believed that although there was a "decided coolness," the greatest threat to Russian-American relations was over and that the dark diplomatic cloud would dissipate with the departure of its chief architect.[111] Indeed, on February 5, 1872, Eugene Schuyler announced that Catacazy had at last been officially recalled and that Baron Henri Offenberg would be the new minister.[112] Offenberg arrived in the United States and presented his papers on April 30, 1872. At last, Fish was rid of the meddlesome minister who had consumed so much of his time over the past three years. Now, Catacazy was Russia's problem.

8

"He … Smirked Too Much to Be Dignified":
The Departure of Constantin Catacazy

Catacazy would not go quietly into that good night. In addition to his repeated declarations of innocence he also continued to launch accusations at others. On December 7, 1871, an article appeared in the *New York Sun* saying that the secretary of state resented Catacazy because he did not buy Fish's land for the construction of a Greek Orthodox Church in New York City. The article was subsequently published in other papers across the country, much to Fish's dismay. The article suggested, without subtlety, that it was "a noteworthy circumstance that Catacazy's conduct did not become objectionable to the secretary and president until after he was found unwilling to engage in this peculiar kind of official land speculation."[1] Fish was certain that Catacazy was behind the article.

It is true that Fish had offered to sell Catacazy some of his own land for the establishment of a Greek Church in New York. On April 30, 1870, the secretary of state wrote to the Russian minister about some lots he owned on 14th and 15th Streets between 2nd and 3rd Avenues in New York City, including a sketch of the lots and indicating that the neighboring lots belonged to someone else who was willing to consider a sale.[2] Though Catacazy declined Fish's offer, the subject of the church land would resurface a year later. In mid-June 1871, Frank Turk paid a call to Fish's home and declared that Catacazy had defrauded his government in purchasing land for the construction of a church. According to Turk, Catacazy had purchased the lots for $17,000 but charged the Russian government $20,000, after pressuring the seller to put the false price in the deed.[3] Soon after this meeting with Turk, Fish wrote to George Sharpe, marshal of the Southern District of New York, asking him to explore this story quickly, but with the utmost discretion. He cautioned, "The investigation should be conducted carefully, and so as not to attract attention or excite a suspicion as to the quarter for which it is desired."[4] Fish also had asked Curtin to explore the matter and in early November, Curtin indicated to Fish that he was investigating the church purchase from his end. He wrote, "I have made some examination and believe the sum paid for the ground in New York for the Russian Church was $20,000. I will however get definite information and write you again."[5] A month later, on December 18, 1871, Fish mentioned the church in his diary and the article in the *New York Sun* of December 7 that attributed his ill feeling toward Catacazy to this conflict. Fish addressed his concerns about these rumors to Gorlov and told him, "I understand from what I think to be good authority the C. purchased the lots for $17,000 and caused $20,000 to be inserted in the deed, and probably charged that to his Govt.; that C. pays for the U.S. Revenue Stamps, for the $3000 between the real and the expressed consideration."[6] It is unclear whether Fish ever got the definitive proof of his suspicions, but Catacazy would later address the church fraud in his published defense.

Even as he was preparing to depart the United States, Catacazy continued to pursue actions that exacerbated tensions between himself and members of the American administration, for example, threatening to sue George Adams of *The World*. Shirkov and Fish discussed the matter in a meeting in early January 1872. Fish informed the acting Russian minister, Shirkov, that this would be an unwise decision, for if Catacazy threatened American citizens with legal proceedings "it will be a waiver of his Diplomatic privilege of 'extraterritoriality,' and I should be forced to consider whether I should not immediately terminate his immunities, and allow any citizens who have been aggrieved by him, or who have claims against him, to bring him before the courts, before he may leave the Country." Fish cited the situation regarding Mrs. Andrews, who had already appealed to him more than once about rent owed to her by Catacazy. Fish declared that he had refused to get involved in the matter, but if Catacazy attempted to sue Adams, then Mrs. Andrews could proceed with a claim against him. Several hours later, Shirkov informed Fish that the whole matter was a misunderstanding, and that Catacazy had no intention of pursuing legal action against any American citizen.[7]

But it appears that Catacazy could not resist the urge to defend himself in the public eye, using the newspapers once again as his vehicle. A Washington correspondent claimed to have spoken with Catacazy, who repeated his denials regarding the publication of newspaper articles and had even offered to deposit $3000 in a local bank to be used for charity if "one scintilla of proof" could be produced that he was responsible in any way for the publication of the article mentioned by Fish in his report to Congress.[8] No one seems to have attempted to exonerate him, however.

Catacazy also continued to lie to his own government. On January 10, 1872, Curtin wrote to Fish about an unpleasant meeting he had with Gorchakov in which the latter read the most recent letter from the recalled minister. Curtin described this "most extraordinary communication" which, among other things, declared that in the United States the press was crowing about the defeat of Russia in the recent scandal and the "humiliation of the Imperial Government." The letter referred to rumors that the Perkins claim would now be paid out "as a million of dollars" and accused the State Department of planting these articles in papers that supported the administration. Curtin had denied knowledge of any such documents or articles and assured Gorchakov that the whole thing was false and ludicrous.[9]

In the third week of January, as Grand Duke Alexis enjoyed a buffalo hunt in Nebraska with General George Armstrong Custer, Buffalo Bill Cody, and General Philip Sheridan, celebrating each kill with bottles of champagne, the dismissed Russian minister auctioned off the belongings of his home. According to contemporary descriptions, the sale included horses, carriages, and interior furnishings, the majority of which had been imported at great expense from Paris and Berlin. There was a large crowd, and there was such competition for the much-coveted items that the selling prices were 30–50 percent above actual value. Still, one paper noted, even in the midst of the gawkers and bargain hunters, there was a sense of melancholy over the departure of Mrs. Catacazy, who had been such a gracious hostess.[10]

Catacazy departed the United States on January 20, 1872, sailing aboard the *Atlantic*, a steamer of the relatively new White Star Line.[11] The exit of the controversial minister was quiet and without pomp or circumstance. According to the *New York World*, the Catacazys boarded the steamer, along with their friends and traveling companions, Mr. and Mrs. August Vogue. A few sailors from Grand Duke Alexis's frigate, the *Svetlana*, helped carry the Catacazys' baggage, while the former minister carried the Russian flag himself. The only notable person mentioned by name who came out to say goodbye to the forlorn diplomat was William Aspinwall, the prominent New York businessman who had been actively involved in the Grand Duke's reception in New York. Finally, when the ship signaled its impending departure, Catacazy "quietly turned on his heel and evaded the party of friends who were crowding around his wife." As Olga Catacazy joined many other guests in enthusiastically waving handkerchiefs to those remaining behind, her husband chose not to partake in the celebrations, but rather "screwed himself into a corner of the lookout bridge, [and] merely surveyed the scene in the calmest manner." The paper concluded that Catacazy seemed "heartily glad at the prospect of soon being quite out of sight of the United States."[12]

Catacazy arrived in Liverpool on January 31 and proceeded to Paris, arriving on February 5.[13] In a letter to Gorchakov, he complained about the "deplorable state" of his health and asked for understanding in his need for rest and a few days of "treatment." This letter was but the first of many written in a tone of martyrdom, as he remarked on his need to preserve his personal honor while being condemned "without remission or hearing."[14] Catacazy also asked Gorchakov to grant him some sort of hearing, the exclusion of which, he declared, would be interpreted "by the whole world, as a tacit acknowledgement of the infamous charges against me."[15]

Catacazy eventually reached St. Petersburg and pled his innocence before Gorchakov and the tsar, but to no avail. The former Russian minister also now presented a new claim, that his home had been robbed before he left Washington, DC. In early February, Schuyler wrote to Fish that Catacazy had reported to his government that someone had stolen valuable documents and silver from his home; luckily, the documents he needed to defend himself were safely under his pillow, since he had anticipated such a possibility. Catacazy added an unusual detail, that "the tracks left on the carpet were those of small, gentlemanly feet" (underline in the original source).[16] He claimed to have further proof as well. Catacazy had received a letter from Schirkov that seemed to offer a clue as to who might have been involved in the theft. Schirkov described an encounter he had with Waldemar Bodisco, a secretary of the Russian Legation, as he traveled with the Grand Duke's party from St. Louis to Louisville. In a heated confrontation, Bodisco exclaimed that he possessed copies of Catacazy's correspondence and dispatches. Catacazy interpreted this to mean that Bodisco, or someone in his employ, had robbed him.[17] Schuyler said that as far as he could tell no one took these claims seriously. Fish concurred that the story of the robbery was probably false, but believed it was prudent to at least make an inquiry.[18]

Catacazy also began to prepare a detailed defense of his name and honor soon after leaving his diplomatic post in the United States. In late February, Catacazy sent Gorchakov and Alexander II a lengthy report from Paris addressing the charges against him and urged its immediate publication. Having suffered "outrages, insult, and persecution" for nearly a year, Catacazy assured the tsar that he had done everything he could to serve his country well and ensure the successful journey of the Grand Duke Alexis. He suggested that the tsar create a commission to evaluate the evidence and decide whether he should be rehabilitated or expelled from the only career he had ever known and forced to bear the "stigmata of ignominy."[19] Catacazy continued to insist that every accusation against him and every complication surrounding his time in Washington was, in some way, connected to the Perkins claim. If it had been only a personal incident, he pointed out, then the Russian government's assurance of his departure would have been sufficient and Fish would not have persisted.[20]

Meanwhile, Catacazy also appealed to Count Alexander Adlerberg, asking for his help and support in rehabilitating himself and obtaining a new position in the diplomatic service. Adlerberg was one of the officials charged with investigating the scandal and so Catacazy also wrote to him specifically about that process, complaining that the men entrusted with deciding his fate had not seen all of the pertinent documents, questioned him, or allowed him to question them.[21] He also detailed for Adlerberg the appointment of several individuals to new diplomatic posts, underscoring his own sense of urgency about clearing his name.[22] Over the course of several letters, Catacazy declared that Fish's publication of various documents made it critical for the publication of his defense, though he believed the American public understood that each line of Fish's explanation contained "two lies and an insult." Catacazy declared that Gorchakov was contradicting himself in not allowing him to speak out; it was his understanding that the Imperial Cabinet intended to review Catacazy's situation and issue a verdict, so he did not understand why he could not publish his own defense. Catacazy declared, "If I am guilty, we must give the Americans the reparation due to them, excluding me from the service. But if … my memoir completely refutes the charges against me, it is we who are entitled to a reparation." Catacazy argued that the publication of his side of the story must be done in the *Journal of St. Petersburg*, since the "American slanders" had been published in an official message.[23]

Catacazy received his verdict in late March. He was granted a pension of 3,000 rubles a year with the proviso that should he misbehave or publish anything about the scandal it would be withdrawn. This pension came from some source other than the Ministry of Foreign Affairs, so while he remained within the government service, he was no longer employed in the foreign service.[24] He was also granted a leave of absence until June 20.[25] The American press received and disseminated this news with some delight. The *Cleveland Daily Leader*, for example, decided that the verdict on Catacazy had "sustained the right of a friendly government to protect itself against impertinent and interference in private affairs and diplomatic relations with other nations, by meddlesome foreign ministers who have not sense enough to mind their own business."[26] *Harper's Weekly* reported that Catacazy had left St. Petersburg in "utter disgrace."[27] The *New York Herald* was particularly biting in its reaction to Catacazy's ruin, commenting sarcastically, "all his talking and letter writing could avail him nothing when judged impartially by his own countrymen." The *Herald* also rather relished the manner in which Catacazy had been punished. "To be pensioned off and then humiliated with an injunction placed upon his pen is an infliction which a less energetic work than the little mercurial ambassador would find it difficult to bear ... This is the worse cut of all."[28]

Catacazy was not happy with this verdict and believed that he had been treated unfairly and was the victim of a conspiracy. Complaining to anyone who would listen, Catacazy pointed out, more than once, that Fish published the details of his punishment in "4,500 American journals" before he himself had even been told, indicating that the information must have been communicated directly to Fish from the Russian Ministry of Foreign Affairs. Catacazy believed that "thanks to the common action of Mr. Fish and his accomplices in Petersburg," the Russian government had contrived a way to condemn and disgrace him without having to address the accusations against him in an official way.[29] He believed that his case had not been given full consideration, for if it had, "unjust facts and monstrous abuses impeding and undermining our diplomatic service would have been brought to light."[30] Catacazy believed there were several individuals who had been intriguing for some time and misleading Gorchakov, intent on ruining Catacazy. Now, emboldened by their success, they would be looking for other victims to discredit, further undermining the integrity of the Russian Foreign Office. Most infuriating to Catacazy was that these schemers would portray his silence as an acceptance of his situation, leaving him to choose between "misery and ignominy."[31] Elihu Washburne reported to Fish that some people believed that Catacazy was losing his mind. Prince Nikolai Orlov, the Russian minister to France, told Washburne, "He is a very dangerous man, and I tell you this confidentially that I have orders to put him under surveillance."[32]

On May 1, Catacazy wrote to Adlerberg from Paris that he had received a telegram ordering him to return to St. Petersburg at once. Catacazy declared, "I shudder to think about the reasons which could determine a sudden call before the expiration of the leave granted to me." He pleaded exhaustion and "terrible tremors" after a year of unimaginable torture, and begged to postpone his return to Russia until he had recovered. He retained hope that he could resume his place in the diplomatic service and assured Adlerberg that "as long as there remains to me a moment of hope for obtaining justice and restitution, I will observe religiously the absolute reserve which has been presented to me."[33]

Catacazy chaffed under this sentence of silence, and letters to Adlerberg always expressed his frustration at not being permitted to publicly defend himself. More than once he had mentioned a document he had already prepared for publication, but he simultaneously promised to abide by the emperor's orders.[34] It seems likely, however, that the disgraced Russian already was defending himself verbally, spreading stories of his innocence and rumors of a forthcoming book. The *Chicago Tribune* discussed the impending appearance of a "piquant and startling book by Catacazy," though suggesting that its veracity would be uncertain: "Knowing the wonderful capacity of that individual for sensational stories, it is more than likely that he uses a supposed prohibition on the publication as a pretext for circulating stories that he could dare not otherwise publish."[35]

In late May, Catacazy discovered why he had been summoned to St. Petersburg so quickly. Someone had accused him of placing an article in the *Paris-Journal* that spoke ill of Gorchakov and the Russian government. In letters to Peter Shuvalov, a trusted statesman and advisor to the tsar, and Nikolai Orlov, Russian minister to France, Catacazy denied any involvement in the article in question and declared that he intended to ask the editor-in-chief of that newspaper to testify "in the presence of witnesses, whether I have had any direct or indirect relationship with him, or with his newspaper."[36] He asked that someone from the Russian Legation in Paris attend this meeting, but Orlov saw no reason to comply, assuring Catacazy "your Excellency's affirmation is to me much more valuable than the testimonies of persons unknown to me."[37] Catacazy met with the editor nonetheless and obtained a statement of his innocence in contributing in any way to the publication of the article in question and sent a copy to Westmann in late May.[38] It is unclear whether anyone in the Russian Foreign Office believed Catacazy, but he, at the very least, had not at this point gotten into any more trouble. In a letter from Gorchakov to Catacazy of May 23, 1872, the Russian foreign minister granted the disgraced diplomat an extension of his leave to take "the cure" in Vichy, requesting that he return to St. Petersburg after his convalescence.[39]

While still in France, Catacazy wrote to Tsar Alexander as well, pleading his case and invoking the name of Grand Duke Alexis for extra effect. Catacazy declared that while still in the United States, he had written a letter of resignation, but that the Grand Duke had persuaded him not to resign, citing the just and good character of his father who would surely see through the lies and calumnies perpetrated against the Russian representative. Catacazy begged to be restored to the diplomatic service and to be given the post of a minister once more.[40]

Despite all the warnings and prohibitions from the tsar and the Foreign Office, in fact, Catacazy was working on a document that he hoped would vindicate him. In the summer of 1872, several newspapers reported that Catacazy had prepared a pamphlet and was attempting to find a publisher in London.[41] On July 13, Prince Orlov, the Russian minister in France, informed Catacazy that a telegram from Westmann declared once again that the tsar expressly forbade Catacazy from publishing his account of events and demanded that he return to St. Petersburg immediately or else he would be "stricken from service and deprived of pension." Catacazy replied that it was too late, that he had already sent it to the United States, claiming that he could not have imagined that even after submitting his letter of resignation he would be forbidden to "claim a reparation of honor." Nor did Catacazy believe he could return to St. Petersburg since his "persecutors" were clearly still intent on ruining his life. "They want to rob me of the rights I have acquired to a pension after 24 ½ years of service," he declared, service that was "irreproachable … active and useful."[42]

In subsequent letters, Catacazy explained that after receiving the judgment of the tsar's committee, he kept silent and waited four months for "some kind of rehabilitation." When that did not occur, he submitted his letter of resignation so that he would be free to defend himself publicly.[43] He did not wish for his defense to be construed as a criticism or comment on the sovereign's will, but he was determined to decry the "American outrages" and "fight against the hateful fury" of his enemies. He anticipated that both in Washington and in St. Petersburg he would be the target of criticism and would be blamed with negative articles in the press.[44] He also addressed the accusation that he had stolen money from the Russian government while purchasing land for the Russian church. Catacazy denied doing so and complained, "despite all my entreaties, an inquiry has been refused me."[45]

In July 1872, in direct defiance of the orders from the Russian government, Catacazy published an eighty-page refutation in French, entitled, *Un Incident Diplomatique*. Written as an appeal to the chief justice of the United States, Salmon P. Chase, the document was Catacazy's brazen and confrontational attempt to explain all of the charges against him. In it, Catacazy resorted to name-calling, misrepresentations, and outright falsehoods.[46] He repeatedly referred to the excessive rudeness and "malicious slander" of the secretary of state.[47] He declared that the collection of documents submitted by Fish to Congress "was compiled in a manner calculated to conceal the truth completely. The most important papers have been omitted; others have been garbled."[48] He expressed no intent to pursue legal action against Fish for these offenses because

American law would offer him only monetary compensation and "a functionary who has had the distinguished honor to represent His Majesty the Emperor of all the Russias, does not accept pecuniary compensation."[49]

Catacazy's refutation began with two extraordinary sentences that both reflect the personality of the author and set the tone for the remainder of the document: "A diplomat, like a soldier, is sometimes called upon to allow himself to be sacrificed in silence for the benefit of the cause he serves. There are circumstances in which he must expose himself without saying a word to receive the most murderous of grape-shot, that of calumny."[50] Claiming that he previously could not defend himself while serving Russia, he now intended to do so, since the tsar had relieved him of his diplomatic position "at my own request." Catacazy declared that according to Article Three, Section Two of the US Constitution, the Supreme Court oversaw cases involving ambassadors and other ministers, which gave him the right to ask that court to grant him "justice and reparation for the acts against my honor and my interests by Mr. Hamilton Fish." He then laid out in six points the accusations against him.[51]

The first point, of course, was the Perkins claim. Catacazy attempted to demonstrate that his earliest interactions with the president and the secretary of state had been friendly and cordial, and that the difficulties between them were the result of outside parties. He accused the Perkins attorneys and a number of other people of conspiring against him to squeeze money from the Russian government and to ruin him personally and professionally. He blamed them for the false dispatches and Fish for refusing to punish them. He insisted that calling the Perkins attorneys "audacious forgers" and "men capable of anything" was not a violation of his diplomatic immunities.[52]

Catacazy also took issue with the notion that he had interfered in matters not within his purview, with senators and members of Congress, or that he had "annoyed them by steps hampering the free course of legislation."[53] One specific example was his appeal for the reduction of the tariff on Russian hemp. Catacazy argued that Fish was incorrect in assuming that he had irritated these legislators; in fact, he stated, a number of these "eminent statesmen" had "done me the honor of frequenting my house" and exchanged "amiable and sometimes even affectionate letters."[54] Catacazy also addressed the rumors that he stole money from his own government by lying about the actual cost of land purchased for the establishment of an Orthodox church in New York City. Referring to actual correspondence from Fish regarding land he had for sale, Catacazy added this dig: "It was impossible for me to profit by this proposition, the land in question having been appraised by competent persons at half the price demanded."[55]

Catacazy had also been accused of writing or inspiring articles in American newspapers. Denying his involvement in these publications in any way, Catacazy claimed that a group of people had determined to get him expelled from the country, yet Fish had not believed him. Indeed, Fish had told him that he believed that Catacazy was writing abusive letters to himself to discredit the Perkins attorneys in his (Fish's) eyes. Frustrated with the secretary of state in this situation, Catacazy professed, "I was necessarily reduced to ask myself whether I was in the presence of one afflicted with mental aberration, or bent on provocation."[56] He believed that the Department of State was responsible for negative articles about him. He accused Fish of "arbitrary and insulting accusations." He denied having any interaction with George Adams of the *New York World*, the paper where one of the first articles attributed to him had appeared on November 29, 1870.[57] He declared that Fish had threatened to have him arrested if he attempted to prosecute Adams or Turk. He claimed to have "positive proof" that Fish and his assistant Bancroft Davis had "taken part in the writing and the circulation of the outrageous articles" published against him, numbering over eighty in total.[58]

Catacazy also denied any wrongdoing in the matter of the *Alabama* claims. He alleged that he had always had "sympathies in favor of a pacific solution" and had expressed those sympathies to Fish in writing, though the latter had not included those in his published collection of documents.[59] He denied that his visit to the president at Long Branch had been improper or that Grant had received him with coolness.[60] In fact, he emphasized that General Grant was perfectly courteous, and that he was "kind enough to listen attentively to everything I had the honor to say to him."[61] He repeatedly claimed to have evidence that he could not attach and witnesses he could not divulge.[62] Catacazy further declared that many Americans supported him, and that dozens had written him kind letters.[63] To this lengthy refutation, Catacazy attached appendices, nearly two dozen letters and articles. Most of these were correspondence between Fish and Catacazy, but there were also letters from James Gordon Bennett, Jr., of the *New York Herald*, Horace Greeley of the *New York Tribune*, and Charles Dana of the *New York Sun*, all of whom testified to their acquaintance with the Russian minister, but denied any influence or wrongdoing by him.

Catacazy found no sympathy in the American press. The *New York Times* declared that "the shrewd Greek" had published his pamphlet "for the gratuitous enlightenment of the public" but his "'revelations' have fallen with utter flatness." It further suspected that "his pamphlet was undoubtedly gotten up as much for the purpose of piecing out his small salary, as for any other reason."[64] The *Brooklyn*

Eagle summarized the ex-Russian minister's publication, but gave no credit to it. It did, however, spend half its column attributing the entire disagreement to the jealousy between Mrs. Catacazy and Mrs. Fish. Among other things, it accused Mrs. Fish of rescheduling her weekly receptions to coincide with those of Mrs. Catacazy and then of being angry and jealous when her guests stayed too short a time to rush off to her competitor's home. It concluded, "Then the usual social fighting occurred, and the husbands of each were forced into war."[65]

The *New York Herald* dedicated many columns to the pamphlet, publishing a lengthy summary of it. Its multiple headlines to the summary included, "The Bone of Catacazy's Diplomatic Life," "How the Row Began—A Woman at the Bottom of the Quarrel," and "Fish on the Warpath—Must Have the Muscovite's Scalp." A separate article interpreted and commented on the pamphlet, declaring, "we had hoped when the fiery little Graeco-Russian departed from our shores that we had heard the end of his wordy warfare with our somewhat unfortunate Secretary of State." The article was critical of the Grant administration, especially Fish, and remarked that if Catacazy had remained silent, "many at this side of the water would have continued to regard him as an able and in some respects an injured man." But in attempting to defend himself, he had failed, for "nothing in the letter to Chief Justice Chase supports the high pretensions of Catacazy."[66]

In Russia, Catacazy found support in the newspaper, *Golos*. The article gave a lengthy summary of the pamphlet with much supportive commentary, declaring that Catacazy demonstrated the "entire groundlessness" of the accusations against him. The paper's defense of the former minister is worth quoting:

> The proof presented by Catacazy in this brochure in support of all he has said so clearly and categorically that one can barely refute, and therefore it becomes clear that our representative in America, in view of such foul and low intrigues, … despite all his moderation and patience, could not stay in his post any longer. But he left with honor, and undoubtedly, will have on his side public opinion and the respect of all honest people.

> This brochure reveals many dark sides of the political life of the young and powerful republic, the establishment which so they so often love to place as the example and the model, in comparison to the rotting monarchies of old Europe: it shows that … under the protection of free laws, can flourish bribery and theft, and the bribery of judges, the most scandalous market speculation, scarcely less than under the "yoke of tyranny."

The paper concluded that perhaps Catacazy went slightly beyond the standard limits of diplomatic norms in his attempts to serve his country, but only because of his dedication to the honor of his nation. In the end, *Golos* believed that Catacazy acted "as a dignified representative of a great nation."[67]

Catacazy's insistence on defending himself in a public forum, however, got him in serious trouble. The Russian Government dismissed him from service and made it known that the document had not been authorized by way of an article published in the *Journal de St. Petersbourg*.[68] This second disgrace was celebrated by some American newspapers, such as the *New York Times*, which featured the headline, "Exit Catacazy—Dismissal of the Kantankerous Little Greek from Russian Service Destroyed by His Own Spite."[69]

Despite the obvious negative reaction of his own government to his pamphlet, Catacazy continued to appeal particularly to Orlov during August of 1872, bemoaning the "new infamies, which put me in the inevitable obligation to appeal, once again, to the justice of the Emperor." Catacazy understood that fighting these accusations in the press or by means of the American court system would be pointless.[70] Orlov advised Catacazy to remain silent, but the former Russian minister had never been capable of biting his tongue. Now, he feared that his silence would be construed as agreement and that in failing to protest he might lose his rights to a later claim. Most of all, Catacazy believed that his reputation would be permanently marred should he cease his fight against his attackers. Catacazy declared, "even if I can resign myself to the loss of my career, and even to that of my daily bread, I can not resign myself to the loss of my honor."[71] Orlov had also advised Catacazy to cease his appeals to Adlerberg. Catacazy would not listen, however, certain that Adlerberg was a "true and loyal man … too sincerely devoted to the Emperor not to tell Him the truth, and not to signal His Majesty the urgent necessity of elucidating this unhappy and shameful affair by a rigorous and impartial inquiry."[72] With this hope, Catacazy continued to write to Adlerberg, assuring the man he hoped would be his advocate, "At Naples, as at Petersburg, Paris, Washington, and everywhere I shall be, with no pay, I will scrupulously obey the orders of the Emperor, I will not despair of his justice, and I will wait with resignation for His Majesty to deign to grant the inquiry for my reintegration."[73]

Catacazy's appeal for a new inquiry and the ability to defend himself and his performance as minister in Washington persisted into the following years. In April 1873, he accused Count Shuvalov of being the person who had stood in the way of him getting the impartial evaluation he deserved. He had written Shuvalov repeatedly but had apparently received no reply, and now surmised that this "cruel silence" confirmed his conviction that Shuvalov was an enemy "as powerful as he is inflexible."[74] In a subsequent letter, he claimed to have been "indignantly slandered and mistreated" and asked Shuvalov, "is it right to hear the accusers, to stifle the voice of the accused, to say to a man: you will discontinue your career, your heart will rent, your honor will be defiled, but you are forbidden to defend yourself?" He begged for the chance to clear his name. He reminded Shuvalov that he had sacrificed himself "completely to ensure the happy outcome of the Grd Duc Alexis's trip."[75]

Catacazy reached out to Alexis, as well. He recounted the indignities and accusations, penned not in ink, but "in the most acrid filth one could dip his pen in," and asked the Grand Duke for assistance in receiving justice. While he expressed doubts about the trustworthiness of Gorchakov, he expressed faith in the justice of the tsar, comparing it to the light of the sun: "It can be momentarily eclipsed. It cannot be permanently obscured."[76] He asked that the Grand Duke help him obtain the fair inquiry he needed to clear his name. If found guilty, he would accept his punishment; if not, he argued, "it is clear that I am entitled, if not a compensation at least for the rehabilitation of my honor by my readmission to service in a position equivalent to the one I occupied."[77] Catacazy was right to worry about Gorchakov's opinion of him. In March 1873, James Orr, the new American minister in Russia, wrote that Gorchakov had called Catacazy "meddlesome" and "lacking in judgement."[78]

Catacazy never gave up, however. In the summer of 1880, he wrote to Count Mikhail Loris-Melikov, a very important advisor to the tsar, of his unjust dismissal and his denial of a full and fair inquiry. He still held out hope that he could return to diplomatic service, declaring, "If His Majesty deigns to lift the cruel prohibition upon me, I shall be ready to go to your call at St. Petersburg." Loris-Melikov had offered Catacazy a position as an intermediary between the Ministry of the Interior and the Foreign Office, and while he was grateful for the offer, he refused it because it was not equivalent to his previous position.[79] With the same presumptive air that always seemed to get him into trouble, Catacazy suggested that Loris-Melikov could appoint him as Russian minister at Brussels, "a post of unimportant political observation," but from which he could exert "an immediate and daily influence on our unofficial organ 'The North' which publishes in Brussels." He described the need for a minister "who knows how to influence public opinion in favor of our interests." He went so far as to suggest that the current minister at Brussels was in poor health and would probably welcome the opportunity to swap his position with one that would permit him more rest. Catacazy declared that his only desire was to win the tsar's favor again and to serve him—but only in a position equal to that which he held before.[80]

At some point during his time in France, Catacazy became an intelligence agent for the Russian government, operating chiefly from Paris, tasked with reporting anything that might be of interest to his court. He became a supporter of the Pan-Slav movement, as well, a movement that expressed a shared sense of national identity among all Slavs and advocated for the protections of Slavs living under foreign rule.[81] Some sources indicated that he also served as one of the editors of the French newspaper, *Le Figaro*.[82] He continued to seek a higher position, however. In 1882, Catacazy wrote several letters to Minister Nikolai Giers, foreign minister under Alexander III, once again asking for a return to diplomatic service. Tsar Alexander II had been assassinated by terrorists in March of the previous year, so perhaps Catacazy thought his chances might improve under the reign of Alexander III, son of the murdered tsar and brother of Grand Duke Alexis. Catacazy cited "ten years of painful withdrawal," during which he had seized every chance to demonstrate his zeal and devotion; now, Catacazy declared, "The personal considerations which forbade it until now to return to the Ministry of Foreign Affairs no longer exist."[83] Catacazy had submitted to Giers what he labeled his "Proekt dokladnoi zapiske." He explained that this plan, which would result in his reintegration into the service, was not written with personal goals in mind, but rather for the good of Russia.[84] Catacazy was disappointed once again. In July 1882, he received word that the emperor did not wish to bring him back into the diplomatic service. Catacazy was devastated, stating, "It only remains for me to go away and return to silence and idleness."[85]

Silence, however, was not in Catacazy's genetic makeup. He returned to St. Petersburg for a period in 1883–4 and sent several long letters to Giers recounting the many injustices he had endured and asking for a reconsideration of his exile from favor and service. Giers must have given some good news in reply to one of these letters, for Catacazy responded, "It is a great pleasure for me to know that the Emperor, our august master, deigns not to find me unworthy of returning one day to the service." This consoling news gave Catacazy the strength to wait.[86] Returning to France, he maintained an active correspondence with Giers and others, while publishing Pan-Slavist pieces in the French press under a false name.[87] He was, in fact, very active in a number of endeavors. He apparently worked with a cast of other characters to undermine the Russian alliance with Germany in favor of one with France until, after yet another rejection from St. Petersburg, he switched sides and became involved in intrigue yet again.[88] Some sources also point to his association with Jamāl al-Dīn al-Afghānī, a political activist in the late nineteenth century who was involved in the Pan-Islamic movement and one of the founders of the ideology of Islamic Modernism. Al-Afghānī was an Anglophobe because of the British Empire's imperialist ambitions in the Muslim world. The French police file on

Afghānī in Paris contained a document that declared that Catacazy was working as a secret Russian agent, possibly attempting to recruit the Islamic activist. According to this report, "Catacazy … is on a secret mission; he does what the Russian Embassy cannot do; he forged relations which might compromise the Embassy, and his objective was naturally all that had any force that could be used against England."[89]

Catacazy continued to appeal to the Russian government for help in restoring his public image and in securing higher pay. In 1887, he wrote to Giers again, this time referring to information he had received from a friend in St. Petersburg. This unnamed friend warned Catacazy that there were people in the capital who spoke ill of him to Giers and to the tsar. This informant asked Catacazy,

> Did you perhaps do something in your usual zeal to irritate someone? I heard that you made some sharp comments about those who wanted a closer relationship with France and were in favor of the final Break with Germany … You are right, of course; but friend, hasn't experience taught you that it's not helpful to speak the truth when the truth is poking powerful people in the eyes?

Catacazy had also received a devastating letter warning him that the minister of finance refused to grant his allowance for the next year.[90]

In fact, in late 1887 and early 1888, Catacazy was at the center of a scandal once again. In the summer of 1886, Alexander Battenberg, the first Prince of the Principality of Bulgaria, abdicated his throne after a coup d'état, civil unrest, and foreign intervention. The following year, the Bulgarian National Assembly elected Prince Ferdinand of Saxe-Coburg-Gotha as the new Prince of Bulgaria. Russia, which had disapproved of various Bulgarian actions in recent years, was unhappy about the choice of Ferdinand and declared the election irregular. Over the following months, the other powers of Europe were reluctant to declare their support for him publicly, so when Ferdinand finally accepted the throne and was crowned on August 22, 1887, there were suspicions that one of the Great Powers had quietly encouraged him. This seemed to be confirmed when in early fall, while Alexander III and his wife Dagmar were visiting her parents, the King and Queen of Denmark, the tsar received copies of letters that, if true, showed that Otto von Bismarck of Germany had been lying to him and had secretly encouraged Ferdinand to accept the throne. The various signatories denied the veracity of the letters and declared them forgeries. The question then became, who had composed the forged letters?[91]

It should come as no surprise that Catacazy was named as one of those possibly responsible. The stain on his reputation after his removal from Washington certainly contributed to this assumption, as did his general character. In the words of one contemporary, he was known for having "a remarkable spirit of intrigue" and was "as greedy as a merchant in the Constantinople bazaar."[92] The French newspaper, *Le Figaro*, accused Catacazy of authoring the "Ferdinand Letters," as did other contemporaries.[93] According to *Le Temps*, Catacazy denied any involvement in a letter to another newspaper and declared, with no apparent sense of irony, that his position as special adviser to the emperor and as a functionary in the Ministry of Foreign Affairs prohibited him from engaging in arguments in the press. He did, however, add that though he was innocent of the charges against him, he found himself in good company, since he was the seventh person to whom the false documents had been attributed.[94] Not surprisingly, the Russian Embassy in France denied Catacazy's involvement as well.[95]

Still, the suspicions about Catacazy lingered. Francesco Crispi, a major figure in Italian Unification and the prime minister of Italy at this time, hinted in his memoir that Catacazy could have been the guilty party. Though he declared that the author was unknown, he also noted, "It is suspected, however, that he is of Russian extraction and resides, or once resided, in France." Moreover, the form and style of the letters gave clues to their origin. While it was reported that the letters were translations from German to French, Crispi declared, "it is evident they were composed in French. They betray the fact that the author was in the habit not only of perusing diplomatic documents, but also of composing them."[96] Secondary sources would later argue against the former Russian minister as the author, though leaving open the possibility of his assistance.[97]

Soon after the drama of the Ferdinand documents, Catacazy was still asking Giers for help in obtaining financial assistance, specifically "a grant from the Minister's Economic Funds."[98] Recounting the many wrongs done to him, despite his many years of loyal service, Catacazy once again requested that his case be put before the emperor, his honor restored, and his place in the diplomatic service reestablished.[99] Catacazy, however, would never see that wish come to pass. He died in 1890 in Paris after a long illness.[100] The case of the duplicitous diplomat was finally closed.

Conclusion: "The Catfish War" and Its Legacy

When Constantin Catacazy died in 1890, his departure generated little interest in the press, either in the United States or abroad. Very few newspapers marked his death and his obituaries were, by and large, short and unremarkable.[1] Several newspapers in Michigan reported, "M. Catacazy is dead, and probably few know or care who he was."[2] The *New York Sun* declared, "Better men have been forgotten in half of twenty years," suggesting that it was his notoriety, not his ability, that made him memorable. The article then continued on at length with the story of Olga Catacazy and the cold shoulder of female Washington society.[3] The Washington *Evening Star* described his exceptional qualities as a young diplomat but then also digressed into a long history of the scandal involving his recall.[4] The *Pittsburgh Dispatch* honored him even less; failing to even mention his death, the paper left it up to its patrons to read between the lines and simply stated, "Mme. Catacazy, widow of the ex-Russian Ambassador, is still a beautiful woman and retains the glorious golden hair which was the envy of her sex when she was in Washington."[5] Only a few papers were gracious in their final assessments of the former minister, crediting him with the friendly relations that currently existed between Russia and France.[6]

Though Catacazy's death did not make large headlines, the Catacazy Affair would have a far-reaching impact, both in the immediate years after the scandal and in subsequent decades as well. It nearly cost one minister his job. It caused tensions in diplomatic circles and was widely reported in the foreign press. It made it uncomfortable for Americans to visit the court of Russia for some time after. From the standpoint of international law, it became an interesting example of a nation's power to reject or request the removal of a foreign representative who betrayed certain expectations or rules about diplomacy. Finally, it was the beginning of the slow decline in Russian-American relations from friend to foe.[7]

Even as Catacazy's recall was being implemented it was already making itself felt in other diplomatic circles, prompting speculation and gossip, and putting American representatives around the world on the defensive. When Hamilton Fish informed the country's representatives abroad about the reasons for the request for the recall of the Russian minister in November 1871, he had intended for the summary of the facts to dispel rumors and clarify the American government's decision. One diplomat, however, Michael J. Cramer, the US representative in Copenhagen, Denmark, apparently took the secretary's instructions a step further, causing yet another international dust up. Cramer was the husband of President Grant's younger sister, Mary, and, therefore, his brother-in-law. In an administration already plagued with accusations of nepotism and corruption, accusations of Cramer's overzealousness were not a welcome addition to Fish's overflowing cup of diplomatic difficulties.

Oddly enough, the first reports of any possible misconduct by Cramer did not appear until early 1872. At that time, articles in the *Washington Daily National Republican*, the *New York Herald*, and other papers described the American minister's alleged missteps. According to these sources, in early November 1871, the German minister in Copenhagen, Georg von Heydebrand, hosted a diplomatic dinner to which many representatives were invited. At the dinner, Cramer informed the Russian minister, Arthur von Mohrenheim, that he had received a dispatch from Fish regarding the Catacazy case and subsequently proposed to read it to the gathered men. Though Mohrenheim protested, Cramer persisted until the host decried his actions as inappropriate. Cramer then announced that he would call on each of them separately the following day and read the paper to them, which he subsequently did. Mohrenheim relayed this all to his superiors and the Russian cabinet was "vexed" by the entire matter. Several papers reported that Gorchakov had called Cramer "an animal."[8]

As condemning as the story itself was, the commentary in the American press was even worse. The *New York Herald* declared that Cramer's understanding of his duties was "to say the least, remarkable," but other papers went much further in their condemnation. The *Cincinnati Gazette* declared that if one-tenth of what was printed about Cramer was true, "he deserves not only to be dismissed in disgrace, but also to be expelled from the Methodist Church." The *Memphis Daily Appeal* was particularly critical. In response to the news that Gorchakov had called Cramer "an animal," the *Appeal* added, "That it is well deserved we have too much evidence … His tastes and instincts are those of an animal with brutal appetites to be appeased at any cost of dignity and honor." Under a column entitled, "Editor's Appeal," the paper took Cramer to task for not being fluent in Danish and accused him of drunkenness and embarrassing public displays while under the influence of alcohol. It described him as a "consummate blockhead and pompous ass" whose "lack of tact and good breeding are such that the other members of the diplomatic corps hold as little intercourse with him as possible."[9]

Cramer immediately responded to these charges of impropriety in a letter to Fish. He explained that prior to receiving the secretary of state's memo he had frequently been asked by his colleagues, including the German minister, if the newspaper stories about the Catacazy scandal were true. Consequently, once he had Fish's statement, he was prepared to address all inquiries, and when Heydebrand invited him to a dinner, he brought the official document with him. After dinner, in a private conversation, the German minister inquired if he knew anything more about the Catacazy Affair. Cramer acknowledged that he did and asked his host "if he thought that occasion a proper one for me to correct any erroneous impressions that may have been made on the minds of our colleagues by the newspaper reports." Heydebrand was sure they would, but suggested that these conversations should take place separately, at their homes. After everyone had departed, Cramer read an extract from Fish's dispatch to the German minister, who made some negative remarks about Catacazy. Cramer insisted that there was no clash between himself and the Russian minister, in public or in private. In fact, he stated, "during the entire evening no words whatever were exchanged between the Russian Minister and myself on the 'Catacazy Affair.'" Moreover, when Cramer attempted to call on him at home, he was out. He admitted to discussing the matter with the English minister, the Austrian Chargé d'Affaires, and the Danish minister for foreign affairs, but declared that he believed these actions were required by the circumstances, and that his sole object was to "defend the honor and dignity" of the American government.[10]

Apparently, however, this initial defense did not suffice, for two weeks later Cramer sent Fish a similar letter that reiterated the content of his previous report in slightly greater detail. In this letter, Cramer emphasizes that he did not at that dinner or at any other time "speak, read, or propose to read, or write a word to him [the Russian Minister] on the subject; hence he <u>never</u> had the slightest occasion or reason to remonstrate or become offended at me, and he <u>never did</u> remonstrate" (underline in the original source). Cramer claimed that the relations between himself and Mohrenheim were still friendly and cordial, demonstrated by their lengthy conversation at a subsequent dinner only a few days later on "science, psychology, and Christianity," as well as several other social interactions. In this letter to Fish, however, Cramer also recognized that he "may have misapprehended the precise tenor" of the secretary's dispatch and asked forgiveness for his zeal to protect the honor of his country. He also attempted to mitigate the damage to his reputation by noting that the Danish minister of foreign affairs had recently complimented him by expressing his hope that the American government would allow Cramer to stay at his post in Copenhagen "for a long time to come." Cramer concluded that the newspaper stories were "gross exaggerations and stupid misrepresentations," and the abuse heaped upon him was "as unjustified as it is gratuitous."[11]

The matter did not end there, however. In early March, Cramer wrote to Fish again with additional information. He relayed a conversation with Heydebrand, who had expressed his sympathy with Cramer as one who had been "misrepresented and abused" and voluntarily stated that the American minister's actions had been "in accordance with diplomatic usages" and it had been appropriate and necessary for him to correct erroneous impressions being circulated by reports in the press. Cramer also emphasized that any rumors that Gorchakov had complained to the German government about this matter were untrue, since the German minister, who would surely have been called upon to explain himself, had no knowledge of any such correspondence. Cramer concluded that the report of any angry note from Gorchakov to the German government was "probably manufactured for political purposes either in Berlin, or Copenhagen, or St. Petersburg, or New York, or Washington."[12]

One might imagine that Cramer's previous explanation would have sufficiently addressed the concerns of the State Department. Not so. In late March, Cramer again felt compelled to give a "general denial of the slanderous reports" about his actions in Denmark. Some of these articles had apparently appeared in the Danish papers. The stories about him had grown considerably by this point, and he was now accused of visiting "beer saloons and public places of amusement, of having wounded on theses occasions the national pride of the Danish people and its officers by praising the valour displayed by the Germans in the wars of 1864, 1866, and 1870." According to these reports, Cramer reportedly associated exclusively with Germans and generally behaved in an offensive manner. Cramer called these accusations "slanders and infamous calumnies" and denied all of these actions. He admitted that he conversed with the Danish minister of foreign affairs in German, but only out of necessity; the Danish minister did not speak English and Cramer, like most of the other foreign diplomats, did not speak Danish fluently enough to carry on a genuine conversation. (Cramer reminded Fish that he had only been there seven months.) He explained to Fish that he had always been very careful in articulating opinion on international questions, "believing that discretion and silence are some of the principal rules to be followed in diplomacy." He denied visiting public places of amusement, citing his respect for his character, his family, his country, and emphasized that God led him "to act as it becomes a Christian gentleman and an officer of the United States Government." Cramer, however, had his suspicions as to what might have led to these attacks on him. During the previous summer, a group of Americans traveling in Copenhagen had frequented some of these public establishments, consorting with "certain questionable persons." Cramer had recently become aware that when the Americans left, some of them had failed to pay their hotel, wine, restaurant, and other bills. He had been approached, for example, by a restaurant owner seeking to recover his losses and had discovered similar claims elsewhere. Cramer felt certain that someone had accidentally mistaken one of those Americans for him, leading to the false reports of his behavior, or that some "malicious person or persons" had intentionally attributed these things to him for purposes of discrediting him. In general, Cramer declared, "I have seen with great regret that a portion of the Danish press seem to make it a point to publish whatever is derogatory of America and Americans, but seldom if ever to speak of what is praiseworthy and good." Cramer attributed this bad blood to the failure of "the St. Thomas Treaty," an agreement in 1867, by which the United States would have purchased the islands of St. Thomas and St. John from Denmark for seven and a half million dollars. When the US Senate refused to ratify the treaty for various reasons, the deal fell through, apparently angering some parties.[13]

Six weeks later, Cramer addressed the aspersions on his reputation yet again, prompted by "fresh slanders" that had recently circulated about him. Indeed, there were new rumors circulating in the press about his behavior and general inappropriateness for diplomatic service. Several papers reported that Cramer had sought admittance to the Royal Club in Copenhagen, an exclusive club to which all foreign ministers usually belonged. When, however, it became apparent that there were numerous objections to his admittance, he was encouraged to withdraw his name. Cramer angrily refused, it was said, accusing the members of snobbery and seeking to uncover the names of those who had opposed him. According to one paper, "On one occasion, indeed, he became entangled in a personal encounter, and had to be dissuaded from further violence by the efforts of the police." Other reports claimed that the Danish minister of foreign affairs had demanded Cramer's recall.[14]

After making some inquiries, Cramer now believed that the efforts against him had originated not in Copenhagen but in Washington and New York. His source, a local editor in the city, claimed that numerous articles in German-language papers, such as the *Neue Freie Presse* out of Vienna, contained "the most villainous attacks upon the public and private character of the President" and other members of his family. These articles, the editor believed, were inspired by Senator Carl Schurz for the purpose of preventing President Grant's reelection to office. Schurz was the first German-born American to serve in the Senate and had recently broken from Grant's party and was in the process of founding the Liberal Republican Party. Cramer believed that the offending articles were essentially originating in the United States, published in Vienna or other German cities, then republished in Danish newspapers; once in the Danish press, the articles were in turn sent to "libelous journals in New York which with an air of triumph publish them as coming directly from Denmark." As evidence, Cramer offered that many of the locations mentioned in the articles did not exist.[15]

Though Cramer could do little about how he was portrayed in various newspapers, he may have taken some solace in the support of his fellow diplomats and clergymen. In May, the *Daily National Republican* published a letter defending Cramer, written by G. W. Griffin, the US Consul in Copenhagen, who called him a gentleman and denied that the stories about him were true. The letter consumed a whole column on the front page of the paper. The following month, a group of ministers appointed by the Cincinnati Methodist Conference passed a resolution in defense of Cramer's character. Declaring the attacks on him to be "a source of profound regret and mortification to … his brethren in the Christian ministry," they noted that many people had testified to his "blameless and upright official and moral character."[16]

Still, Cramer continued to defend himself. In June, he wrote to Fish about an article he received, purportedly from the *St. Louis Republican* from March, about the rumor that the Danish government was requesting his recall. Cramer appealed to the Danish minister for foreign affairs, who called the charges "as absurd as they are untrue" and indicated that he did not believe they had originated in that city, but rather outside of the Kingdom of Denmark.[17] Several articles from Danish newspapers, translated and republished in American papers, support the foreign minister's argument that the accusations against Cramer were coming from outside of Denmark. These American papers all defended Cramer's honor, declaring him a man of high esteem who was regarded well by his diplomatic colleagues. They called the rumors about him "venomous inventions" and suggested that it was his relation to President Grant that had inspired these slanders against him.[18]

The case of Cramer and his difficulties abroad is illustrative of another aspect of the Catacazy Affair, specifically how it was reported and viewed in Europe. In diplomatic circles, for the most part, there was agreement or at least sympathy with the stance of the American government and its decision to oust a troublesome minister. It would appear Catacazy's reputation had proceeded him and the reports of American ministers serving in Europe indicate no great surprise from their colleagues. The press, however, tended to approach the story less delicately.

The Catacazy Affair attracted a great deal of attention in international news sources. After the fears of a Russian-American alliance during the Alaska purchase and the similar rumors that emerged during the Black Sea crisis, it should be expected that the very public battle between the Russian minister and his American hosts would be keenly observed abroad. Many newspapers in Europe followed the story, though initially often without judgment or significant comment. Papers like the *Belfast News-Letter*, *Aberdeen Journal*, the *London Times*, *Le Temps*, and many others all dedicated a few sentences to Catacazy's recall in November and December of 1871.[19] It was widely known by this point that the Russian minister would only be tolerated by the American government during the visit of Grand Duke Alexis and that he would be departing at the end of that period. The *Montreal Gazette*, however, doubted that the restrictions on the troublemaking diplomat would have much effect, declaring, "his conduct under this ban is not better than it was before and people are growing tired of his 'tolerated' presence, which is now becoming intolerable to them."[20]

Eventually, after the documents from the case were published, and Grant presented his annual address, the foreign press had more to say. A number of papers chose to publish summaries or excerpts of the Fish–Catacazy correspondence; similarly, Grant's speech was redacted, or quoted at length or in full in many journals.[21] British papers in particular appear to have accepted as fact that Catacazy had interfered in the settlement of the *Alabama* claims, perhaps at the instructions of his government. The *Glasgow Herald* stated quite directly, "it is hardly to be supposed that M. Catacazy's intermeddling about the Alabama Treaty was not in accordance with imperial policy."[22] In a similar vein, the *Bristol Mercury* discussed "the plots of the Muscovite schemer" and their ultimate failure.[23] Many British papers believed that Catacazy was trying to destroy the friendly relationship that was developing between the United States and Great Britain in the wake of the Black Sea crisis and with the impending conclusion of the lengthy *Alabama* claims. Russia wanted the exclusive privilege of being America's unofficial ally. But, the *London Daily News* noted, "there are not a few political enthusiasts who believe that Czar and President are destined in the fulness [sic] of time to divide the world between them."[24]

By January 1872, the foreign papers covered Russia's responses to the minister's expulsion and commented particularly on Gorchakov's letter. The Dublin, Ireland *Freeman's Journal and Daily Commercial Advertiser* referred to the "strangely aggressive circular" of the Russian foreign minister, while many other papers quoted Gorchakov's reply to Fish at length.[25] The *Leeds Mercury* suggested that Fish's decision to publish his correspondence with Catacazy for all the world to see probably accounted for the terse tone of Gorchakov's reply. More pointedly, the paper noted, "Mr. Fish invites the world to hear a terrible lecture to Russia on the proprieties of diplomatic intercourse."[26] Still Catacazy found little sympathy in the foreign media. The St. Petersburg correspondent for the *London Telegraph* called Catacazy a "disagreeable ogre" and stated that even in Russia he was known as "a man of a certain ability, but with principles of a very doubtful character," while the *Hamburg Correspondent* accused the ex-minister of being "over-zealous" in following the instruction of his Foreign Office regarding the *Alabama* settlement.[27] Still, according to several French papers, the United States had handled Russia roughly, and they questioned if America believed it could "break a lance with impunity against all the European powers."[28]

The Catacazy Affair evoked strong opinions and passionate debates between papers, as well. In January 1872, the *London Times* and the *Moskovskie Vedomosti* took aim at one another over their respective interpretations of the scandal and how it was being portrayed in their countries. In late January, in the same article that snidely referred to Americans' ability to keep secrets when it suited them, the *Vedomosti* also addressed the origins of the Fish–Catacazy clash. Discussing the various charges against the Russian minister at length, the paper observed that there was nothing to gain for either Russia or America in this dispute. Another country, it suggested, might benefit from the demise of the Russian-American friendship, however—England. Thus, according to the *Gazette*, "not the Americans, but the English interest, would demand that the U.S. Secretary of State should exaggerate the meaning of this altercation with the Russian Minister." The paper assured its readers, however, that the messy affair had done nothing to negatively impact the long-standing relationship, nor had the corrupt actions of its leaders fooled the American people. Citing some critical articles in the American press, the *Vedomosti* concluded that administrators come and go, "but the state remains, the nation remains, its real interests remain, and the Americans understand their own interests very well, and we can be assured of the maintenance of our good relations with them."[29] Curtin subsequently described this article as "doubtless prepared in the Foreign Office and was intended to be accepted as what Prince Gortchakoff would have said if he had not been restrained by his views of official propriety."[30]

The *London Times* took offense at these accusations, first publishing the *Gazette* article and then responding to it at length. On January 24, the *Times* reprinted the offending article declaring that it was, in essence, a "continuation of Prince Gortchakoff's dispatch on the Katakazy case." The following day, it addressed the *Vedomosti*'s version of events and made some scathing comments of its own. Not surprisingly, the *Times* flatly denied the charges of complicity in the publication of the Catacazy correspondence and expressed sympathy with the American administration in its uncomfortable situation. It spared no words in its assessment of Catacazy's behavior in various episodes. In general, the *Times* claimed, Catacazy "allowed himself too much license in his mode of action"; specifically, in the case of the *Alabama* claims, "his intervention was a piece of political impertinence." The *Times* clearly delighted in the embarrassment the Russian government experienced by the exposure of all Catacazy's sins, but declared that it had only itself to blame. By not reining in Catacazy's "zeal," the Russian government had emboldened him, creating the difficulty it now faced.[31]

This was not the end of the war of words, however. A week later, the *Moskovskie Vedomosti* responded, rejecting that its article had any official character whatsoever and declaring that the *Times* has misunderstood its intent. It denied blaming England for the publication of the correspondence, adding sarcastically, "This would be of exactly the same character and quite as strange as the supposition that the Russian Minister could hinder a good understanding between America and England." The article critiqued the so-called evidence against Catacazy, as "petty gossip which clearly showed the personal character of his dispute with Mr. Catacazy … These accusations were supported by proofs of a very doubtful nature." The *Vedomosti* thought it interesting that the *Times* turned a blind eye to these glaring problems, and "sees the whole cause of the dissatisfaction with the Russian Minister in his trying to hinder the negotiations between England and America on the Alabama question." As to its suggestion of the role of Great Britain in the scandal, the paper stated,

> A dispute between Russia and America would be desired by an interest opposed to that of America: This seems to us indisputable. We did not say that Mr. Fish

acted at the suggestion of English diplomacy; we only said, and affirm now, that if there were any political calculation, its success would be profitable not to America but to England.[32]

A week later, the *Vedomosti* complained that "some English gazettes still continued their efforts to represent as something serious the diplomatic disagreement between America and Russia," but it appears that the direct sparring died out at this point.[33]

The appearance of Catacazy's pamphlet in the summer of 1872 garnered a new wave of coverage in the European news. The *Pall Mall Gazette*, among others, gave lengthy summaries of the ex-minister's defense. The *Birmingham Daily Post* had much to say about the publication. It noted with sarcasm that Catacazy denied all the allegations and "exculpates himself with a charming ingenuousness." The paper found it surprising, however, that someone with such a reputation of candor did not choose to tell the whole truth. Harkening back to the rumor that had been circulated for well over a year, the *Daily Post* stated, "in this, as in all other muddles, there was a woman at the bottom, and if Madame Catacazy had been old or ugly, it is quite probable that her husband might have continued to represent the Czar at Washington."[34]

There were other reverberations of the Catacazy Affair as well. Although the American and Russian press both praised the reception of Grand Duke Alexis by the American people, there had been snide comments and bitterness in Russia about his treatment at the hands of the American president. In early 1872, the secretary to the American Legation in St. Petersburg, Eugene Schuyler, found it difficult because of "a little ill-feeling against General Grant, on account of the Catacazy affair … to procure a proper reception for General Sherman, because he was accompanied by one of the President's sons as aide-de-camp."[35] Schuyler also reported that there was a feeling of hostility toward the reelection of Grant in St. Petersburg, in both official and unofficial circles, "a feeling apparently called out by the Catacazy affair."[36] The following year, when Marshall Jewell replaced Andrew Curtin as minister to Russia, he experienced this as well. Upon his arrival in St. Petersburg, it took much longer than usual before he was presented to the tsar. This, combined with the cool interactions of the courtiers, made him keenly aware that he was being punished for his countrymen's sins. When he finally met Alexander II, who was on his way out for a ride, the tsar barely paused, did not remove his gloves or extend his hand, but simply said, "Your Government did not treat my son Alexis well."[37] In fact, the hard feelings persisted for some years after the royal visit and made for some tense interactions in subsequent visits of Americans.

When President Grant and his wife traveled around the world in 1877–9 after the conclusion of his second term in office, they visited Russia as well. Fish did not think this was a good idea and had warned against it. In a letter to Grant of July 1878, Fish had suggested that the president should only go to Russia if he was invited by the tsar himself. Specifically, Fish was concerned that Gorchakov had not yet forgiven the dismissal of "his pet, that scamp Catacazy" and that he had convinced the tsar that Grant had not sufficiently welcomed Alexis. Fish believed that Gorchakov would not "lose the opportunity of doing something disagreeable."[38] The American minister to Russia at that time, George Boker, felt the same way. Grant, however, was determined to see Russia and insisted that it made no difference to him if the tsar received him.[39] Various sources report that while the Grants were politely received and able to renew their acquaintance with Grand Duke Alexis, "the Catacazy ouster lay like a shadow around them all." The tsar was polite and engaged in pleasant conversation with Grant, but did not invite him to dinner.[40]

The Catacazy Affair left its mark on international law as well. In the century following Catacazy's removal, the case of the errant Russian minister was cited by many treatises of international law and practice in discussions of the rights and duties of foreign ministers and their governments, as well as the distinctions between requesting the recall of a minister by his home government versus dismissing him outright. Francis Wharton's *Digest of the International Law of the United States*, first published in 1886, dedicates several pages to the Catacazy Affair. Subsequent compilations of international law discuss the case as well, in varying lengths, though with little commentary. For the most part, the episode is seen as an example of one of the hazards of the practice of using ministers to conduct international diplomacy.[41] However, Fish's explanation for why Russia should have recalled its minister without question was incorporated into a number of law digests as the new standard according to which this particular situation should be handled. This explanation, drawn from his November 16, 1871, letter to Curtin, stated,

> The official or authorised statement that a Minister has made himself unacceptable or even that he has ceased to be persona grata to the Government to which he is accredited is sufficient to invoke the deference to a friendly power and the observance of the courtesy and the practice regulating the Diplomatic Intercourse of the Powers of Christendom for the recall of an objectionable

minister. The declaration of this authorised representative of minister is accredited is all that can properly be asked and all that a self respecting Power could give.[42]

Indeed, in 1895, when President Grover Cleveland requested the recall of Lorrin Thurston, minister from Hawaii, the *New York Times* and the Washington *Evening Star* recognized that it was based on this principle.[43]

Finally, and most importantly, the Catacazy Affair was a significant blemish on the unusual friendship between Russia and the United States. While under Alexander II, there was mutual interest and mutual admiration—expressions of gratitude (for Russia's support during the Civil War); congratulations (for Alexander's escape from an assassination attempt); and condolences (on Lincoln's assassination)—in subsequent years, the situation would change dramatically due to a variety of factors. The harsh feelings created by the recall process itself, the frequent misunderstandings and misinterpretations due to Catacazy's intentionally altered or exaggerated reports, and the complications of overseas communications made the execution of sensitive diplomatic matters even more difficult. Under the best of circumstances, the request to have a minister removed could provoke outrage and an interruption of normal friendly relations. In this sense, Catacazy's recall was successfully completed with less drama than might have occurred; there had been rumors that Russia would demand the recall of Andrew Curtin in retaliation, but those proved to be false. The fact that Russia chose not to retaliate is an indication of the goodwill that had been built up between the two nations over the previous decades. Throughout the entire episode, both nations, in private and public communications, emphasized the history and value of the Russian-American relationship. Nonetheless, the Catacazy scandal and its impact on the visit of Grand Duke Alexis left its mark, as we have seen, and was but the first of many growing differences over the next years.

One issue that complicated the feelings of the United States for Russia was the latter nation's treatment of its Jewish population. This problem already had been a subject of American concern at the time of Catacazy's appointment. Fish recorded in his diary in November 1869, "The President had rec'd a memorial from some Israelites, complaining of an Ukase of the Russian Gov. expatriating a large number of Jews, on account of their faith, & asking usual interference in their behalf. He directs that the subject be mentioned to the Russian Minister."[44]

There were, of course, other events in which America supported Russia. The Russo-Turkish War of 1877–8 garnered much attention in the American press, for the most part, sympathetic to Russia and its desire to protect fellow Christians.[45] Similarly, during the Russian famine of 1891–2. Americans offered assistance, both private endeavors and others led by Clara Barton of the American Red Cross resulting in five American vessels traveled to Russia in the spring of 1892 carrying flour, cornmeal, and grain.[46] Though some Americans complained about the passivity, fatalism, and inertia of Russians, in the end the famine also resurrected that sentiment repeated so often during Alexis's visit, that Russia and America were friends. The *New York Times* emphasized that American generosity had "stimulated a feeling between the two nations which will last so long as they both endure." As one historian wrote, "In 1892, we still clung to this cherished myth of traditional friendship despite a growing antipathy to autocracy and all it stood for in our eyes."[47]

Despite American sympathy and generosity, public opinion about Russia became gradually more negative. The Senate expressed sympathy for Russia when Alexander II died at the hands of terrorists in 1881, declaring in a resolution "its sincere condolence in this sad national bereavement," but the subsequent reactionary stance of his son, Alexander III, proved difficult to reconcile and it was more difficult to find common ground. This allowed for the less generous assessments of Russia to drown out those that had focused on similarities and Russia's ability to change.[48] Now, American public opinion began to view Russia not as a friend but as a repressive state. This view was reinforced by the October Revolution of 1917. The Russian-American relationship could not continue under the circumstances created by the Bolshevik victory. To be sure, there would still be moments of détente and cooperation—the notable example being the alliance of the Second World War—but these brief interludes were driven largely by self-interest, ulterior motives, and need, not the feeling of mutual goodwill that had been palpable in the 1860s and 1870s. The scandal of the meddling minister and his scandalously beautiful wife certainly was part of this shift from diplomatic friendship to uneasy coexistence.

The Catacazy Affair is also a clear example of the power that individuals have to impact diplomacy and international relations. Despite the lofty ideals about democracy and the system of checks and balances in the American government, it was (and, one might argue, still is) possible for personal clashes between individuals to influence and shape policy. Though Constantin Catacazy certainly violated protocol in a variety of ways and overstepped his role as minister, there was clearly a personal dimension to his conflict with Fish and Grant. Catacazy was haughty, abrasive, and pushy; he was officious, duplicitous, and prone to exaggeration. All of the primary sources by and about Catacazy paint the portrait of a thoroughly irritating individual, and he clearly got under Fish's skin soon after his arrival. In contrast, his wife Olga was universally described as a charming and lovely woman, with a remarkable beauty that was the envy of all the other ladies of Washington. Her perfect skin, however, could not overshadow a blemished past, and she was ostracized from polite society at a time when the social and political worlds overlapped considerably. Combined, the two Catacazys had many social strikes against them.

In Russia, where domestic and foreign policy were more personal in nature to begin with, the importance of individuals was even more evident. Catacazy had been appointed as minister to the United States only because Gorchakov had pushed his cause, repeatedly asking the tsar to agree. When Fish requested Catacazy's recall in the summer of 1871, Gorchakov attempted to protect his favorite for several months until so much evidence of Catacazy's lies and obnoxious behavior appeared that he could support him no more. The tsar, who had never cared much for Catacazy, was less concerned about the destruction of that diplomat's career as he was about the perceived snubbing of his son, Alexis, by President Grant during the young Russian's visit to Washington. Many years later, he apparently still held a grudge.

Finally, Catacazy's utilization of American newspapers as a venue and medium for his intrigue is a reminder that long before cable news channels and 24/7 internet news coverage the media could influence and shape events in remarkable ways. In his book, *Mightier Than the Sword: How the News Media Have Shaped American History*, historian and journalism professor Rodger Streitmatter examines the way journalistic coverage can shape events, focusing on a selection of milestones in American history, from the American Revolution to Watergate. Streitmatter emphasizes that the media does not create the events in question, but "the news media can place an issue on the public agenda … can move it to the front burner … can get people talking about the issue."[49] The Russian minister clearly understood this and took advantage of the freedom of the American press to promote his interests and manipulate public opinion. In Russia, the press and, in fact, all publications were limited in what they could publish by state censorship. Throughout the nineteenth century, the Russian periodical press, be it newspapers or journals, was strictly regulated and monitored and was not permitted to print anything negative about the government or the Russian Empire. Journals were temporarily closed by the government and editors were jailed. Though some of these restrictions were lifted during the period of Alexander II's reforms, the state still kept an eye on Russia's growing mass-circulation newspaper industry.[50] Catacazy grew up in and worked in this world of state control and state censorship, yet, once in the United States, made the most of the opportunity provided by the American right of freedom of the press. As it turned out, he also learned that freedom of speech does not mean freedom from consequences. Although he complained about the "unlimited liberty the press enjoys in the United States," he was more than willing to utilize the freedom of the press when he thought it might serve his needs.[51]

The meddling of the Russian minister in affairs of the American government in general and his use of the press, in particular, is also particularly interesting in the twenty-first century as the United States once again faces the potential of interference by Russia(ns) in internal affairs. The Catacazy scandal foreshadows more recent events, specifically Russian exploitation of social media to disseminate disinformation and create divisiveness in the already polarized American public. In December 2018, a report produced by the cybersecurity firm New Knowledge for the Senate Intelligence Committee explained the ways in which Russian "trolls" had utilized various social media platforms to influence American popular opinion around the time of the 2016 US presidential election.[52] As the 2020 election approached, both researchers and respected news outlets sounded the alarm again. In March 2020, the *Associated Press* revealed that the social media platforms Facebook and Twitter had removed dozens of fake accounts, but declared that Russian efforts to interfere in the upcoming election were "getting more sophisticated and harder to detect." Concerns intensified in the weeks before the election.[53] But Russian meddling in American politics was not an entirely new phenomenon. Constantin Catacazy had made similar efforts over a century earlier.[54]

Notes

1 "There is a great sympathy between the people of the two countries which is a delusion": Russian-American Relations before 1869

1 Title quote from Telegram from Curtin to Moran, September 9, 1871, Despatches from US Ministers to Russia, 1808–1906, Roll 23.

2 This chapter has been reprinted, with some alterations, with the permission of Louisiana State University Press, from my book *Alexis in America: A Russian Grand Duke's Tour, 1871–72* (2014).

3 Norman E. Saul, *Distant Friends: The United States and Russia, 1763–1867* (Lawrence: University Press of Kansas, 1991), 3–13. See also David M. Griffiths, "Nikita Panin, Russian Diplomacy and the American Revolution," *Slavic Review*, vol. 28, no. 1 (March 1969): 1–24.

4 Saul, *Distant Friends*, 13–18.

5 Ibid., 22–5. For more on this, see Lincoln Lorenz, *The Admiral and the Empress: John Paul Jones and Catherine the Great* (New York: Bookman Associate, 1954).

6 Saul, *Distant Friends*, 25–8.

7 Ibid., 48–51.

8 Ibid., 74–8.

9 Ibid., 80–1.

10 Ibid., 111–12.

11 Ibid.

12 Ibid. See also Walther Kirchner, *Studies in Russian-American Commerce, 1820–1860* (Leiden: E. J. Brill, 1975).

13 Saul, *Distant Friends*, 132–4.

14 Ibid., 184; Albert L. Weeks, *Russia's Life-Saver; Lend-Lease Aid to the U.S.S.R. in World War II* (Lanham, MD: Lexington Books, 2004), 68–9; Alexandre Tarsaidze, "American Pioneers in Russian Railroad Building," *Russian Review*, vol. 9, no. 4 (October 1950): 286–95.

15 Saul, *Distant Friends*, 198–200; 209–10, 217–18; Frank Golder, "Russian American Relations during the Crimean War," *American Historical Review*, vol. 31, no. 3 (April 1926): 462–76; Richard W. Van Alstyne, "John F. Crampton, Conspirator or Dupe?" *American Historical Review*, vol. 41, no. 3 (April 1936): 492–502.

16 Saul, *Distant Friends*, 198.

17 Ibid., 218–22.

18 Ibid., 210–15, 222–3; Eufrosina Dvoichenko-Markov, "Americans in the Crimean War," *Russian Review*, vol. 13, no. 2 (April 1954): 137–45; Albert Parry, "American Doctors in the Crimean War," *South Atlantic Quarterly*, vol. 54, no. 4 (October 1955): 478–90.

19 Saul, *Distant Friends*, 235.

20 Ibid., 251–7.

21 Ibid., 237, 243, 251–7, 264.

22 Ibid., 316–17, 321; Frank Golder, "The American Civil War through the Eyes of a Russian Diplomat," *American Historical Review*, vol. 26, no. 3 (April 1921): 454–63.

23 Saul, *Distant Friends*, 333.

24 Ibid., 336–9; Harold Blinn, "Seward and the Polish Rebellion of 1863," *American Historical Review*, vol. 45, no. 4 (July 1940): 828–33.

25 Saul, *Distant Friends*, 340–52; William E. Nagengast, "The Visit of the Russian Fleet to the United States: Were Americans Deceived?" *Russian Review*, vol. 8, no. 1 (January 1949): 46–55; Frank A. Golder, "The Russian Fleet and the Civil War," *American Historical Review*, vol. 20, no. 2 (1915): 801–12; Thomas A. Bailey, "The Russian Fleet Myth Re-Examined," *Mississippi Valley Historical Review*, vol. 38, no. 1 (June 1951): 81–90; C. Douglas Kroll, *"Friends in Peace and War": The Russian Navy's Landmark Visit to Civil War San Francisco* (Washington, DC: Potomac Books, 2007).

26 Norman E. Saul, *Concord and Conflict; The United States and Russia, 1867–1914*. Lawrence: University Press of Kansas, 1996. *Distant Friends*, 360–70. For more on Kennan, see, George Kennan, *Tent Life in Siberia* (Honolulu: University Press of the Pacific, 2001); Frederick F. Travis, *George Kennan and the American-Russian Relationship, 1865–1924* (Athens: Ohio University Press, 1990).

27 Saul, *Distant Friends*, 370–7. For more on Karakozov, see Claudia Verhoeven, *The Odd Man Karakozov: Imperial Russia, Modernity, and the Birth of Terrorism* (Ithaca, NY: Cornell University Press, 2011).

28 Mark Twain, *The Innocents Abroad*. Edited by Shelley Fisher Fishkin. Introduction by Mordecai Richler. Afterword by David E. E. Sloan (New York: Oxford University Press, 1996), 390–8.

29 Saul, *Concord and Conflict*, 18, 103; Charles L. Lewis, *David Glasgow Farragut: Admiral in the Making* (Annapolis: United States Naval Institute, 1980), 339–42.

30 Saul, *Distant Friends*, 388–96; Saul, *Concord and Conflict*, 2–13. See also Ronald Jensen, *The Alaska Purchase and Russian-American Relations* (Seattle: University of Washington Press, 1975); Paul Holbo, *Tarnished Expansion: The Alaska Scandal, the Press and Congress* (Knoxville: University of Tennessee Press, 1983), N. N. Bolkhovitinov, *Russian-American Relations and the Sale of Alaska, 1834–1867* (Kingston, ON: Limestone Press; distributed by the University of Alaska Press, 1996), Thomas Bailey, "Why the United States Purchased Alaska," *Pacific Historical*

Review, vol. 3 (1934): 39–49; Frank Golder, "The Purchase of Alaska," *American Historical Review*, vol. 25 (1920): 411–25; William Dunning, "Paying for Alaska," *Political Science Quarterly*, vol. 38 (1912): 385–98; and David H. Miller, "Russian Opinion on the Cession of Alaska," *American Historical Review*, vol. 48 (April 1943): 526–31.

31 *Claim of Captain Benjamin W. Perkins against the Government of Russia, in the Matter of Two Contracts Entered into in the Years 1855 and 1856* [Washington, 1860].

32 Ibid.

33 Ibid.

34 Ibid.

35 Ibid.

36 Ibid.

37 *Brooklyn Eagle*, June 18, 1856.

38 Summons for a money demand on contract, to Lilienfeldt, Supreme Court, City and County of New York, June 7, 1856; Court order for cost bond, New York, June 18, 1856; Offer of Judgement between Perkins and Lilienfeldt, New York, March 21, 1857; Acceptance of Judgment between Perkins and Lilienfeldt, New York, March 21, 1857; Judge's order to enter judgment in Supreme Court of New York, March 21, 1857; Records of Boundary and Claims Commissions and Arbitrations, 1716–1979, Record Group 76, Box 1, National Archives, Washington, DC; *Claim of Captain Benjamin W. Perkins*.

39 *Claim of Captain Benjamin W. Perkins*; Letter from Counsel of Perkins, H. L. Stevens and J. B. Stewart, July 1858, Records of Boundary and Claims Commissions and Arbitrations, 1716–1979, Record Group 76, Box 1, National Archives, Washington, DC.

40 *Senate Journal*, 35th Cong., 1st sess., June 15, 1858, 724–5; *Congressional Globe*, Special Session of the Senate, 35th Cong., 1st sess., June 15, 1858, 3051–2.

41 *Baltimore Sun*, May 25, 1859; also *Weekly Wisconsin Patriot*, May 28, 1859; *New York Herald*, June 16, 1858; *Daily Evening Bulletin* (San Francisco, CA), June 18, 1859; *Weekly San Joaquin Republican* (Stockton, CA), July 17, 1858; *Pittsfield Sun* (MA), February 3, 1859.

42 In the Matter of Benjamin W. Perkins against the Russian Government. Report of William Evarts to William Seward, March 1, 1861, Records of Boundary and Claims Commissions and Arbitrations, 1716–1979, Record Group 76, Box 1, National Archives, Washington, DC.

43 John Bassett Moore and Francis Wharton, *A Digest of International Law: As Embodied in Diplomatic Discussions, Treaties and Other International Agreements, International Awards, the Decisions of Municipal Courts, and the Writings of Jurists* … (U.S. Government Printing Office, 1906), VII: 652, 705, 2–3, 37, 615–16, 708–9.

44 *The Russian Contracts* (Washington, DC, 1861), Obtained from the Western Reserve Historical Society, Cleveland, OH; *The Perkins claim against the Russian government. Letter of Mr. Seward to Mr. Clay* (McGill & Witherow Printers and Stereotypers, 1861), Records of Boundary and Claims Commissions and Arbitrations, 1716–1979, Record Group 76, Box 1, National Archives, Washington, DC.

45 Memo in the Bureau of Claims by E. Peshine Smith, October 24, 1867, Records of Boundary and Claims Commissions and Arbitrations, 1716–1979, Record Group 76, Box 2, National Archives, Washington, DC.

46 *Petition of Anna B. Perkins, of Worcester, Mass, Administratrix of the Late B. W. Perkins: Praying That Out of the Sums of Money to Be Paid to the Imperial Government of Russia, under the Terms of the Recent Treaty between the Government and the United States* ... (Washington: Intelligencer Printing House, 1867).

47 Memo in the Bureau of Claims by E. Peshine Smith.

48 Miller, "Russian Opinion on the Cession of Alaska," 167.

49 Bolkhovitnov, *Russian-American Relations*, 294.

50 *Washington Daily Morning Chronicle*, February 4, 1868.

51 *Journal of the House of Representatives*, 40th Cong., 3rd sess., January 13, 1869, 148.

52 Letter from Catacazy to Fish, New York, August 12/24, 1870, Notes from the Russian Legation in the US to the Department of State, 1809–1906, National Archives and Records Administration, Washington, DC (NARA), Record Group 59, roll 5; *In the Matter of the Claim of Captain B. W. Perkins, against the Russian Government, for Alleged Breach of Contract. Statement of Mr. C. Catacazy, Minister, &c., of His Majesty, the Emperor of Russia*, 18–24, and *Russian Testimony Presented and Filed by His Excellency C. Catacazy, Minister, & c. Of His Majesty the Emperor of Russia with His "Statement" in Opposition to the Claims of Mrs. Anna B. Perkins, Administratrix, & c.*, Records of Boundary and Claims Commissions and Arbitrations, 1716–1979, Record Group 76, Box 2, National Archives, Washington, DC.

53 *Fish, Diaries*, reel 1 (vol. 2), October 14, 1870.

54 In the matters of the claim of Mrs. Anna B. Perkins, administratrix, etc., etc., against the government of Russia. Documents relatifs a la reclamation de la dame Anna B. Perkins, adminitratrice etc. etc, contre le gouvernement de Russie, 1871.

55 Ibid.

56 Ibid.

57 Hamilton Fish to Andrew Curtain, June 26, 1871. Diplomatic Instructions, Roll 137.

58 Letter from Prince Gorchakov to Andrew Curtin, St. Petersburg, December 4, 1871, in Andrew Curtin to Hamilton Fish, December 18, 1871, Despatches from the US Ministers to Russia, 1808–1906, Roll 23.

59 Ibid.

60 *Fish, Diaries*, reel 1 (vol. 3), January 17, 1872; Draft of note to Russian Legation, c. 1881, Records of Boundary and Claims Commissions and Arbitrations, 1716–1979, Record Group 76, Box 2, National Archives, Washington, DC.

61 Draft of note to Russian Legation, c. 1881.

2 "Two-Penny Machiavelli": The Early Life and Career of Constantin Catacazy

1 William Miller, "Modern Greek Historians of Modern Greece," *History*, vol. 10, no. 38 (July 1925): 115; Barbara Jelavich, *Russia and the Greek Revolution of 1843* (Munich: Verlag R. Oldenbourg, 1966), 18, 26–7, 30.

2 John Anthony Petropulos, *Politics and Statecraft in the Kingdom of Greece, 1833–1843* (Princeton, NJ: Princeton University Press, 1968), 296, 449–50.

3 Adam Badeau says Brazil: Adam Badeau, *Grant in Peace: From Appomattox to Mount McGregor, A Personal Memoir* (Hartford: S. S. Scranton, 1887), 375. So does Ronald Jensen, *The Alaska Purchase and Russian-American Relations* (Seattle: University of Washington Press, 1975), 137.

4 Divorced: *New York Sun*, August 15, 1871; Ran off: Badeau, 374–5.

5 Badeau claims she did not go with him at this time, but other primary sources disagree. See also *Cleveland Daily Plain Dealer*, October 31, 1871.

6 *Register of the Department of State,* In Four Parts (Washington: Government Printing Office, 1874), 121; *Russkii Biograficheskii slovar'* (Idak'-Kliucharev') (Saint Petersburg, 1897; reprint, Moscow: Aspect Press, 1994), 545–6.

7 *The Papers of Hamilton Fish, Diaries,* 1869–76, Reel 1 (vol. 1), September 16, 1869; September 19, 1869; September 24, 1869, microfilmed from manuscript collection in the Library of Congress, Manuscript Division, MSS 17, 634 (Washington, DC: Library of Congress, Photoduplication Service, 1979).

8 The accusation from the title of this chapter is but one example. *Leavenworth Daily Commercial*, November 28, 1871.

9 Badeau, *Grant in Peace*, 374–5.

10 Amos S. Hershey, *The Essentials of International Public Law* (New York: Macmillan, 1919), 277.

11 M. S. Anderson, *The Rise of Modern Diplomacy, 1450–1919* (London: Longman, 1993), 103–48.

12 Francis Wharton, *A Digest of the International Law of the United States, Taken from Documents Issued by Presidents and Secretaries of State, and from Decisions of Federal Courts and Opinions of Attorneys-General* (Washington, DC: Government Printing Office, 1887), 628–9.

13 There are various examples of correspondence regarding congregations in New York and New Orleans; Arkhiv Vneshnei Politiki Rossiiskoi Imperii (Archive of Foreign Policy of the Russian Empire), Moscow, Russia (henceforth AVPRI), f. 170, op. 512/3, d. 106, ll. 285–6, and others.

14 *New York World*, November 10, 1871.

15 Rutger B. Miller to Catacazy, January 7, 1872, AVPRI, f. 170, op. 512/3, d. 107, ll. 8–10, 23.

16 Frederick Smith to Catacazy, March 22, 1871, AVPRI, f. 170, op. 512/3, d. 106, ll. 134–5 ob.; George Merrill to Catacazy, December 11, 1871, AVPRI, f. 170, op. 512/3, d. 106, ll. 121–2; Hermann Lentz to Catacazy, February–, 1871, AVPRI, f. 170, op. 512/3, d. 106, ll. 238–9; J. P. Quimby to Catacazy, January 29, 1871, AVPRI, f. 170, op. 512/3, d. 106, ll. 252–2 ob.; L. H. Pingnee to Catacazy, January 27, 1871, AVPRI, f. 170, op. 512/3, d. 106, ll. 257–8.

17 John M. Kinney to Catacazy, January 7, 1871, AVPRI, f. 170, op. 512/3, d. 106, ll. 277–8.

18 *Hamilton Fish Diaries*, January 6, 1870, Reel 1 (vol. 1); Moore, VII: 706.

19 *Hamilton Fish Diaries*, November 4, 1869, Reel 1 (vol. 1); *Washington Daily Morning Chronicle*, April 27, 1870.

20 Catacazy to Fish, May 27/June 8, 1871, Library of Congress, Washington, DC (henceforth LOC), Notes from the Russian Legation in the United States to the Department of State, 1806–1905, Roll 5; *Washington Daily Morning Chronicle*, October 21, 1869.

21 Hershey, *The Essentials of International Public Law*, 289–90.

22 William Hunter, Acting Secretary of State, to Catacazy, July 1, 1871, Notes to Foreign Legations, Roll 83, and from J. C. B. Davis, Acting Secretary of State, to Catacazy, July 26, 1871, National Archives and Records Administration, College Park, MD (henceforth NARA), Record Group (RG) 59, Notes to Foreign Legations, Roll 83.

23 Wharton, *A Digest of the International Law of the United States*, 638–66; Hershey, *The Essentials of International Public Law*, 286–95.

24 Wharton, *A Digest of the International Law of the United States*, 586, 628–9, 696.

3 "The Intermeddling of the Russian Minister"

1 *Hamilton Fish Diaries*, Reel 1 (vol. 1), July 12, 1869.

2 Elihu B. Washburne to Grant, August 25, 1869, Hamilton Fish Papers, LOC, Container 64, Doc. 8668–9.

3 *Washington Daily Morning Chronicle*, September 7, 1869; *Hamilton Fish Diaries*, Reel 1 (vol. 1), September 19, 1869 and September 24, 1869.

4 Curtin to Fish, October 6, 1869, Hamilton Fish Papers, LOC, Container 65, Doc. 8946.

5 *Washington Daily Morning Chronicle*, November 24, 1869.

6 *Washington Daily Morning Chronicle*, February 3, 1870 and February 4, 1870.

7 *New York Herald*, January 2, 1870.

8 Curtin to Fish, January 8/20, 1870, Hamilton Fish Papers, LOC, Container 67, Doc. 9436–7.

9 *Hamilton Fish Diaries*, January 6, 1870 and January 27, 1870, Reel 1 (vol. 1).

10 *National Republican*, February 26, 1870.

11 Stewart to Dent, March 2, 1870, Hamilton Fish Papers, LOC, Container 68, Doc. 9635–7.

12 Stewart to Fish, March 8, 1870, Hamilton Fish Papers, LOC, Container 68, Doc. 9670.

13 *Hamilton Fish Diaries*, Reel 1 (vol. 1), March 3, 1870.

14 Stewart to Dent, March 2, 1870, Hamilton Fish Papers, LOC, Container 68, Doc. 9635–7, 11313–14, 11315–16.

15 *Washington Daily Morning Chronicle*, March 11, 1870.

16 Catacazy to Gorchakov, March 21/April 2, 1870, AVPRI, f. 340, op. 813, d. 45, ll. 3–11 ob.

17 Fish to Catacazy, March 19, 1871, Notes to Foreign Legations, Roll 83.

18 *Hamilton Fish Diaries*, Reel 1 (vol. 1), March 14, 1870; Letter of Fish to Catacazy, March 13, 1870, Hamilton Fish Papers, LOC, Container 68, Doc. 9698.

19 Catacazy to Fish, March 13, 1870, Hamilton Fish Papers, LOC, Container 68, Doc. 9694–7.

20 Catacazy to Gorchakov, March 21/April 2, 1870, AVPRI, f. 340, op. 813, d. 45, ll. 3–11 ob.

21 Catacazy to Fish, April 26, 1870, Hamilton Fish Papers, LOC, Container 69, Doc. 9891–2.

22 Memorandum, April 9, 1870, Hamilton Fish Papers, LOC, Container 68, Doc. 9832–3.

23 Ibid.

24 Memorandum signed by Frank Turk, n.d., Hamilton Fish Papers, LOC, Container 69, Doc. 9893–4.

25 Curtin to Fish, May 11, 1870, Hamilton Fish Papers, LOC, Container 69, Doc. 9969–74.

26 Barbara Jelavich, *The Ottoman Empire, the Great Powers, and the Straits Questions, 1870-1887* (Bloomington: Indiana University Press, 1973), 3–85; Nihan Ünlü, *The Legal Regime of the Straits* (The Hague: Martins Nijhoff, 2002), 10–30.

27 Quoted from the Treaty.

28 W. E. Moss, "The End of the Crimean System: England, Russia and the Neutrality of the Black Sea, 1870–71," *Historical Journal*, vol. 4, no. 2 (1961): 164.

29 Chester W. Clark, "Gorchakov and the Black Sea Question, 1866: A Russian Bomb That Did Not Explode," *American Historical Review*, vol. 48, no. 1 (October 1942): 52–60.

30 *Golos*, November 5/17, 1870.

31 Charles Tuckerman to Hamilton Fish, December 2, 1870, Despatches from US Ministers to Greece, 1868–1906, NARA, T 159, Roll 2.

32 Wayne MacVeagh to Fish, October 18, 1870, Despatches from US Ministers to Turkey, 1818–1906, NARA, RG 59, M 46, Roll 23.

33 Michael Cramer to Hamilton Fish, December 1, 1870, Despatches from US Ministers to Denmark, 1811–1906, NARA, RG 59, M 41, Roll 13.

34 Ibid. American newspapers feared war, as well: *New York World*, November 24, 1870.

35 Moss, "The End of the Crimean System," 171–2.

36 For example, *New York Sun*, November 17, 1870, November 18, 1870, November 19, 1870, November 21, 1870, November 25, 1870, November 29, 1870.

37 Moss, "The End of the Crimean System," 172–4.

38 *Hamilton Fish Diaries*, Reel 1 (vol. 2) November 13, 1870.

39 *Hamilton Fish Diaries*, Reel 1 (vol. 2), November 17, 1870.

40 Draft note written by Catacazy for Gortchakov, November 1870, AVPRI, f. 340, op. 813, d. 26, l. 66.

41 Quoted in Jean Haythorne Braden, "The Eagle and the Crescent: American Interests in the Ottoman Empire, 1861–1870" (PhD Dissertation, Ohio State University, 1973), 366.

42 William W. Murphy to William Seward, May 23, 1867, Despatches from U.S. Consuls in Frankfort on the Main, Germany, 1829–1906, NARA, M161 (Roll 17). A full discussion of international reaction to the Alaska purchase can be found in Lee A. Farrow, *Seward's Folly: A New Look at the Alaska Purchase* (Fairbanks: University of Alaska Press, 2016).

43 *National Republican*, November 22, 1870.

44 Curtin to Fish, December 19, 1870, Despatches from the US Ministers to Russia, 1808–1906, NARA.

45 Ibid.

46 Curtin to Fish, December 18, 1870, Hamilton Fish Papers, LOC, Container 74, Doc. 11203.

47 *New York World*, December 3, 1870.

48 *New York Evening Post*, November 26, 1870, December 1, 1870. The paper stated that Catacazy was hoping to persuade Sumner to advocate for intervention, presumably because then the United States could weigh in on the Black Sea question as well.

49 *New York World*, November 17, 1870.

50 Curtin to Fish, December 19, 1870, Despatches from the US Ministers to Russia, 1808†Note1906, NARA.

51 Department of State Memo on Black Sea, December 21, 1870, Hamilton Fish Papers, LOC, Container 74, Doc. 11213–26.

52 *Golos*, November 17/25, 1870.

53 Eugene Schuyler to Eva Schuyler, November 14, 1870, Papers of Eugene Schuyler, LOC, Box II:1, Folder 7.

54 Eugene Schuyler to Eva Schuyler, December 8, 1870, Papers of Eugene Schuyler, LOC, Box II:1, Folder 7.

55 Curtin to Fish, December 9, 1870, Papers of Hamilton Fish, LOC, Box 68? 69? 74?, Doc. 11128–29.

56 John Lothrop Motley to Fish, November 15, 1870, Despatches from US Ministers to Great Britain, NARA, RG 59, M 30, Roll 102.

57 Cramer to Fish, November 19, 1870, Despatches from US Ministers to Denmark, NARA, RG 59, M 41, Roll 13.

58 Cramer to Fish, January 5, 1871, Despatches from US Ministers to Denmark, NARA, RG 59, M 41, Roll 13.

59 *The London Times*, January 9, 1872.

60 William Marvel, *The Alabama and the Kearsarge* (Chapel Hill: University of North Carolina Press, 1996); Adrian Cook, *The Alabama Claims: American Politics and Anglo-American Relations, 1865–1872* (Ithaca, NY: Cornell University Press, 1975).

61 Cook, *The Alabama Claims*, 80–2, 124–7.

62 Ibid., 136–8.

63 *Hamilton Fish Diaries*, Reel 1 (vol. 2), November 19, 1870.

64 *New York World*, November 29, 1870.

65 *Hamilton Fish Diaries*, Reel 1 (vol. 2), November 30, 1870.

66 Buchanan to Granville, December 14, 1870, Foreign Office and Foreign and Commonwealth Office: Embassy and Consulates, Union of Soviet Socialist Republics (formerly Russian Empire). Political from Sir Andrew Buchanan, FO 181/480, British National Archives, London (henceforth BNA).

67 Buchanan to Granville, December 21, 1870, Foreign Office and Foreign and Commonwealth Office: Embassy and Consulates, Union of Soviet Socialist Republics (formerly Russian Empire). Political from Sir Andrew Buchanan, FO 181/480, BNA.

68 *Hamilton Fish Diaries*, Reel 1 (vol. 2), February 20, 1871.

69 Buchanan to Granville, February 4, 1871, Foreign Office and Foreign and Commonwealth Office: Embassy and Consulates, Union of Soviet Socialist Republics (formerly Russian Empire): General Correspondence. Political from Sir Andrew Buchanan, FO 181/487, BNA.

70 Buchanan to Granville, March 21, 1871, Foreign Office and Foreign and Commonwealth Office: Embassy and Consulates, Union of Soviet Socialist Republics (formerly Russian Empire): General Correspondence. Political from Sir Andrew Buchanan, FO 181/487, BNA.

71 Buchanan to Granville, April 4, 1871, Foreign Office and Foreign and Commonwealth Office: Embassy and Consulates, Union of Soviet Socialist

Republics (formerly Russian Empire): General Correspondence. Political from
Sir Andrew Buchanan, FO 181/487, BNA.

72 Buchanan to Granville, May 17, 1871, Foreign Office and Foreign and
Commonwealth Office: Embassy and Consulates, Union of Soviet Socialist
Republics (formerly Russian Empire): General Correspondence. Political from
Sir Andrew Buchanan, FO 181/488, BNA.

73 *Hamilton Fish Diaries*, Reel 1 (vol. 3), May 25, 1871.

74 Translation of letter from Catacazy (New York) to Fish, May 31/June 12, 1871—
Hamilton Fish Papers, LOC, Container 80, Doc. 12403–6.

75 *Harper's Weekly*, November 11, 1871; *Cleveland Daily Leader*, January 20, 1872; *New
Orleans Times*, January 20, 1872.

76 *Detroit Free Press*, December 13, 1871.

77 Andrew Lang, *Life, Letters, and Diaries of Sir Stafford Northcote, First Earl of
Iddesleigh*, vol. II (Edinburgh: William Blackwood, 1890), 23–4.

78 Edmond Fitzmaurice, *The Life of Granville George Leveson Gower, Second Earl
Granville, K. G., 1815–1891* (London: Longmans, Green, 1905), II: 88.

79 *Hamilton Fish Diaries*, Reel 1 (vol. 3), November 17, 1871.

80 Translation of *Russian World*, December 1/13, 1871, contained in letter from Curtin
to Fish, December 14, 1871; with article and translation from *Russian World*,
Despatches from the US Ministers to Russia, 1808–1906, Roll 23.

81 *London Times*, December 6, 1871, quoted in *Buffalo Commercial Advertiser*,
December 22, 1871.

82 Cook, *The Alabama Claims*, 207–29.

83 Translation of an editorial article in the *Moscow Gazette* of January 21/February
2 contained in Despatch of Eugene Schuyler to Hamilton Fish, February 5, 1872,
Despatches from the US Ministers to Russia, 1808–1906, Roll 23. The newspaper
Golos, monitored the British press as well; January 21/February 2, 1872.

84 Article "Russian Diplomacy in America," quoted in journal, *The Living Age*, vol. 112,
no. 1443 (February 3, 1872), 319–20.

85 Cook, *The Alabama Claims*, 232–44.

4 "Falsehood, Intrigue and Hostility": Catacazy's Breaches of Protocol

1 Philip H. Melanson with Peter F. Stevens, *The Secret Service: The Hidden History
of an Enigmatic Agency* (New York: Carroll and Graf, 2002), 3–19; *Hamilton Fish
Diaries*, Reel 1 (vol. 2), November 30, 1870.

2 *Hamilton Fish Diaries*, Reel 1 (vol. 2), December 1, 1870.

3 Catacazy to Fish, December 1, 1870, Hamilton Fish Papers, LOC, Container 74,
Doc. 11096–9.

4 Catacazy to Fish, December 3, 1870, Hamilton Fish Papers, LOC, Container 74, Doc. 11102.

5 *Hamilton Fish Diaries*, Reel 1 (vol. 2), December 22, 1870. Two weeks later, Catacazy had contacted Fish again with new information and allegations. Catacazy claimed to have tracked down the journalist who had questioned him, and this man alleged that the trail of leaked information could be traced directly back to the State Department. These men, the Russian minister added, were planning new "machinations" against him, insinuating that he (Catacazy) had influenced Charles Sumner in his views of the proposed annexation of St. Domingo. Catacazy concluded, "It is scarcely necessary to say how utterly false and absurd is such as assertion." Catacazy to Fish, December 24, 1870/January 5, 1871, AVPRI, f. 340, op. 813, d. 26, ll. 69–70 ob.

6 *New York Herald*, December 24, 1870.

7 Wharton, *A Digest of the International Law of the United States*, 586.

8 H. C. Whitley to Fish, February 1, 1871, Hamilton Fish Papers, LOC, Container 76, Doc. 11583–606.

9 Ibid.

10 Ibid.

11 Ibid.

12 *Hamilton Fish Diaries*, April 1, 1871, Hamilton Fish Papers, LOC, Reel 4.

13 *Hamilton Fish Diaries*, Reel 1 (vol. 2), February 20, 1871.

14 *Hamilton Fish Diaries*, Reel 1 (vol. 2), February 26, 1871 and March 2, 1871.

15 Catacazy to Fish, March 12, 1871, Hamilton Fish Papers, LOC, Container 77, Doc. 11809–10.

16 Fish to Catacazy, March 14, 1871, AVPRI, f. 340, op. 813, d. 19, ll. 72–4.

17 Fish to Catacazy, March 19, 1871, NARA, Notes to Foreign Legations, Roll 83.

18 *Hamilton Fish Diaries*, Reel 1 (vol. 3), April 29, 1871.

19 Fish to Catacazy, March 24, 1871, NARA, Notes to Foreign Legations in the United States, Roll 83.

20 *Hamilton Fish Diaries*, May 2, 1871.

21 William E. Huntzicker, *The Popular Press, 1833–1865* (Westport, CN: Greenwood Press, 1999), 1–36; Ted Curtis Smythe, *The Gilded Age Press, 1865–1900* (Westport, CT: Praeger, 2003), 1–24; and Gerald J. Baldasty, *The Commercialization of News in the Nineteenth Century* (Madison: University of Wisconsin Press, 1992), 36–7.

22 Huntzicker, *The Popular Press, 1833–1865*, 15; Smythe, *The Gilded Age Press, 1865–1900*, 1–2, 17–24; Baldasty, *The Commercialization of News in the Nineteenth Century*, 117–25; David Paul Nord, *Communities of Journalism: A History of American Newspapers and Their Readers* (Urbana: University of Illinois Press, 2001), 109–28; Mark Wahlgren Summers, *The Press Gang: Newspapers and Politics, 1865–1878* (Chapel Hill: University of North Carolina Press, 1994), 5–27; and Richard L. Kaplan, *Politics and the American Press: The Rise of Objectivity, 1865–1920* (Cambridge: Cambridge University Press, 2002), 184–5.

23 *Hamilton Fish Diaries*, Reel 1 (vol. 3), May 25, 1871.

24 Ibid.

25 Catacazy to Fish, May 31, 1871/June 11, 1871, NARA, Notes from the Russian Legation in the US to the Department of State, M 39, Roll 5.

26 Catacazy to Fish, May 31/June 12, 1871, Hamilton Fish Papers, LOC, Container 80, Doc. 12403–6.

27 *Hamilton Fish Diaries*, Reel 1 (vol. 3), May 31, 1871.

28 Turk to Fish, June 2, 1871, Hamilton Fish Papers, LOC, Container 80, Doc. 12365.

29 *Bancroft Davis Diary*, June 6, 1871, Papers of J. C. Bancroft Davis, LOC, Container 65.

30 Turk to Fish, June 12, 1871, Hamilton Fish Papers, LOC, Container 80, Doc. 12409–10.

31 *Hamilton Fish Diaries*, June 1, 1871, Hamilton Fish Papers, Reel 4.

32 Curtin to Fish, June 2, 1871, Hamilton Fish Papers, LOC, Container 80, Doc. 12418–19.

33 *Hamilton Fish Diaries*, June 16, 1871, Reel 1 (vol. 3).

34 *New York Post*, June 10, 1871.

35 *Philadelphia Inquirer*, May 29, 1871.

36 *New York World*, June 19, 1871, July 26, 1871.

5 "She Had a Story and a Past": Olga Catacazy and the Washington Wives

1 Quote from title of this chapter found in online version of book, Ishbel Ross, *The General's Wife: The Life of Mrs. Ulysses S. Grant* (New York: Dodd, Mead, 1959), n.p.

2 https://www.geni.com/people/Olga-de-Fitz-James-Greuther-Grutther-o-Grutter/6000000030252500060 (accessed April 4, 2021).

3 Adam Badeau says Brazil: Badeau, 375. So does Jensen, *The Alaska Purchase and Russian-American Relations*, 137.

4 Divorced: *New York Sun*, August 15, 1871; Ran off: Badeau, 374–5.

5 Arlie Hochschild, "The Role of the Ambassador's Wife: An Exploratory Study," *Journal of Marriage and Family*, vol. 31, no. 1 (February 1969): 73.

6 Molly M. Wood, "Wives, Clerks, and 'Lady Diplomats': The Gendered Politics of Diplomacy and Representation in the U.S. Foreign Service, 1900–1940," *European Journal of American Studies*, vol. 10, no. 1 (2015): 2.

7 Carolyn James and Glenda Sluga, "Introduction: The Long International History of Women and Diplomacy," in *Women, Diplomacy and International Politics since 1500* (Oxford: Routledge, 2016), 7.

8 *New York World*, November 6, 1870.

9 *New York Sun*, August 15, 1871.

10 *Washington Daily Morning Chronicle*, January 21, 1870; *Evening Star* (Washington, DC), January 28, 1870.

11 *Washington Daily Morning Chronicle*, February 4, 1870.

12 *New York Sun*, August 15, 1871.

13 *Washington Daily Morning Chronicle*, February 3, 1870.

14 *Harper's Weekly*, March 12, 1870.

15 *New York Sun*, August 15, 1871.

16 *Cincinnati Daily Enquirer*, January 3, 1872; *Wheeling Daily Intelligencer* (WV), February 1, 1870.

17 *Nashville Union and American*, March 16, 1870.

18 *Memphis Public Ledger*, March 16, 1871.

19 Thomas Keneally, *American Scoundrel: The Life of the Notorious Civil War General Dan Sickles* (New York: Doubleday, 2002), 71.

20 Badeau, *Grant in Peace*, 376.

21 Ibid., 375–6.

22 Undated newspaper clippings, Hamilton Fish Letters and Miscellany, Manuscripts and Archives Division, New York Public Library, New York.

23 Emily Edson Briggs, *The Olivia Letters: Being Some History of Washington City for Forty Years as Told by the Letters of a Newspaper Correspondent* (New York: Neale, 1906), 259.

24 Kathryn Allamong Jacob, *Capital Elites: High Society in Washington, D. C., after the Civil War* (Washington, DC: Smithsonian Institution Press, 1995), 98–9.

25 *Milwaukee Sentinel*, October 30, 1871.

26 Ibid.

27 *Cleveland Daily Plain Dealer*, October 19, 1871.

28 Ibid.

29 *Hamilton Fish Diaries*, Reel 1 (vol. 2), December 22, 1870.

30 *Daily National Republican*, December 3, 1871.

31 *Golos*, February 13/25, 1871.

32 Harriet Blaine, *Letters of Mrs. James G. Blaine*, edited by Harriet S. Blaine Beale, vol. I (New York: Duffield, 1908), 49–50, 81–7, 126.

33 Ibid., 81.

34 Marian Adams, *The Letters of Mrs. Henry Adams*, edited by War Thoron (Boston, MA: Little, Brown, 1936), 344.

35 John F. Marszalek, *The Petticoat Affair: Manners, Mutiny, and Sex in Andrew Jackson's White House* (Baton Rouge: Louisiana State University Press, 2000), 107; Jacob, *Capital Elites*, 2–3, 68–69.

36 Marszalek, *The Petticoat Affair*, 111–12.

37 Madeleine Vinton Dahlgren, *Etiquette of Social Life in Washington* (Washington, DC: [J. A. Wineberger], 1873), 14.

38 Jacob, *Capital Elites*, 2, 10.

39 Ibid., 68–9.

40 Dahlgren, *Etiquette of Social Life in Washington*, 27.

41 Quoted in Jacob, *Capital Elites*, 112.

42 Jacob, *Capital Elites*, 73.

43 *New York World*, January 31, 1871.

44 *New York World*, January 11, 1871.

45 *New York Evening Post*, February 8, 1871; *New York World*, February 12, 1871.

46 *New York World*, March 9, 1871; *Evening Star*, March 29, 1871.

47 *New York World*, April 2, 1871.

48 *New York Herald*, April, 17, 1871.

49 *New York World*, April 23, 1871.

50 *Hamilton Fish Diaries*, Reel 1 (vol. 3), May 25, 1871.

51 Fish to Curtin, May 29, 1871, Papers of Hamilton Fish, LOC, Manuscript Division, Box 189.

52 *New York World*, May 28, 1871.

53 *New York World*, July 22, 1871.

54 *Chicago Tribune*, August 30, 1871; *Daily Dispatch* (Richmond, VA), August 24, 1871; *Memphis Public Ledger*, October 17, 1871; *Louisiana Democrat*, November 8, 1871.

55 *New York Herald*, October 7, 1871, October 8, 1871.

56 *New York Times*, November 17, 1871.

57 *Hamilton Fish Diaries*, Reel 1 (vol. 3), November 17, 1871.

58 Buchanan to Granville, September 20, 1871—Foreign Office and Foreign and Commonwealth Office: Embassy and Consulates, Union of Soviet Socialist Republics (formerly Russian Empire): General Correspondence. Political from Sir Andrew Buchanan (May 17, 1871–October 4, 1871), FO 181/488, BNA.

59 *Chicago Times*, December 9, 1871.

60 *Buffalo Commercial Advertiser*, December 19, 1871.

61 *Chicago Times*, December 12, 1871. The *New York World* had reported this on October 26, 1871, as well.

62 *New York Times*, November 17, 1871.

63 *New York Sun*, August 15, 1871.

64 *Chicago Times*, January 3, 1872.

65 *Kansas City Times*, January 17, 1872.

66 *Detroit Free Press*, December 13, 1871.

67 *Cincinnati Daily Enquirer*, January 16, 1872; *Memphis Daily Appeal*, December 12, 1871.

68 *Kansas City Times*, December 14, 1871.

69 *Milwaukee Sentinel*, November 16, 1871.

70 *Cincinnati Daily Enquirer*, November 25, 1871.

71 *Cleveland Daily Leader*, December 21, 1871, January 24, 1872.

72 *Brooklyn Eagle*, November 1, 1871.

73 *Cleveland Daily Plain Dealer*, November 25, 1871.

74 *Cleveland Daily Plain Dealer*, November 23, 1871.

75 *Montreal Gazette*, November 3, 1871; *Daily News* (London), December 8, 1871.

76 *Freeman's Journal and Daily Commercial Advertiser* (Dublin), January 8, 1872.

77 *Toronto Globe*, November 22, 1871.

78 *New York Times*, November 17, 1871.

79 This story is told in detail in Marszalek, *The Petticoat Affair*.

80 Ibid., 239.

81 Ibid., 56.

82 *Leavenworth Daily Commercial*, November 28, 1871.

83 *Detroit Free Press*, January 6, 1872.

84 *Cincinnati Daily Enquirer*, October 19, 1871.

85 Marszalek, *The Petticoat Affair*, 64.

86 Ibid., 166–88.

87 *Boston Herald*, December 7, 1871.

88 Lori Ginzberg, *Women and the Work of Benevolence: Morality, Politics, and Class in Nineteenth-Century United States* (New Haven, CT: Yale University Press, 1990), 1–5, 11–13, 177.

89 Jon Grinspan, *The Virgin Vote: How Young Americans Made Democracy Social, Politics Personal, and Voting Popular in the Nineteenth Century* (Chapel Hill: University of North Carolina Press, 2016), 8, 43–5, 100.

90 Jacob, *Capital Elites*, 74.

91 Esther B. Aresty, *The Best Behavior: The Course of Good Manners—from Antiquity to the Present—as Seen through Courtesy and Etiquette Books* (New York: Simon and Schuster, 1970), 199, 259.

92 Adams, *The Letters of Mrs. Henry Adams*, xi.

93 Blaine, *Letters of Mrs. James G. Blaine*, 50.

94 Fish to Washburne, *Papers of Ulysses S. Grant*, vol. 22: 148.

95 John W. Foster, *Diplomatic Memoirs*, vol. II (Boston, MA: Houghton Mifflin, 1909), 318–19.

6 "A Thorough Mischief Maker": The Recall of Catacazy

1 Ron Chernow, *Alexander Hamilton* (New York: Penguin, 2005), 431–47.

2 Ibid., 431–47. The *Boston Herald* mentioned the Genêt case in its reporting of the Catacazy Affair, December 7, 1871.

3 Wharton, *A Digest of the International Law of the United States*, 596.

4 Marcus Daniel, *Scandal and Civility: Journalism and the Birth of American Democracy* (Oxford: Oxford University Press, 2010), 226–7.

5 Sandra Sealove, "The Founding Fathers as Seen by the Marqués de Casa-Irujo," *The Americas*, vol. 20, no. 1 (July 1963): 38.

6 Ibid., 40.

7 James Monroe to James Madison, April 16, 1805, footnote in online source, https://founders.archives.gov/documents/Madison/02-09-02-0273#JSMN-02-09-02-0273-fn-0008 (accessed April 1, 2020).

8 Letter from James Madison to Carlos Martínez de Yrujo, January 15, 1806, https://founders.archives.gov/documents/Madison/02-11-02-0060 (accessed April 1, 2020).

9 Rufus Rockwell Wilson, *Washington: The Capital City, and Its Part in the History of the Nation*, vol. 1 (Philadelphia and London: J. B. Lippincott, 1902), 71.

10 Wharton, *A Digest of the International Law of the United States*, 598.

11 Fish to Curtin, June 16, 1871, Hamilton Fish papers, LOC, Container 80, Doc. 12427–8.

12 Fish to Catacazy, June 16, 1871, Notes to Foreign Legations, Roll 83.

13 Catacazy to Westmann, June 22, 1871/July 4, 1871, AVPRI, f. 170, op. 512/3, d. 107, ll. 279–80 ob.

14 Curtin to Fish, July 7/19, 1871, Dispatches from the United States Ministers to Russia, 1808–1906 (Roll 23); Dispatch from Curtin to Fish, July 7/19, 1871, Dispatches from the United States Ministers to Russia, 1808–1906 (Roll 23).

15 Curtin to Fish, July 9/21, 1871, Dispatches from the United States Ministers to Russia, 1808–1906 (Roll 23).

16 *Buffalo Commercial Advertiser*, December 19, 1871.

17 See Thomas Keneally, *American Scoundrel: The Life of the Notorious Civil War General Dan Sickles* (New York: Doubleday, 2002).

18 Cassius Clay, *The Life of Cassius Marcellus Clay. Memoirs, Writings and Speeches* (New York: Negro Universities Press, 1969), 463–77.

19 Saul, *Concord and Conflict*, 16–17.

20 *Cleveland Daily Plain Dealer*, December 21, 1871.

21 Jeremiah Curtin, *Memoirs of Jeremiah Curtin*, edited by Joseph Schafer (Madison: State Historical Society of Wisconsin, 1940), 209.

22 Curtin to Fish, October 5, 1871, Hamilton Fish Papers, LOC, Container 83, Doc. 13014–19.

23 Fish to Davis, August 17, 1871, Bancroft Davis papers, LOC, Container 10, Doc. 2228; Davis to Curtin, August 18, 1871, Hamilton Fish Papers, LOC, Container 82, Doc. 12764–6.

24 Curtin to Fish, August 15/27, 1871, Dispatches from the United States Ministers to Russia, 1808–1906 (Roll 23).

25 Ibid.

26 Ibid.

27 Curtin to Fish, September 1, 1871, Dispatches from the United States Ministers to Russia, 1808–1906 (Roll 23).

28 Curtin to Schenck, August 27, 1871, Enclosure in Dispatch from Moran to Curtin, September 2, 1871, Despatches from US Ministers to Great Britain, 1791–1906, NARA, RG 59, M 30, Roll 107.

29 Fish to Curtin, September 5, 1871, Diplomatic Instructions, Roll 137.

30 *New York Herald*, September 5, 1871; *Chicago Tribune*, September 6, 1871.

31 *Evening Star* (DC), September 8, 1871; *New York Herald*, October 6, 1871; *Golos*, October 17, 1871.

32 Curtin to Fish, September 10, 1871, Despatches from US Ministers to Russia, 1808–1906, Roll 23.

33 Curtin to Fish, September 9, 1871, via Moran in London, Despatches from US Ministers to Russia, 1808–1906, Roll 23.

34 Curtin to Moran, September 9, 1871, Despatches from US Ministers to Russia, 1808–1906, Roll 23; Curtin to Fish, September 10, 1871, Despatches from US Ministers to Russia, 1808–1906, Roll 23.

35 Curtin to Fish, September 10, 1871, Hamilton Fish Papers, LOC, Container 82, Doc. 12864–5.

36 George Pomutz to Hamilton Fish, September 11/23, 1871, Despatches from US Ministers to Russia, 1808–1906, Roll 23.

37 G. F. Pyle, "The Diffusion of Cholera in the United States in the Nineteenth Century," *Geographical Analysis*, vol. 1: 59–75.

38 *New York World*, August 20, 1871.

39 *New York World*, November 14, 1871.

40 Catacazy to Westmann, September 1/13, 1871, AVPRI, f. 170, op. 512/3. d. 107, ll. 386–95 ob.

41 Fish to Grant, September 15, 1871, Hamilton Fish Papers, LOC, Container 82, Doc. 12891–3.

42 Ibid.

43 Fish to Davis, September 18, 1871, Bancroft Davis Papers, LOC, Container 10, Doc. 2344–5.

44 Grant to Fish, September 19, 1871, contained in The Papers of Ulysses S. Grant, p. 147.

45 Westmann to Catacazy, September 6/18, 1871, AVPRI, f. 170, op. 512/3, d. 106, ll. 56–66 ob.

46 *Golos*, August 15, 1871.

47 *Russkii Mir*, September 21, 1871, October 20, 1871; *Golos*, September 29, 1871, October 17, 1871.

48 *Golos*, October 21, 1871.

49 Ibid.

50 Catacazy to Westmann, September 21/October 3, 1871, AVPRI, f. 170, op. 512/3, d. 107, ll. 431–8 ob.

51 Ibid.

52 Catacazy to Westmann, October 22/November 3, 1871, AVPRI, f. 170, op. 512/3, d. 107, ll. 478–9 ob.

53 Catacazy to Stremaoukov, October 1/13, 1871, AVPRI, f. 170, op. 512/3, d. 107, ll. 456–7.

54 Catacazy to Gorchakov, October 19/31, 1871, AVPRI, f. 340, op. 813, d. 45, ll. 185–90 ob.

55 Ibid.

56 Ibid.

57 Ibid.

58 Catacazy to George B. Cowlan, October 3, 1871, AVPRI, f. 170, op. 512/3, d. 107, ll. 460–460 ob.

59 Catacazy to Simon Cameron, October 9, 1871, AVPRI, f. 170, op. 512/3, d. 107, 461–2 ob.

60 Catacazy to T. L. Cottman, October 12, 1871, AVPRI, f. 170, op. 512/3, d. 107, l. 471.

61 *Golos*, October 21, 1871; also, November 11, 1871.

62 *New York World*, October 6, 1871.

63 Anonymous Death Threat, October 7 (1871?), AVPRI, f. 340, op. 813, d. 19, ll. 104.

64 *New York Times*, December 5, 1871, November 19, 1871, December 1, 1871.

65 *Leavenworth Daily Commercial*, January 25, 1872.

66 *Brooklyn Eagle*, January 4, 1872.

67 *Aberdeen Journal*, December 13, 1871.

68 *Daily News* (London), December 8, 1871.

69 *Hamilton Fish Diaries*, October 6, 1871.

70 Catacazy to Fish, October 26, 1871, AVPRI, f. 340, op. 813, d. 26, ll. 57–57a.

71 Curtin to Fish, October 5, 1871, Hamilton Fish Papers, LOC, Container 83, Doc. 13014–19.

72 Wharton, *A Digest of the International Law of the United States*, 585–6, 591–2.

73 *Hamilton Fish Diaries*, October 9, 1871, Reel 1 (vol. 3).

74 Bancroft Davis Diary, October 25, 1871, Papers of J. C. Bancroft Davis, LOC, Container 65.

75 Hamilton Fish Diary, December 1, 1871, Papers of Hamilton Fish, Diaries, Reel 4, Manuscript Division, LOC.

76 *Journal de St. Petersbourg*, November 1, 1871.

77 For example, see *Evening Star* (DC), November 2, 1871; *New Orleans Republican*, November 2, 1871; *New York Herald*, November 2, 1871, November 3, 1871; *Chicago Tribune*, November 3, 1871; *New York Sun*, November 3, 1871; *Washington*

Daily Morning Chronicle, November 3, 1871; *New York Times*, November 3, 1871; *Philadelphia Inquirer*, November 3, 1871; *London Times*, November 4, 1871; *Golos*, November 11, 1871.

78 *New York Times*, November 3, 1871.

79 Fish to Curtin, November 16, 1871, Diplomatic Instructions, Roll 137, LOC, Box 233.

80 Fish to Washburne, contained in Paper of Ulysses S. Grant, vol. 22: 148.

81 Dispatch from Elihu Washburne, October 27, 1871, Despatches from US Ministers to France, 1789–1906, NARA, RG 59, M 34, Roll T 74.

82 Cramer to Fish, November 3, 1871, Despatches from US Ministers to Denmark, NARA, M 41, Roll 13.

83 Cramer to Fish, November 9, 1871, Despatches from US Ministers to Denmark, NARA, RG 59, M 41, Roll 13; Letter from Curtin to Fish, July 7/19, 1871, Despatches from the US Ministers to Russia, 1808–1906, NARA, Roll 23.

84 Cramer to Fish, November 11, 1871, Despatches from US Ministers to Denmark, NARA, RG 59, M 41, Roll 13.

85 George Marsh to Hamilton Fish, October 27, 1871, Despatches from US Ministers to the Italian States, 1832–1906, NARA, RG 59, M 90, Roll 15.

86 Bancroft to Fish, November 4, 1871, Despatches from US Ministers to the German States and Germany, 1799–1906, NARA, RG 59, M 44, Roll 19.

87 Charles T. Gorham to Fish, January 1, 1872, Despatches from U.S. Ministers to the Netherlands, NARA, M. 42, Roll 24.

88 *Hamilton Fish Diaries*, November 24, 1871, Reel 1 (vol. 3).

89 Curtin to Fish, November 10, 1871, Despatches from US Ministers to Russia, Roll 23; Curtin to Fish, December 10, 1871, Hamilton Fish Papers, LOC, Container 84, Doc. 13314–21.

90 George Adams to Fish, October 28, 1871, Diplomatic Instructions, Roll 137.

91 Catacazy to Fish, November 2, 1871, Notes from the Russian Legation in the US to the Department of State, 1809–1906, Roll 5.

92 Moran to Schenck, November 4, 1871, Despatches from US Ministers to Great Britain, 1791–1906, NARA, RG 59, M 30, Roll 107.

93 Catacazy to Cameron, October 9, 1871, AVPRI, f. 170, op. 512/3, d. 107, ll. 461–2 ob.

94 Fish to Catacazy, November 10, 1871, Notes to Foreign Legations, Roll 83.

95 *Hamilton Fish Diaries*, November 15, 1871, Reel 1 (vol. 3).

96 *Hamilton Fish Diaries*, November 23, 1871, Reel 1 (vol. 3).

97 Moran to Fish, September 9, 1871.

98 Curtin to Fish, September 10, 1871, Hamilton Fish papers, LOC, Container 82, Doc. 12864–5; Curtin to Fish, October 5, 1871, Hamilton Fish Papers, LOC, Container 83, Doc. 13014–19; Fish to Curtin, September 20, 1871, Hamilton Fish Papers, LOC, Container 82, Doc. 12905.

99 Catacazy to Westmann, September 12/October 3, 1871, AVPRI, f. 170, op. 512/3, d. 107, ll. 431–8 ob.; Letter from Catacazy to Simon Cameron, October 9, 1871, AVPRI, f. 170, op. 512/3, d. 107, ll. 461–2 ob.

100 Washburne to Fish, October 27, 1871, Despatches from US Ministers to France, 1789–1906, NARA, RG 59, M 34, Roll T 74; Hamilton Fish Diaries, November 14, 1871, November 15, 1871, November 17, 1871, Reel 1 (vol. 3).

101 Report of Eugene Schuyler of a conversation with Mr. de Westmann, November 2, 1871, Despatches from the US Ministers to Russia, 1808–1906, NARA, Roll 23.

102 Ibid.

103 Telegram to Fish from Schuyler, November 4, 1871 (via Moran in London), Despatches from US Ministers to Great Britain, 1791–1906, NARA, RG 59, M 30, Roll 107.

104 Curtin to Fish, November 10, 1871, Despatches from US Ministers to Russia, 1808–1906, Roll 23. Pomutz, indeed, also had heard Westmann say tolerate; Despatch of George Pomutz to Hamilton Fish, September 11/23, 1871, Despatches from US Ministers to Russia, 1808–1906, Roll 23.

105 Curtin to Fish, November 10, 1871, Despatches from US Ministers to Russia, 1808–1906, Roll 23.

106 *New York Herald*, October 8, 1871.

107 *Philadelphia Inquirer*, October 9, 1871.

108 *Brooklyn Eagle*, December 8, 1871.

109 *Brooklyn Eagle*, December 7, 1871.

110 Quoted in the *Cincinnati Daily Enquirer*, December 17, 1871.

111 *Cincinnati Daily Enquirer*, December 6, 1871.

112 *Chicago Times*, December 12, 1871.

113 *New York Times*, November 13, 1871.

114 *New York Times*, November 27, 1871.

115 *New York World*, November 10, 1871.

116 *New York Times*, November 1, 1871.

117 *New York Times*, December 1, 1871.

7 The "Industrious Flea": Catacazy and the Visit of Grand Duke Alexis

1 "Quote in the title of this chapter can be found in *New York Times*, November 17, 1871. A full exploration of the visit of Grand Duke Alexis and its diplomatic and domestic implications can be found in Lee A. Farrow, *Alexis in America: A Russian Grand Duke's Tour, 1871–72* (Baton Rouge: LSU Press, 2014).

2 Catacazy to Robert B. Roosevelt, January 9/21, 1871, AVPRI, f. 170, op. 512/3, d. 107, ll. 43. There are many similar letters in this folder.

3 Report by Catacazy to Court, f. 170, op. 512/2, d. 36, ll. 370–6.

4 Gorchakov to Catacazy, April 5, 1871, AVPRI, f. 170, op. 512/3, d. 106, ll. 414-414 ob.

5 Silvanus Macy to Catacazy, April 26, 1871, AVPRI, f. 170, op. 512/3, d. 106, ll. 359–62; New York Alexis Committee to Catacazy, 170, op. 512/3, d. 106, ll. 358–9.

6 Catacazy to Macy, April 21/May 6, 1871, AVPRI, f. 170, op. 512/3, d. 107, l. 190; Catacazy to Macy, April 16/28, 1871, f. 170, op. 512/3, d. 107, ll. 183, 184–5; Catacazy to J. Bennett, June 29/July 11, 1871, AVPRI, f. 170, op. 512/3, d. 107, l. 285. There are many letters from Catacazy to various people concerning the Grand Duke's visit in this folder.

7 April 6, 1871, *Hamilton Fish, Diaries*, Reel 1 (vol. 2); January 26, 1870, *Hamilton Fish, Diaries*, Reel 1 (vol. 1); William S. McFeely, *Grant: A Biography* (New York: W. W. Norton, 1981), 335.

8 *New York World*, May 22, 1871.

9 *Philadelphia Inquirer*, August 23, 1871.

10 Alvey Augustus Ader, to Davis, July 10, 1871, Bancroft Davis Papers, LOC, Container 9, Doc. 2170–1.

11 Fish to Catacazy, September 22, 1871, Hamilton Fish Papers, LOC, Container 82, Doc. 12939–40.

12 Fish to Davis, September 29, 1871, Bancroft Davis Papers, LOC, Container 10, Doc. 2392–6.

13 Curtin to Fish, October 5, 1871, Hamilton Fish Papers, LOC, Container 83, Doc. 13014–19.

14 (ill.) to (ill.), September 16/28, 1871, AVPRI, f. 170, op. 512/3, d. 107, ll. 428–30; Catacazy to Westmann, September 6/18, AVPRI, f. 170, op. 512/3, d. 107, ll. 411–12 ob.

15 Saul, *Distant Friends*, 337.

16 Edmund G. Olszyk, *The Polish Press in America* (Milwaukee: Marquette University Press, 1940), 7; Ninth U.S. Census, vol. 1, June 1, 1870 (Washington: Government Printing Office, 1872), 390–1.

17 Saul, *Distant Friends*, 338.

18 For more on Lincoln's assassination, see Kathryn Canavan, *Lincoln's Final Hours: Conspiracy, Terror, and the Assassination of America's Greatest President* (Lexington: University Press of Kentucky, 2015). Again, for more on Karakozov, see Verhoeven, *The Odd Man Karakozov*.

19 Catacazy to Fish, September 16/28, 1871, Notes from the Russian Legation in the United States to the Department of State, 1809–1906, NARA, RG 59, M 39, Roll 5; Catacazy to Westmann, September 30/October 12, 1871, AVPRI, f. 170, op. 512/3, d. 107, ll. 454–5 ob.; J. B. Stewart to Fish, November 3, 1871, Hamilton Fish Papers, LOC, Container 83, Doc. 13125–6.

20 Fish to Catacazy, October 3 and October 31, 1871, Notes to Foreign Legations, NARA, RG 59, M99, Roll 83.

21 *New York Tribune*, October 15, 1871.

22 *Chicago Times*, November 24, 1871; *Kansas Daily Commonwealth*, November 25, 1871.

23 *Chicago Times*, January 7, 1872.

24 *Cleveland Daily Leader*, December 9, 1871.

25 *Cincinnati Daily Enquirer*, December 1, 1871.

26 *New York Times*, September 16, 1871, November 12, 1871.

27 *New York Times*, November 4, 1871, November 5, 1871, November 12, 1871.

28 *New York Times*, November 5, 1871.

29 *New York Times*, November 12, 1871.

30 Catacazy to Westmann, October 15/27, 1871, AVPRI, f. 170, op. 512/3, d. 107, ll. 476–77 ob., and Catacazy to McCormick, October 24, 1871, AVPRI, f. 170, op. 512/3, d. 107, l. 472.

31 *New York Times*, November 1, 1871.

32 *New York World*, November 4, 1871.

33 Fish to Catacazy, November 10, 1871, Notes to Foreign Legations, NARA, RG 59, M99, Roll 83.

34 *Hamilton Fish Diaries*, November 15, 1871, Reel 1 (vol. 3).

35 Fish to Curtin, November 16, 1871, LOC, Diplomatic Instructions, Roll 137, Box 233.

36 Fish to Catacazy, November 16, 1871, Notes to Foreign Legations, NARA, RG 59, M99, Roll 83.

37 *Hamilton Fish Diaries*, November 17, 1871, Reel 1 (vol. 3).

38 Fish to Catacazy, November 24, 1871, Notes to Foreign Legations, NARA, RG 59, M99, Roll 83.

39 Fish to Catacazy, November 1871, Hamilton Fish papers, LOC, Container 84, Doc. 13201–3.

40 *Hamilton Fish Diaries*, November 24, 1871, Reel 1 (vol. 3).

41 Fish to Gorlov, December 1, 1871, Notes to Foreign Legations, NARA, RG 59, M99, Roll 83.

42 Curtin to Fish, December 10, 1871, Hamilton Fish papers, LOC, Container 84, Doc. 13314–21.

43 Curtin to Fish, December 8, 1871, Despatches from US Ministers to Russia, 1808–1906, Roll 23.

44 Curtin to Fish, December 22, 1871, Despatches from the US Ministers to Russia, 1808–1906, Roll 23.

45 *New York Herald*, November 17, 1871, November 21, 1871.

46 *Hamilton Fish Diaries*, November 14, 1871, Reel 1 (vol. 3).

47 *Hamilton Fish Diaries*, November 22, 1871, Reel 1 (vol. 3).

48 *New York Times*, November 23, 1871; Thomas Carrier, *Washington, D.C.: A Historical Walking Tour* (Charleston: Arcadia, 2005), 77.

49 Farrow, *Alexis in America*, 64; *New York Times*, November 24, 1871; Betty
   C. Monkman, *The White House: Its Historic Furnishings and First Families*
   (New York and London: Abbeville Press, 2000), 120, 143–4.

50 Farrow, Alexis in *America*, 64; *New York Times*, November 24, 1871; *New York
   Times*, November 24, 1871; Monkman, 30, 38, 101, 132, 150; Julia Dent Grant, *The
   Personal Memoirs of Julia Dent Grant*, edited, with notes and foreword by John
   Y. Simon, with an introduction by Bruce Catton (New York: G.P. Putnam's Sons,
   1975), 187.

51 Farrow, *Alexis in America*, 65.

52 *The Nation* (NY), January 18, 1872.

53 *Washington Daily Morning Chronicle*, January 18, 1872.

54 *Cheyenne Daily Leader*, January 17, 1872.

55 Cited in *Cleveland Daily Leader*, February 14, 1872.

56 Farrow, *Alexis in America*, 66–7.

57 Farrow, *Alexis in America*, 95.

58 Farrow, *Alexis in America*, 104–6.

59 *New York Times*, December 5, 1871.

60 *Cleveland Daily Plain Dealer*, December 8, 1871.

61 Curtin to Fish, December 10, 1871, Hamilton Fish Papers, LOC, Container 84, Doc.
   13314–21.

62 *Russkii Mir*, of December 1/13, 1871, included in Letter from Andrew Curtin to
   Hamilton Fish, December 14, 1871, Despatches from the US Ministers to Russia,
   1808–1906, Roll 23.

63 Catacazy to Fish, November 12/24, 1871, Notes from the Russian Legation in the US
   to the Department of State, 1809–1906, Roll 5.

64 *Hamilton Fish Diaries*, Reel 1 (vol. 3), November 24, 1871.

65 Fish to Gorlov, December 19, 1871, AVPRI, f. 170, op. 512/3, d. 106, ll. 42-42 ob.

66 *New York World*, November 27, 1871.

67 *Buffalo Commercial Advertiser*, December 7, 1871.

68 *Cleveland Daily Leader*, January 1, 1872.

69 John Y. Simon, ed., *The Papers of Ulysses S. Grant* (Carbondale: Southern Illinois
   University Press, 1988), vol. 22: 270–1.

70 Curtin to Fish, December 10, 1871, Hamilton Fish Papers, LOC, Container 84, Doc.
   13314–21.

71 Curtin to Fish, December 13, 1871, Despatches from the US Ministers to Russia,
   1808–1906, Roll 23; Letter from Andrew Curtin, St. Petersburg, to Hamilton Fish,
   Washington DC, December 22, 1871, Despatches from the US Ministers to Russia,
   1808–1906, Roll 23.

72 Wharton, *A Digest of the International Law of the United States*, 589.

73 Curtin to Fish, December 10, 1871, Hamilton Fish Papers, LOC, Container 84, Doc.
   13314–21.

74 Curtin to Fish, December 22, 1871, Despatches from the US Ministers to Russia, 1808–1906, Roll 23.

75 *New York Times*, December 6, 1871; Journal of the Senate, December 6, 1871, United States Congressional Series Set, vol. 1477, page 22.

76 *Washington Daily Morning Chronicle*, December 8, 1871.

77 *Chicago Republican*, December 7, 1871. Other papers quoted the letters as well: *New York Sun*, December 7, 1871.

78 *Cleveland Leader*, December 7, 1871.

79 *Washington Daily Morning Chronicle*, December 12, 1871.

80 *Philadelphia Inquirer*, December 8, 1871 and December 11, 1871.

81 *New Orleans Republican*, December 20, 1871.

82 John H. Clifford to Fish, December 18, 1871, Hamilton Fish Papers, LOC, Container 84, Doc. 13284–7.

83 William H. Crosby to Fish, December 18, 1871, Hamilton Fish Papers, LOC, Container 84, Doc. 13288–9.

84 William W. Campbell to Hamilton Fish, December 20, 1871, Hamilton Fish Papers, LOC, Container 84, Doc. 13304–5.

85 Haight to Fish, December 21, 1871, Hamilton Fish Papers, LOC, Container 84, Doc. 13310–11.

86 Francis Lieber to Fish, December 21, 1871, Hamilton Fish Papers, LOC, Container 84, Doc. 13312.

87 Robert C. Winthrop to Fish, December 31, 1871, Hamilton Fish Papers, LOC, Container 84, Doc. 13369–70.

88 Jacob D. Cox, December 21, 1871, Hamilton Fish Papers, LOC, Container 84, Doc. 13306–9.

89 Eugene Schuyler to Fish, January 17, 1872, Despatches from the US Ministers to Russia, 1808–1906, Roll 23.

90 Translation of article from *Russian World*, December 1/13, 1871, contained in letter from Curtin to Fish, December 14, 1871; with article and translation from *Russian World*, Despatches from the US Ministers to Russia, 1808–1906, Roll 23.

91 Curtin to Fish, December 14, 1871; with article and translation from *Russian World*, Despatches from the US Ministers to Russia, 1808–1906, Roll 23.

92 Curtin to Fish, December 13, 1871, Despatches from the US Ministers to Russia, 1808–1906, Roll 23.

93 *New York Herald*, December 17, 1871.

94 *Hamilton Fish Diaries*, December 18, 1871, Reel 1 (vol. 3).

95 Catacazy to Gorchakov, November 16/28, 1871 and December 22/January 3, 1872, cited in Saul, *Concord and Conflict*, 36. Saul also says that Danzas was suffering from a mental breakdown due to the stress of the diplomatic situation and to being nearly trampled by a crowd welcoming Alexis.

96 Curtin to Fish, December 22, 1871, Despatches from the US Ministers to Russia, 1808–1906, Roll 23.

97 Catacazy to Fish, December 21, 1871/ January 2, 1872, Notes from the Russian Legation in the US to the Department of State, 1809–1906, Roll 5; *Hamilton Fish Diaries*, January 2, 1872, Reel 1 (vol. 3).

98 Fish to Valerien Schirkov, January 6, 1872, Notes to Foreign Legations, Roll 83.

99 Schirkov to Fish, January 11, 1872, Notes from the Russian Legation, Roll 5.

100 *Biographic Register of the Department of State* (Washington, DC: Government Printing Office, 1872), 87.

101 Curtin to Fish, January 6, 1872, Despatches from the US Ministers to Russia, 1808–1906, Roll 23.

102 Translation of *Moscow Gazette* article, December 23, 1871/January 4, 1872, by Eugene Schuyler, attached to letter from Curtin to Fish, January 6, 1872, Despatches from the US Ministers to Russia, 1808–1906, Roll 23.

103 *New York Herald*, January 12, 1872; *New Orleans Daily Picayune*, January 31, 1872.

104 *New York Herald*, January 12, 1872; *Cleveland Daily Plain Dealer*, January 15, 1872; *Chicago Times*, January 14, 1872; *New Orleans Daily Picayune*, January 18, 1872.

105 *New Orleans Daily Picayune*, January 18, 1872; *Harper's Weekly*, February 3, 1872.

106 *New Orleans Daily Picayune*, January 19, 1872.

107 *Chicago Times*, January 3, 1872, January 14, 1872.

108 *Cleveland Daily Leader*, January 6, 1872.

109 *Cleveland Daily Plain Dealer*, January 13, 1872.

110 *Washington Daily Morning Chronicle*, January 18, 1872.

111 *Kansas City Times*, January 16, 1872; *Leavenworth Daily Commercial*, January 21, 1872; *Cleveland Daily Leader*, January 15, 1872.

112 Schuyler to Fish, February 5, 1872, Despatches from the US Ministers to Russia, 1808–1906, Roll 23.

8 "He … Smirked Too Much to Be Dignified": The Departure of Constantin Catacazy

1 *Chicago Times*, December 8, 1871; *Cleveland Daily Plain Dealer*, December 11, 1871; *Cincinnati Daily Enquirer*, December 8, 1871; *New Orleans Times*, December 15, 1871.

2 Fish to Catacazy, April 30, 1870, AVPRI, f. 340, op. 813, ll. 78–9.

3 *Hamilton Fish Diaries*, June 12, 1871, Reel 1 (vol. 3).

4 Fish to George Sharpe, June 17, 1871, Papers of Hamilton Fish, LOC, Manuscript Division, Box 189.

5 Curtin to Fish, October 5, 1871, Hamilton Fish Papers, LOC, Container 83, Doc. 13014–19; Curtin to Fish, November 10, 1871, Despatches from the US Ministers to Russia, 1808–1906, Roll 23.

6 *Hamilton Fish Diaries*, December 18, 1871, Reel 1 (vol. 3).

7 *Hamilton Fish Diaries*, January 5, 1872, Reel 1 (vol. 3).

8 *New Orleans Daily Picayune*, January 23, 1872.

9 Curtin to Fish, January 10, 1872, Hamilton Fish Papers, LOC, Container 84, Doc. 13413–14.

10 *Indianapolis News*, January 20, 1872; *Leavenworth Daily Commercial*, January 18, 1872.

11 *Kansas Daily Commonwealth*, January 21, 1872; *Harper's Weekly*, February 10, 1872; *New York Times*, January 21, 1872.

12 *New York World*, January 21, 1872.

13 *Golos*, January 21/February 2, 1872; *Memphis Daily Appeal*, February 7, 1872.

14 Catacazy to Gorchakov, February 3, 1872, AVPRI, f. 340, op. 813, d. 27, ll. 3-3ob.

15 Catacazy to Gorchakov, February 4/16, 1872, AVPRI, f. 340, op. 813, d. 27, ll. 4-4ob.

16 Schuyler to Fish, February 5, 1872, Hamilton Fish Papers, LOC, Container 85, Doc. 13554-5.

17 Schirkov to Catacazy, January 21/February 2, 1872, AVPRI, f. 340, op. 813, d. 45, pp. 195–6 ob.

18 *Hamilton Fish Diaries*, March 5, 1872, Reel 1 (vol. 3).

19 Catacazy to Alexander II, February 21/March 4, 1872, AVPRI, f. 340, op. 813, d. 27, ll. 9-9ob; Catacazy to Gorchakov, February 21/March 4, 1872, AVPRI, f. 340, op. 813, d. 27, ll. 7-8ob.

20 Catacazy to Alexander II, February 21/March 4, 1872, AVPRI, f. 340, op. 813, d. 27, ll. 9-9ob.

21 Catacazy to Adlerberg, March 10, 1872, AVPRI, f. 340, op. 813, d. 45, ll. 202-202ob.

22 Catacazy to Adlerberg, February 21, 1872, AVPRI, f. 340, op. 813, d. 27, ll. 5-6ob; Catacazy to Adlerberg February 21/March 4, 1872, AVPRI, f. 340, op. 813, d. 45, ll. 197-197ob.

23 Catacazy to Adlerberg, February 21, 1872, AVPRI, f. 340, op. 813, d. 27, ll. 5-6ob; Catacazy to Adlerberg February 21/March 4, 1872, AVPRI, f. 340, op. 813, d. 45, ll. 197-197ob.

24 Schuyler to Fish, March 31, 1872, Hamilton Fish Papers, LOC, Container 86, Doc. 13779.

25 Gorchakov to Catacazy, May 23, 1872, AVPRI, f. 340, op. 813, d. 19, ll. 113-144ob.

26 *Cleveland Daily Leader*, April 20, 1872.

27 *Harper's Weekly*, May 4, 1872.

28 *New York Herald*, April 24, 1872.

29 Catacazy to Adlerberg, April 23/May 5, 1872, AVPRI, f. 340, op. 813, d. 27, ll. 15-15ob.

30 Catacazy to Adlerberg, April 23/May 5, 1872, AVPRI, f. 340, op. 813, d. 27, ll. 10-11ob.

31 Ibid.

32 Quoted in Saul, *Concord and Conflict*, 38.

33 Catacazy to Adlerberg, May 1/13, 1872, AVPRI, f. 340, op. 813, d. 27, ll. 17-17ob.

34 Ibid.

35 *Chicago Tribune*, May 3, 1872.

36 Catacazy to Shuvalov, May 11/23, 1872, AVPRI, f. 340, op. 813, d. 27, 22-22ob.

37 Orlov to Catacazy, May 15/27, 1872, AVPRI, f. 340, op. 813, d. 19, ll. 29-29ob.

38 Catacazy to Westmann, May 19/31, 1872, AVPRI, f. 340, op. 813, d. 45, ll. 206-7.

39 Gorchakov to Catacazy, May 23, 1872, AVPRI, f. 340, op. 813, d. 19, ll. 113–14.

40 Catacazy to Alexander II, June 25/July 7, 1872, AVPRI, f. 340, op. 813, d. 27, ll. 29–30.

41 *Appleton's*, June 1, 1872; *New York Times*, July 10, 1872; *New York Times*, July 16, 1872.

42 Catacazy to Orlov, July 2/14, 1872, AVPRI, f. 340, d. 27, ll. 31-31ob.

43 Catacazy to Orlov, July 23/August 4, 1872, AVPRI, f. 340, d. 27, ll. 33-34ob.

44 Ibid.

45 Catacazy to Adlerberg, August 3/15, 1872, AVPRI, f. 340, d. 27, ll. 36-37ob.

46 Constantin de Catacazy, *Un Incident Diplomatique* (Paris: Amyot, 1872).

47 Ibid., 2.

48 Ibid., 22.

49 Ibid., 2.

50 Ibid., i.

51 Ibid., 2.

52 Ibid., 5–14.

53 Ibid., 4.

54 Ibid., 17–18.

55 Ibid., 15.

56 Ibid., 23.

57 Ibid., 26.

58 Ibid., 28-9.

59 Ibid., 41.

60 Ibid., 32–4.

61 Ibid., 36.

62 Ibid., 37, 39.

63 Ibid., 46.

64 *New York Times*, July 16, 1872, July 22, 1872.

65 *Brooklyn Eagle*, July 16, 1872.

66 *New York Herald*, July 16, 1872.

67 *Golos*, August 5, 1872.

68 *Brooklyn Eagle*, July 26, 1872; *Golos*, August 5, 1872; *Harper's Weekly*, August 10, 1872; *New York Tribune*, May 10, 1890.

69 *New York Times*, July 16, 1872.

70 Catacazy to Orlov, August 3/15, 1872, f. 340,, op. 813, d. 27, ll. 40-40 ob.

71 Catacazy to Orlov, August 7/19, 1872, f. 340,, op. 813, d. 27, ll. 41-41 ob.

72 Ibid.

73 Catacazy to Adlerberg, September 16/28, 1872, f. 340, op. 813, d. 27, ll. 45–48 ob.

74 Catacazy to Shuvalov, April 16/28, 1873, f. 340, op. 813, d. 28, ll. 3-3ob.

75 Catacazy to Shuvalov, May 11/23, 1874, f. 340, op. 813, d. 29, ll. 2–4 ob; Catacazy to Shuvalov, May 18/30, 1874, f. 340, op. 813, d. 29, ll. 5–6; Catacazy to Shuvalov, August 15/27, 1874, f. 340, op. 813, d. 29, ll. 9-9 ob.

76 Catacazy to Grand Duke Alexis, May 22/June 3, 1873, f. 340, op. 813, d. 28, ll. 4–5.

77 Catacazy to Grand Duke Alexis, November 14/26, 1873, f. 340, op. 813, d. 28, ll. 22–23 ob.

78 Quoted in James L. Orr and Joseph O. Baylen (ed.), "A Letter of James L. Orr, Minister to Russia, 1873," *South Carolina Historical Magazine*, vol. 61, no. 4 (October 1960): 225.

79 Catacazy to Loris Melikov, July 2/14, 1880, f. 340, op. 813, d. 35, ll. 36–7.

80 Catacazy to Miliutin, August 24/September 2, 1880, f. 340, op. 813, d. 35, ll. 41–2 ob.

81 Saul, *Concord and Conflict*, 39; *Truth*, vol. 28 (December 11, 1890): 1217; *Le Petit Journal*, May 6, 1890.

82 *New York Tribune*, May 10, 1890.

83 Catacazy to Giers, July 1, 1882, f. 340, op. 813, d. 45, ll. 55-55 ob.

84 Catacazy to Vlangali, June 23, 1882, f. 340, op. 813, d. 45, ll. 48–9.

85 Catacazy to Giers, July 5, 1882, f. 340, op. 813, d. 45, ll. 58-58 ob.

86 Catacazy to Giers, July 18/30, 1883, f. 340, op. 813, d. 45, ll. 59–60 ob; Catacazy Giers, August 27/September 8, 1883, f. 340, op. 813, d. 45, ll. 63–4.

87 Saul, *Concord and Conflict*, 262.

88 Ibid., 263.

89 Quoted in Elie Kedourie, "Afghānī in Paris: A Note," *Middle Eastern Studies*, vol. 8, no. 1 (January 1972): 103–5.

90 Catacazy to Giers, September 30/October 12, 1887, f. 340, op. 813, d. 45, ll. 98–9 ob.

91 George F. Kennan, "The Mystery of the Ferdinand Documents," *Jahrbucher fur Geschichte Osteuropas*, vol. 26, no. 3 (1978): 321–52; Joseph Vincent Fuller, *Bismarck's Diplomacy at Its Zenith* (Cambridge, MA: Harvard University Press, 1922), 294.

92 Elie de Cyon, *Histoire de l'entente Franco-Russe, 1886–1894: Documents et souvenirs* (Paris: A. Charles, 1895), 322–3, quoted in Saul, *Concord and Conflict*, 263 n102.

93 *Le Figaro*, January 16, 1888; *Le Temps*, January 17, 1888; Fuller, *Bismarck's Diplomacy at Its Zenith*, 297.

94 *Le Temps*, January 18, 1888.

95 *Le Petite Presse*, January 18, 1888.

96 Francesco Crispi, *The Memoirs of Francesco Crispi*. Translated by Mary Prichard-Agentti. Edited by Thomas Palamenghi-Crispi. In two volumes (New York: Hodder and Stoughton, 1912), II, 268.

97 Fuller, *Bismarck's Diplomacy at Its Zenith*, 297; Kennan, "The Mystery of the Ferdinand Documents," 344.

98 Catacazy to Giers, September 13/25, 1889, f. 340, op. 813, d. 45, ll. 111–12.

99 Ibid.

100 *New York Tribune*, May 10, 1890; *Le Petit Journal*, May 6, 1890.

Conclusion: "The Catfish War" and Its Legacy

1 *New York Tribune*, May 10, 1890; *Le Petit Journal*, May 6, 1890.

2 *Telegram-Herald* (Grand Rapids, MI), May 26, 1890; *Buchanan Record* (MI), May 29, 1890.

3 *New York Sun*, May 19, 1890.

4 *Evening Star*, May 10, 1890.

5 *Pittsburgh Dispatch*, May 28, 1890.

6 *Watertown Republican* (WI), May 14, 1890.

7 Quote from the title of this chapter found in *Cleveland Leader*, November 27, 1871.

8 *Washington Daily National Republican*, January 16, 1872; *New York Herald*, February 7, 1872; *Memphis Daily Appeal*, February 11, 1872.

9 *New York Herald*, February 7, 1872; *Cincinnati Gazette* quoted in *Belmont Chronicle* (St. Clairsville, OH), April 25, 1872; *Memphis Daily Appeal*, February 11, 1872.

10 Cramer to Fish, February 3, 1872, Despatches from U.S. Ministers to Denmark, NARA, M 41, Roll 13.

11 Cramer to Fish, February 15, 1872, Despatches from U.S. Ministers to Denmark, NARA, M 41, Roll 13.

12 Cramer to Fish, March 4, 1872, Despatches from U.S. Ministers to Denmark, NARA, M 41, Roll 13.

13 Cramer to Fish, March 23, 1872, Despatches from U.S. Ministers to Denmark, NARA, M 41, Roll 13.

14 *Chicago Tribune*, March 27, 1872; *Charleston Daily News*, April 6, 1872; *Alexandria Gazette*, April 19, 1872.

15 Cramer to Fish, May 4, 1872, Despatches from U.S. Ministers to Denmark, NARA, M 41, Roll 13.

16 *Daily National Republican*, May 27, 1782; *Wheeling Daily Intelligencer*, June 20, 1872.

17 Cramer to Fish, June 13, 1872, Despatches from U.S. Ministers to Denmark, NARA, M 41, Roll 13.

18 *New National Era*, June 20, 1872.

19 *Belfast News-Letter*, December 7, 1871; *Liverpool Mercury*, November 27, 1871; *The Graphic* (London), December 30, 1871; *Aberdeen Journal*, December 13, 1871; *Manchester Times*, December 9, 1871; *Pall Mall Gazette*, November 25, 1871; *Glasgow Herald*, November 27, 1871; *Leeds Mercury*, November 28, 1871; *Le Temps*, December 19, 1871; *Le Constitutionnel*, November 4, 1871 and November 26, 1871.

20 *Montreal Gazette*, November 3, 1871.

21 Papers that published the correspondence in some fashion include, *Reynold's Newspaper* (London), December 31, 1871. Papers that published Grant's speech in some form include, *The Graphic* (London), December 2, 1871; *Pall Mall Gazette*, December 5, 1871; *Leeds Mercury*, December 6, 1871; *Belfast News-Letter*, December 5, 1871; *Glasgow Herald*, December 5, 1871; *Liverpool Mercury*, December 5, 1871; *Le Temps*, December 19, 1871; *Le Courrier du Gard*, December 8, 1871; *Le Constitutionnel*, December 18, 1871; *Vossische Zeitung*, December 6, 1871.

22 *Glasgow Herald*, December 27, 1871.

23 *Bristol Mercury*, December 9, 1871.

24 *London Daily News*, December 8, 1871; see also *Leeds Mercury*, December 7, 1871; *Glasgow Herald*, December 7, 1871.

25 *Freeman's Journal and Daily Commercial Advertiser*, January 8, 1872; *Leeds Mercury*, January 5, 1872; *Manchester Times*, January 6, 1872; *Derby Mercury*, January 10, 1872; *Le Temps*, January 6, 1872; *Journal des Debats politique et litteraires*, January 10, 1872.

26 *Leeds Mercury*, January 2, 1872; see also *Birmingham Daily Post*, February 3, 1872; *Glasgow Herald*, February 6, 1872; *The Graphic* (London), February 10, 1872.

27 *New York Times*, March 5, 1872. Article from *Hamburg Correspondent* quoted in the *Pall Mall Gazette*, December 28, 1871 and the *Cleveland Daily Leader*, January 20, 1872.

28 French press quoted in *Leeds Mercury*, February 10, 1872.

29 Translation of *Moskovskie Vedomosti* article, December 23, 1871/January 4, 1872, by Eugene Schuyler, contained in Curtin to Fish, January 6, 1872, Despatches from the US Ministers to Russia, 1808–1906, Roll 23.

30 Curtin to Fish, January 10, 1872, Hamilton Fish Papers, LOC, Container 84, Doc. 13413–14.

31 *London Times*, January 24, 1872, January 25, 1872.

32 Translation of *Moskovskie Vedomosti* of January 21/February 2, 1872, in Schuyler to Fish, February 5, 1872, Despatches from the US Ministers to Russia, 1808–1906, Roll 23.

33 Translation of *Moskovskie Vedomosti*, January 28/February 9, 1872, Schuyler to Fish, February 12, 1872, Despatches from the US Ministers to Russia, 1808–1906, Roll 23.

34 *Birmingham Daily Post*, August 13, 1872; see also *Pall Mall Gazette*, July 20, 1872; *Journal des Debats politique et litteraires*, July 29, 1872; *Le Pays: journal des volontes de la France*, July 28, 1872.

35 Eugene Schuyler, *Selected Essays; with a Memoir by Evelyn Schuyler Schaeffer* (London: Sampson, Low, Marston, 1901), 130.

36 Schuyler to Fish, May 5, 1872, Hamilton Fish papers, LOC, Container 87, Doc. 14027–14027a.

37 Badeau, *Grant in Peace*, 379.

38 Fish to Grant, July 12, 1872, quoted in *The Papers of Ulysses S. Grant*, 28: 455–6.

39 Badeau, *Grant in Peace*, 379–80.

40 Ross, *The General's Wife*, 266; Badeau, *Grant in Peace*, 381.

41 Wharton, *A Digest of the International Law of the United States*, 611–12; Hannis Taylor, *A Treatise on International Public Law* (Chicago: Callaghan and Company, 1901), 353; John Bassett Moore, *History and Digest of the International Arbitrations to which the United States has been a Party* (Washington: Gov't Print Off., 1898), 6: 26–27; Arnold Bennett Hall, *Outline of International Law* (Chicago: LaSalle Extension University, 1915), 55; Amos A. Hershey, *The Essentials of International Public Law* (New York: Macmillan, 1919), 282.

42 Fish to Curtin, November 16, 1871, Diplomatic Instructions, Roll 137, LOC, Box 233; this passage is quoted in B. Sen, *A Diplomat's Handbook of International Law and Practice* (The Hague: Martinus Nijhoff, 1965), 187; Jesse S. Reeves, comp., "Diplomatic Privileges and Immunities," *American Journal of International Law*, vol. 26, no. 1, Supplement: Research on International Law (1932), 78. (all pages are 15–192).

43 *New York Times*, March 21, 1895; *Evening Star* (Washington, DC), March 20, 1895.

44 *Hamilton Fish Diaries*, Reel 1 (vol. 1), November 30, 1869. See also *Washington Daily Morning Chronicle*, December 2, 1869, January 19, 1870, February 1, 1870; M. Y. Isaacs to Hamilton Fish, January 31, 1870, Hamilton Fish Papers, Container 67, Doc. 9500–1, LOC, Manuscripts Division, Washington, DC; *New York Herald*, October 29, 1871. For more on this, see Ann E. Healy, "Tsarist Anti-Semitism and Russian-American Relations," *Slavic Review*, vol. 42, no. 3 (Autumn 1983): 408–25.

45 *Harper's Weekly*, May 26, 1877; Saul, *Concord and Conflict*, 116–23.

46 Richard Robbins, *Famine in Russia, 1891–1892* (New York: Columbia University
     Press, 1975), 2–10; Charles Emory Smith, "The Famine in Russia," *North American
     Review*, vol. 154, no. 426 (May 1892): 541–51; George S. Queen, "American Relief in
     the Russian Famine of 1891–1892," *Russian Review*, vol. 14, no. 2 (April 1955): 140–
     50; *New York Times*, January 30, 1892; see also Harold F. Smith, "Bread for
     Russians: William C. Edgar and the Relief Campaign of 1892," *Minnesota History*,
     42, no. 2 (Summer 1970): 54–62.

47 Farrow, *Alexis in America*, 224; *New York Times*, December 25, 1892; Queen,
     147. Even in 1917, albeit before the worst excesses of the Russian Revolution
     had occurred, Francis Reeves wrote about the famine and warmly referred to the
     continuing friendship between the two nations. See *Russian Then and Now, 1892–
     1917: My Mission to Russia During the Famine of 1891–1892 with Data Bearing
     Upon Russia of Today* (New York: G. P. Putnam's, 1917).

48 Senate Resolution No. 631, "Mr. Blaine to Mr. Bartholomei, Department of State,
     Washington, March 15, 1881," Papers Relating to the Foreign Relations of the
     United States (Washington: U.S. Government Printing Office, 1882), 1038.

49 Rodger Streitmatter, *Mightier than the Sword: How the News Media Have Shaped
     American History* (Boulder, CO: Westview Press, 1997), 1–2.

50 Marianna Tax Choldin, *A Fence around the Empire: Russian Censorship of Western
     Ideas under the Tsars* (Durham, NC: Duke University Press, 1985), 1–2; W. Bruce
     Lincoln, *Nicholas I: Emperor and Autocrat of All the Russias* (Dekalb: Northern
     Illinois Press, 1989), 236, 296, 300–1, 300–1; Abbott Gleason, *Young Russia: The
     Genesis of Russian Radicalism in the 1860s* (Chicago: University of Chicago Press,
     1980), 174–5, 226; Louise McReynolds, *The News under Russia's Old Regime: The
     Development of a Mass-Circulation Press* (Princeton, NJ: Princeton University Press,
     1991), 4, 23–4, 40–1, 52–4, 63.

51 Catacazy to Fish, May 31, 1871/June 11, 1871, NARA, Notes from the Russian
     Legation in the US to the Department of State, M 39, Roll 5.

52 Nicholas Thompson, "How Russian Trolls Used Meme Warfare to Divide
     America," *Wired* (December 12, 2018), https://www.wired.com/story/
     russia-ira-propaganda-senate-report/.

53 "Russian Meddling in the United States: The Historical Context of the Mueller
     Report," Center for Strategic and International Studies (March 27, 2019), https://
     www.csis.org/analysis/russian-meddling-united-states-historical-context-mueller-
     report; Barbara Ortutay, "Facebook Takedowns Reveal Sophistication of Russian
     Trolls," *Associated Press News* (March 12, 2020), https://apnews.com/d97d4820bd
     d801b3cc72d6d18a3a43b6; Jeremy Herb, "Russian Meddling Efforts Intensifying
     as US Election Nears," *CNN News* (September 12, 2020), https://www.cnn.

com/2020/09/12/politics/russian-meddling-2020-us-election/index.html. There are too many news articles of a similar content to list here.

54 William Englund, "When Russian Meddling in the US Got So Bad the Ambassador Got the Boot," *Washington Post*, November 12, 2017, https://www.washingtonpost.com/news/retropolis/wp/2017/11/12/ when-russian-meddling-in-the-u-s-got-so-bad-the-ambassador-got-the-boot/.

Bibliography

Arkhiv Vneshnei Politiki Rossiiskoi Imperii (Archive of Foreign Policy of the Russian Empire), Moscow, Russia (AVPRI)

   Fond 170 (Embassy in Washington), Opis 512/1 and 512/2

   Fond 340 (Collection of Manuscripts from the Personal Archives of Officials of MID), Opis 813 (Catacazy, C. G.)

Library of Congress, Manuscripts Division, Washington, DC (LOC)

   J. C. Bancroft Davis Papers

   Eugene Schuyler Papers

   The Papers of Hamilton Fish

National Archives and Records Administration, College Park, MD (NARA)

   General Records of the Department of State, Record Group 59

      —Despatches from U.S. Consuls in St. Petersburg, Russia, 1803–1906

      —Despatches from U.S. Ministers to Russia, 1866–9

      —Diplomatic Instructions of the Department of State, 1801–1906

      —Notes of the Russian Legation in the U.S. to the Department of State, 1809–1906

      —Notes to Foreign Legations in the United States from the Department of State, 1834–1906: Russia

   Records of Boundary and Claims Commissions and Arbitrations, 1716–1979, Record Group 76

The New York Public Library, Manuscripts and Archives Division, New York

   Hamilton Fish Letters and Miscellany

British National Archives, London (BNA)

   Foreign Office and Foreign and Commonwealth Office: Embassy and Consulates, Union of Soviet Socialist Republics (formerly Russian Empire): General Correspondence. Political from Sir Andrew Buchanan, FO 181/480, FO 181/487, FO 181/488

Newspapers

Aberdeen Journal

Alexandria Gazette

Appleton's

Baltimore Sun

Belfast News-Letter

Belmont Chronicle (St. Clairsville, OH)

Birmingham Daily Post

Boston Herald

Bristol Mercury

Brooklyn Eagle

Buchanan Record (MI)

Buffalo Commercial Advertiser

Charleston Daily News

Cheyenne Daily Leader

Chicago Republican

Chicago Times

Chicago Tribune

Cincinnati Daily Enquirer

Cincinnati Gazette

Cleveland Daily Plain Dealer

Daily Dispatch (Richmond, VA)

Daily Evening Bulletin (San Francisco, CA)

Daily Morning Chronicle (Washington, DC)

Daily National Republican

Daily News (London)

Derby Mercury

Detroit Free Press

Evening Star (Washington, DC)

Freeman's Journal and Daily Commercial Advertiser (Dublin)

Glasgow Herald

Golos

The Graphic (London)

Harper's Weekly

Journal de St. Petersbourg

Journal des Debats politique et litteraires

Kansas City Times

Le Constitutionnel

Le Courrier du Gard

Le Figaro

Le Pays: journal des volontes de la France

Le Petit Journal

Le Petite Presse

Le Temps

Leavenworth Daily Commonwealth

Leeds Mercury

Liverpool Mercury

London Times

Louisiana Democrat

Manchester Times

Memphis Daily Appeal

Memphis Public Ledger

Milwaukee Sentinel

Montreal Gazette

Nashville Union and American

The Nation (New York)

New National Era

New Orleans Daily Picayune

New Orleans Republican

New Orleans Times

New York Herald

New York Post

New York Sun

New York Times

New York World

Pall Mall Gazette

Philadelphia Enquirer

Pittsburgh Dispatch

Pittsfield Sun (Massachusetts)

Reynold's Newspaper (London)

Russkii Mir

Toronto Globe

Truth

Vossische Zeitung

Washington Daily Morning Chronicle

Watertown Republican (Wisconsin)

Weekly San Joaquin Republican (Stockton, CA)

Weekly Wisconsin Patriot

Wheeling Daily Intelligencer (West Virginia)

Published Primary and Secondary Sources

Adams, Marian. *The Letters of Mrs. Henry Adams*, edited by War Thoron. Boston, MA: Little, Brown, 1936.

Anderson, M. S. *The Rise of Modern Diplomacy, 1450–1919*. London: Longman, 1993.

Aresty, Esther B. *The Best Behavior: The Course of Good Manners—from Antiquity to the Present—as Seen through Courtesy and Etiquette Books*. New York: Simon and Schuster, 1970.

Badeau, Adam. *Grant in Peace: From Appomattox to Mount McGregor. A Personal Memoir*. Hartford: S.S. Scranton, 1887; Kessinger, 2010.

Bailey, Thomas A. *A Diplomatic History of the American People*. New York: Appleton-Century-Crofts, 1964.

Bailey, Thomas A. "The Russian Fleet Myth Re-Examined," *Mississippi Valley Historical Review*, vol. 38, no. 1 (June 1951): 81–90.

Bailey, Thomas A. "Why the United States Purchased Alaska," *Pacific Historical Review*, vol. 3 (1934): 39–49.

Baldasty, Gerald J. *The Commercialization of News in the Nineteenth Century*. Madison: University of Wisconsin Press, 1992.

Ball, Alan M. *Imagining America: Influence and Images in Twentieth-Century Russia*. Lanham, MD: Rowman & Littlefield, 2003.

Biographic Register of the Department of State. Washington, DC: Government Printing Office, 1872.

Blaine, Harriet S., ed. *Letters of Mrs. James G. Blaine*. New York: Duffield, 1908.

Blinn, Harold. "Seward and the Polish Rebellion of 1863," *American Historical Review*, vol. 45, no. 4 (July 1940): 828–33.

Bolkhovitinov, N. N. *Russian-American Relations and the Sale of Alaska, 1834–1867*. Kingston, ON: Limestone Press. Distributed by the University of Alaska Press, 1996.

Bowers, Claude G. *The Tragic Era: The Revolution after Lincoln*. Cambridge: Houghton Mifflin, 1929.

Briggs, Emily Edson. *The Olivia Letters: Being Some History of Washington City for Forty Years as Told by the Letters of a Newspaper Correspondent*. New York: Neale, 1906.

Canavan, Kathryn. *Lincoln's Final Hours: Conspiracy, Terror, and the Assassination of America's Greatest President*. Lexington: University Press of Kentucky, 2015.

Carew, Joy Gleason. *Blacks, Reds, and Russians: Sojourners in Search of the Soviet Promise*. New Brunswick, NJ: Rutgers University Press, 2008.

Carrier, Thomas. *Washington, D.C.: A Historical Walking Tour*. Charleston: Arcadia, 2005.

Catacazy, Constantin Gavrilovich. *Un Incident Diplomatique. Lettre a Chief Justice S. Chase*. Paris, 1872.

Chase, Salmon P. *The Salmon P. Chase Papers*, edited by John Niven, 5 vols. Kent, OH: Kent State University Press, 1993.

Chernow, Ron. *Alexander Hamilton*. New York: Penguin, 2005.

Choldin, Marianna Tax. *A Fence around the Empire: Russian Censorship of Western Ideas under the Tsars*. Durham, NC: Duke University Press, 1985.

Claim of Captain Benjamin W. Perkins against the Government of Russia, in the Matter of Two Contracts Entered into in the Years 1855 and 1856. Washington, 1860.

Clay, Cassius. *The Life of Cassius Marcellus Clay. Memoirs, Writings and Speeches*. New York: Negro Universities Press, 1969.

Congressional Globe, Special Session of the Senate, 35th Cong., 1st sess., June 15, 1858, 3051–2.

Cook, Adrian. *The Alabama Claims: American Politics and Anglo-American Relations, 1865–1872*. Ithaca, NY: Cornell University Press, 1975.

Cook, Adrian. "A Lost Opportunity in Anglo-American Relations: The Alabama Claims, 1865–1867," *Australian Journal of Politics and History*, vol. 12, no. 1 (1966): 54–65.

Correspondence Relating to the Recall of Mr. Motley, Transmitted to the Senate January 9, 1871 in Compliance with a Resolution. Washington, DC: Government Printing Office, 1871.

Crispi, Francesco. *The Memoirs of Francesco Crispi*, translated by Mary Prichard-Agentti and edited by Thomas Palamenghi-Crispi, 2 vols. New York: Hodder and Stoughton, 1912.

Curtin, Jeremiah. *Memoirs of Jeremiah Curtin*. Madison: State Historical Society of Wisconsin, 1940.

Dahlgren, Madeleine Vinton. *Etiquette of Social Life in Washington*. Washington, DC: J. A. Wineberger, 1873.

Daniel, Marcus. *Scandal and Civility: Journalism and the Birth of American Democracy.* Oxford: Oxford University Press, 2010.

Dunning, William. "Paying for Alaska," *Political Science Quarterly*, vol. 38 (1912): 385–98.

Dvoichenko-Markov, Eufrosina. "Americans in the Crimean War," *Russian Review*, vol. 13, no. 2 (April 1954): 137–45.

Farrow, Lee A. *Alexis in America: A Grand Duke's Tour, 1871–72*. Baton Rouge: Louisiana State University Press, 2014.

Foster, John W. *Diplomatic Memoirs*. Two volumes in one. Boston: Houghton Mifflin, 1909.

Frame, Arthur Thomas. The U.S. Military Commission to the Crimean War and Its Influence on the U.S. Army before the American Civil War. PhD Dissertation, University Press of Kansas, 1993.

Frary, Lucien J. *Russia and the Making of Modern Greek Identity*. Oxford: Oxford University Press, 2015.

Fuller, Joseph Vincent. *Bismarck's Diplomacy at Its Zenith.*Cambridge, MA: Harvard University Press, 1922.

Ginzberg, Lori D. *Women and the Work of Benevolence: Morality, Politics, and Class in the Nineteenth-Century United States*. New Haven, CT: Yale University Press, 1992.

Gleason, Abbott. *Young Russia: The Genesis of Russian Radicalism in the 1860s.* Chicago: University of Chicago Press, 1980.

Golder, Frank. "The American Civil War through the Eyes of a Russian Diplomat," *American Historical Review*, vol. 26, no. 3 (April 1921): 454–63.

Golder, Frank. "The Purchase of Alaska," *American Historical Review*, vol. 25 (1920): 411–25.

Golder, Frank. "Russian American Relations during the Crimean War," *American Historical Review*, vol. 31,no. 3 (April 1926): 462–76.

Grant, Julia Dent. *The Personal Memoirs of Julia Dent Grant*, edited, with notes and foreword, by John Y. Simon, with an introduction by Bruce Catton. New York: G. P. Putnam's Sons, 1975.

Griffiths, David M. "Nikita Panin, Russian Diplomacy and the American Revolution," *Slavic Review*, vol. 28, no. 1 (March 1969): 1–24.

Grinspan, Jon. *The Virgin Vote: How Young Americans Made Democracy Social, Politics Personal, and Voting Popular in the Nineteenth Century*. Chapel Hill: University of North Carolina Press, 2016.

Hall, Arnold Bennett. *Outline of International Law*. Chicago: LaSalle Extension University, 1915.

Healy, Ann E. "Tsarist Anti-Semitism and Russian-American Relations," *Slavic Review*, vol. 42, no. 3 (Autumn 1983): 408–25.

Hershey, Amos S. *The Essentials of International Public Law*. New York: Macmillan, 1919.

Hochschild, Arlie. "The Role of the Ambassador's Wife: An Exploratory Study," *Journal of Marriage and Family*, vol. 31, no. 1 (February 1969): 73–87.

Holbo, Paul. *Tarnished Expansion: The Alaska Scandal, the Press and Congress*. Knoxville: University of Tennessee Press, 1983.

Huntzicker, William E. *The Popular Press, 1833–1865*. Westport, CT: Greenwood Press, 1999.

Jacob, Kathryn Alamong. "High Society in Washington during the Gilded Age: 'Three Distinct Aristocracies.'" PhD Dissertation. Johns Hopkins University, 1986.

James, Carolyn, and Glenda Sluga, ed., "Introduction: The Long International History of Women and Diplomacy," in *Women, Diplomacy and International Politics since 1500*. Oxford: Routledge, 2016, pp. 1–12.

Jelavich, Barbara. *Russia and the Greek Revolution of 1843*. Munich: Verlag R. Oldenbourg, 1966.

Jelavich, Barbara. *The Ottoman Empire, the Great Powers, and the Straits Questions, 1870–1887*. Bloomington: Indiana University Press, 1973.

Jensen, Ronald. *The Alaska Purchase and Russian-American Relations*. Seattle: University of Washington Press, 1975.

Journal of the House of Representatives, 40th Cong., 3rd sess., January 13, 1869.

Kaplan, Richard L. *Politics and the American Press: The Rise of Objectivity, 1865–1920*. Cambridge: Cambridge University Press, 2002.

Kedourie, Elie. "Afghānī in Paris: A Note," *Middle Eastern Studies*, vol. 8, no. 1 (January 1972): 103–5.

Keneally, Thomas. *American Scoundrel: The Life of the Notorious Civil War General Dan Sickles*. New York: Doubleday, 2002.

Kennan, George F. *Tent Life in Siberia*. Honolulu: University Press of the Pacific, 2001.

Kennan, George F. "The Mystery of the Ferdinand Documents," *Jahrbucher fur Geschichte Osteuropas*, vol. 26, no. 3 (1978): 321–52.

Keys, Barbara. "An African-American Worker in Stalin's Soviet Union: Race and the Soviet Experiment in International Perspective," *The Historian* (2009): 31–54.

Kirchner, Walther. *Studies in Russian-American Commerce, 1820–1860*. Leiden: E. J. Brill, 1975.

Klein, Axel. *O'Kelly: An Irish Musical Family in Nineteenth-Century France* (Books on Demand). Accessed May 5, 2014.

Kroll, C. Douglas. *"Friends in Peace and War": The Russian Navy's Landmark Visit to Civil War San Francisco*. Washington, DC: Potomac Books, 2007.

Leder, Mary M. *My Life in Stalinist Russia: An American Woman Looks Back*. Bloomington: Indiana University Press, 2001.

Lewis, Charles L. *David Glasgow Farragut: Admiral in the Making*. Annapolis: United States Naval Institute, 1980.

Lewy, Guenter. *The Cause That Failed: Communism in American Political Life*. New York: Oxford University Press, 1990.

Lincoln, W. Bruce. *Nicholas I: Emperor and Autocrat of All the Russias*. Dekalb: Northern Illinois Press, 1989.

Logan, Mrs. John A. *Reminiscences of a Soldier's Wife: An Autobiography*. New York: C. Scribner's Sons, 1913; reprint, Carbondale: Southern Illinois University Press, 1997.

Lorenz, Lincoln. *The Admiral and the Empress: John Paul Jones and Catherine the Great*. New York: Bookman Associate, 1954.

Marszalek, John F. *The Petticoat Affair: Manners, Mutiny, and Sex in Andrew Jackson's White House*. Baton Rouge: Louisiana State University Press, 2000.

Marvel, William. *The Alabama and the Kearsarge*. Chapel Hill: University of North Carolina Press, 1996.

McFeely, William S. *Grant: A Biography*. New York: W. W Norton, 1982.

McReynolds, Louise. *The News under Russia's Old Regime: The Development of a Mass-Circulation Press*. Princeton, NJ: Princeton University Press, 1991.

Melanson, Philip H., and Peter F. Stevens, *The Secret Service: The Hidden History of an Enigmatic Agency*. New York: Carroll and Graf, 2002.

Miller, David H. *The Alaska Treaty*. Kingston, ON: Limestone Press, 1981.

Miller, David H. "Russian Opinion on the Cession of Alaska," *American Historical Review*, vol. 48 (April 1943): 526–31.

Miller, William. "Modern Greek Historians of Modern Greece," *History*, vol. 10, no. 38 (July 1925): 110–23.

Monkman, Betty C. *The White House: Its Historic Furnishings and First Families*. New York: Abbeville Press, 2000.

Moore, John Bassett. *History and Digest of the International Arbitrations to which the United States has been a Party*. In 6 vols. Washington: Government Print Off., 1898.

Moore, John Bassett, and Francis Wharton. *A Digest of International Law: As Embodied in Diplomatic Discussions, Treaties and Other International Agreements, International Awards, the Decisions of Municipal Courts, and the Writings of Jurists …* U.S. Government Printing Office, 1906.

Nagengast, William E. "The Visit of the Russian Fleet to the United States: Were Americans Deceived?" *Russian Review*, vol. 8, no. 1 (January 1949): 46–55.

Ninth U.S. Census, Vol. 1, June 1, 1870. Washington, DC: Government Printing Office, 1872.

Olszyk, Edmund G. *The Polish Press in America*. Milwaukee: Marquette University Press, 1940.

Orr, James L., and Joseph O. Baylen, ed., "A Letter of James L. Orr, Minister to Russia, 1873," *South Carolina Historical Magazine*, vol. 61, no. 4 (October 1960): 225–31.

Parry, Albert. "American Doctors in the Crimean War," *South Atlantic Quarterly*, vol. 54, no. 4 (October 1955): 478–90.

Petition of Anna B. Perkins, of Worcester, Mass, Administratrix of the Late B. W. Perkins: Praying That Out of the Sums of Money to Be Paid to the Imperial Government of Russia, under the Terms of the Recent Treaty between the Government and the United States ... Washington, DC: Intelligencer Printing House, 1867.

Petropulos, John Anthony. *Politics and Statecraft in the Kingdom of Greece, 1833–1843*. Princeton, NJ: Princeton University Press, 1968.

Pyle, G. F. "The Diffusion of Cholera in the United States in the Nineteenth Century," *Geographical Analysis*, vol. 1: 59–75.

Queen, George S. "American Relief in the Russian Famine of 1891–1892," *Russian Review*, vol. 14, no. 2 (April 1955): 140–50.

Reeves, Francis. *Russian Then and Now, 1892–1917: My Mission to Russia during the Famine of 1891–1892 with Data Bearing Upon Russia of Today*. New York: G. P. Putnam's Sons, 1917.

Reeves, Jesse S., comp., "Diplomatic Privileges and Immunities," *American Journal of International Law*, vol. 26, no. 1, Supplement: Research on International Law, 1932.

Register of the Department of State. In Four Parts. Washington, DC: Government Printing Office, 1874.

Robbins, Richard. *Famine in Russia, 1891–1892*. New York: Columbia University Press, 1975.

Robinson, Harlow. *Russians in Hollywood, Hollywood's Russians: Biography of an Image*. Boston, MA: Northeastern, 2007.

Robson, Maureen M. "The Alabama Claims and the Anglo-American Reconciliation, 1865–1871," *Canadian Historical Review*, vol. 42, no. 1 (March 1961): 1–22.

Ross, Ishbel. *The General's Wife: The Life of Mrs. Ulysses S. Grant*. New York: Dodd, Mead, 1959.

Rumbold, Sir Horace. *Recollections of a Diplomatist*. London: Edward Arnold, 1903.

The Russian Contracts. Washington, DC, 1861.

Russkii Biograficheskii slovar' (Idak'-Kliucharev'), Saint Petersburg, 1897; reprint, Moscow: Aspect Press, 1994.

Saul, Norman E. *Concord and Conflict; The United States and Russia, 1867–1914*. Lawrence: University Press of Kansas, 1996.

Saul, Norman E. *Distant Friends: The United States and Russia, 1763–1867*. Lawrence: University Press of Kansas, 1991.

Schuyler, Eugene. *Selected Essays; with a Memoir by Evelyn Schuyler Schaeffer*. London: Sampson, Low, Marston, 1901.

Scott, John. *Behind the Urals: An American Worker in Russia's City of Steel*. Bloomington: Indiana University Press, 1973.

Sealove, Sandra. "The Founding Fathers as Seen by the Marqués de Casa-Irujo," *The Americas*, vol. 20, no. 1 (July 1963): 37–42.

Senate Journal, 35th Cong., 1st sess., June 15, 1858, 724–5.

Senate Resolution No. 631, "Mr. Blaine to Mr. Bartholomei, Department of State, Washington, March 15, 1881," Papers Relating to the Foreign Relations of the United States. Washington: U.S. Government Printing Office, 1882.

Senelick, Laurence, ed. *Wandering Stars: Russian Émigré Theatre, 1905–1940*. Iowa City: University of Iowa Press, 1992.

Sen, Biswaneth. *A Diplomat's Handbook of International Law and Practice*. The Hague: Martinus Nijhoff, 1965.

Simon, John Y., ed. *The Papers of Ulysses S. Grant*. Carbondale: Southern Illinois University Press, 1988.

Smith, Charles Emory. "The Famine in Russia," *North American Review*, vol. 154, no. 426 (May 1892): 541–51.

Smith, Harold F. "Bread for Russians: William C. Edgar and the Relief Campaign of 1892," *Minnesota History*, vol. 42, no. 2 (Summer 1970): 54–62.

Smythe, Ted Curtis. *The Gilded Age Press, 1865–1900*. Westport, CT: Praeger, 2003.

Solomon, Mark I. *Red and Black: Communism and Afro-Americans, 1929–1935*. New York: Garland, 1988.

Stites, Richard. *Revolutionary Dreams: Utopian Vision and Experimental Life in the Russian Revolution*. New York: Oxford University Press, 1989.

Stults, Taylor. "Russian Persecution of Jews, and American Public Opinion," *Jewish Social Studies*, vol. 33, no. 1 (January 1971): 13–22.

Summers, Mark Wahlgren. *The Press Gang: Newspapers and Politics, 1865–1878*. Chapel Hill: University of North Carolina Press, 1994.

Sumner, Charles, and Hamilton Fish. *Personal Relations with the President and Secretary of State: An Explanation in Reply to an Assault*. Washington, DC, 1871.

Tarsaidze, Alexandre. "American Pioneers in Russian Railroad Building," *Russian Review*, vol. 9, no. 4 (October 1950): 286–95.

Taylor, Hannis. *A Treatise on International Public Law*. Chicago: Callaghan, 1901.

Travis, Frederick F. *George Kennan and the American-Russian Relationship, 1865–1924*. Athens: Ohio University Press, 1990.

Twain, Mark. *The Innocents Abroad*, edited by Shelley Fisher Fishkin, introduction Mordecai Richler. Afterword by David E. E. Sloan. New York: Oxford University Press, 1996.

Tzouliadis, Tim. *The Forsaken: An American Tragedy in Stalin's Russia*. New York: Penguin, 2008.

Van Alstyne, Richard W. "John F. Crampton, Conspirator or Dupe?" *American Historical Review*, vol. 41, no. 3 (April 1936): 492–502.

Verhoeven, Claudia. *The Odd Man Karakozov: Imperial Russia, Modernity, and the Birth of Terrorism*. Ithaca, NY: Cornell University Press, 2011.

Washburne, Mark. *A Biography of Elihu Benjamin Washburne, Congressman, Secretary of State, Envoy Extraordinary*. In 4 vols. Bloomington, IN: Xlibris, 2005.

Weeks, Albert L. *Russia's Life-Saver; Lend-Lease Aid to the U.S.S.R. in World War II*. Lanham, MD: Lexington Books, 2004.

Wettlin, Margaret. *Fifty Russian Winters: An American Woman's Life in the Soviet Union*. New York: Pharos Books, 1992.

Wharton, Francis. *A Digest of the International Law of the United States, Taken from Documents Issued by Presidents and Secretaries of State, and from Decisions of Federal Courts and Opinions of Attorneys-General*. Washington, DC: Government Printing Office, 1887.

White, Andrew Dickson. *Autobiography of Andrew Dickson White*. New York: Century, 1907.

Williams, Robert C. "The Quiet Trade: Russian Art and American Money," *Wilson Quarterly*, vol. 3, no. 1 (Winter 1979): 162–75.

Wilson, Rufus Rockwell. *Washington: The Capital City, and Its Part in the History of the Nation*, vol. 1. Philadelphia: J. B. Lippincott, 1902.

Wood, Molly M. "Wives, Clerks, and 'Lady Diplomats': The Gendered Politics of Diplomacy and Representation in the U.S. Foreign Service, 1900–1940," *European Journal of American Studies*, vol. 10, no. 1 (2015). document 1.6; online since March 2015. http://ejas.revues.org/10562.

Internet Sources

Herb, Jeremy. "Russian Meddling Efforts Intensifying as US Election Nears," *CNN News* (September 12, 2020), https://www.cnn.com/2020/09/12/politics/russian-meddling-2020-us-election/index.html.

"Russian Meddling in the United States: The Historical Context of the Mueller Report," Center for Strategic and International Studies (March 27, 2019),https://www.csis. org/analysis/russian-meddling-united-states-historical-context-mueller-report.

Ortutay, Barbara. "Facebook Takedowns Reveal Sophistication of Russian Trolls," *Associated Press News* (March 12, 2020), https://apnews.com/d97d4820bdd801b3cc7 2d6d18a3a43b6.

https://www.geni.com/people/Olga-de-Fitz-James-Greuther-Grutther-o-Grutter/6000000030252500060. Accessed April 5, 2021.

https://founders.archives.gov/documents/Madison/02-09-02-0273#JSMN-02-09-02-0273-fn-0008. Accessed July 5, 2020.

Index

Adams, George W. 53–5, 95, 126, 134
Adams, John 79
Adams, John Quincy 8, 9, 53
Adlerberg, Count Alexander 129, 130, 131, 136
Alabama Claims 2, 7, 38, 39, 43–9, 57, 64, 86, 89, 91, 98, 104, 134, 147, 148
Alaska Purchase 3, 15, 19, 20, 23, 32, 34, 40, 43
Alexander I 9–10
Alexander II 4, 8, 11, 12, 13, 14, 37, 42, 46, 96, 106, 112, 115, 128, 131, 138, 150, 152, 153, 154
Alexander III 138, 139, 153
Alexis, Grand Duke 2, 4, 8, 12, 71, 80, 83, 85, 86, 87, 88, 96, 97, 101–24, 127, 128, 131, 137, 138, 147, 150, 151, 152, 153, 154
Aspinwall, William 127
assassination 14, 90, 105, 106, 138, 152
assassination plots 105–7

Bennett, James Gordon, Jr. 134
Black Sea Crisis 4, 36–42, 43–4, 48, 52, 55, 147
Bodisco, Alexander de 26, 31, 103
Bodisco, Waldemar de 31, 35, 36, 55, 128

Cameron, Simon 67, 90, 96, 118
Campbell, William 119
Catacazy, Constantin, Russian Minister to the United States (1869–71)
  background, 25–6
  comments about his Greek heritage 25, 90–1, 92, 116, 119, 134, 135, 136, 146
  death 140
  duties as Minister 26–9
  father, Gavril 25
  later life 137–40
  use of the American press 56–7
Catacazy, Olga 4, 25–6, 61–75, 127, 141, 154
Catherine the Great 8, 9
Chase, Salmon P. 132, 135
Clay, Cassius 14, 19, 36, 81, 82, 83
Constantin, Grand Duke 15
Cox, Jacob 120
Cramer, Michael 38, 42, 94, 142–7
Crampton, John F. 11
Crispi, Francesco 140
Curtin, Jeremiah 82
Custer, George Armstrong 111, 127

Dana, Francis 8
Danzas, Boris 120–1
Dashkov, Andrei 9
Davis, Bancroft, Assistant Secretary of State 47, 59, 82, 83, 84, 87, 89, 92, 103, 104, 115, 134

Eaton, Margaret "Peggy" 3

"Ferdinand Documents" 139–40
Fish, Hamilton, Secretary of State
  accused of corruption 125–6, 133
  early career 63
Fish, Julia Kean 63, 64, 66, 67, 68, 70–1

Giers, Nikolai 138–9
Gladstone, William 39
Gorchakov, Alexander, Prince 17, 20, 22, 31, 32, 33, 34, 35, 36, 37, 38, 39, 42, 46, 59, 80, 81, 82, 83, 89, 91, 92, 94, 96, 97, 101, 108, 110, 115, 116, 117, 118, 120, 121, 122, 123, 127, 128, 129, 130, 131, 137, 142, 144, 148, 151, 154
Gorlov, Alexander 47, 68, 70, 96, 108, 109, 116, 121, 126

Grant, Ulysses S. 1, 2, 3, 21, 26, 31, 33, 41, 44–8, 51–60, 63, 65–7, 69–70, 80, 82, 85–7, 89–96, 98, 102–4, 106, 108–18, 120, 122–3, 134, 135, 142, 146–7, 150–1, 153–4
Granville, Earl (George Leveson Gower) 38, 46, 47, 68
Greeley, Horace 134

Hamilton, Alexander 77–8
Harris, Levett 10
Harrison, Joseph 10

Jackson, Andrew 3, 56, 71–3, 74
Jefferson, Thomas 9, 77–9
Jones, John Paul 9

Lieber, Francis 119
Lincoln, Abraham 14, 73, 106, 114
Loris-Melikov, Mikhail 8

MacVeagh, Wayne 38
Macy, Silvanus 102
Marcy, William 18, 117–18
Morris, Edward Joy 40
Murphy, William 40

Nicholas I 10, 11

Offenberg, Baron Henri de 121, 123
Orlov, Prince Nikolai 130, 131, 132, 136

Perkins, Benjamin (Perkins Claim) 1, 3, 15–23, 31–6, 51, 52, 55, 56, 57, 58, 71, 80, 81, 84, 87, 89, 92, 121, 127, 129, 133, 134
"Petticoat Affair" 3, 71–4
Poland (Polish exiles in the United States) 13, 28, 105–7
Pomutz, George 85, 86, 97
Possiet, Constantin 102, 105, 113, 120

Roslov, Nikolai 9, 10
Russian press, reactions 85, 88, 90, 115, 120, 122, 135–6, 148–50

Schirkov, Valerien 121, 128
Schuyler, Eugenem 41, 42, 95, 96, 97, 123, 128, 150
Shuvalov, Peter 131, 136, 137
Sickles, Dan 81–2
Stewart, J. B. 33, 35, 56, 92
Stoeckl, Edward de 11, 12, 15, 16, 18, 19, 20, 21, 22, 23, 26, 103

Tasistro, Louis 33, 35, 56, 64
Tuckerman, Charles 38
Turk, Frank 35, 38, 54, 55, 59, 125, 134
Twain, Mark 15

Washburne, Elihu B. 31, 74, 93–4, 130
Washington Treaty, see *Alabama* Claims
Westmann, Vladimirm 80, 81, 83, 84, 85, 86, 87, 88, 89, 91, 96, 97, 106, 108, 131, 132
Whistler, James 10
Whitley, H.C. 51, 53, 54
Winthrop, Robert C. 119